PENGUIN BOOKS

PATH OF BLOOD

Dr Peter Becker has won international repute as an author and authority on African history, languages and cultures. Born of English parentage, he was reared in a Transvaal rural area where most of his childhood companions were Africans. His entire adult life has been devoted to a close, on-the-spot study of all African peoples, and this has called for countless research trips into all tribal territories bounded by the Cape in the south, the Zambezi River in the north, and the Indian and Atlantic Oceans.

Peter Becker's fluency in Zulu and related dialects, as well as his intimate understanding of tribal custom and etiquette, have earned him the unique privilege of witnessing, and indeed taking part in, closely guarded rituals and ceremonies, of attending tribal courts, of being admitted into royal villages and kraals of African Kings, Paramount Chiefs and other African dignitaries, and of acquiring first-hand knowledge of African occultism.

In recent times, Becker's researches have been extended to peoples beyond the shores of Africa, namely the inhabitants of Mauritius, the nomadic Bedouin of the Middle East, and the Indians of North America.

Dr Becker has written *Sandy Tracks to the Kraals*; *The Peoples of South Africa* (three volumes); *Path of Blood: The Rise and Conquests of Mzilikazi, Founder of the Matabele of Southern Africa*; *Rule of Fear: The Life and Times of Dingane, King of the Zulu*; *Hill of Destiny: The Life and Times of Moshesh, Founder of the Basotho*; *Peoples of Southern Africa*; *Tribe to Township*; *Trails and Tribes in Southern Africa*; *Mauritius '62*; and *Inland Tribes of Southern Africa*.

He is also the author and presenter of the award-winning television series *The Tribal Identity*.

PETER BECKER

PATH OF BLOOD

The Rise and Conquests of
MZILIKAZI
Founder of the Matabele tribe of
Southern Africa

PENGUIN BOOKS

Penguin Books Ltd, Harmondsworth, Middlesex, England
Penguin Books, 625 Madison Avenue, New York, New York 10022, U.S.A.
Penguin Books Australia Ltd, Ringwood, Victoria, Australia
Penguin Books Canada Ltd, 2801 John Street, Markham, Ontario, Canada L3R 1B4
Penguin Books (N.Z.) Ltd, 182–190 Wairau Road, Auckland 10, New Zealand

—

First published by Allen Lane 1962
Published in Penguin Books 1979

—

Copyright © Peter Becker, 1962
All rights reserved

—

Made and printed in Great Britain by
Hazell Watson & Viney Ltd, Aylesbury, Bucks
Set in Linotype Juliana

TO CONNIE

Mzilikazi kaMashobane
Inkosi yamaNdebele
Intaba yadilika
Ngomhla vzi – 5 kuMandulo, 1868.
Zonke Izizwe zithi: BAYETE!

No one in Zululand suspected the birth of Mzilikazi – the Great Road – to be an ominous event; not even the witch-doctors predicted that he would grow to become a fearsome warrior, a tyrant who would carve a path of blood through Southern Africa and conquer half a million square miles of territory.

CONTENTS

9

Part Two

Part Three

ACKNOWLEDGEMENTS

WE are indebted to Chatto and Windus Ltd for
permission to reproduce extracts from *Matabele
Journals of Robert Moffat* and *Matabele Mission
of J. S. and E. Moffat*, edited by J. P. R.
Wallis.

For permission to reproduce illustrations we are
indebted to the following:

The Africana Museum, Johannesburg for
plate 23; the National Archives of Rhodesia
and Malawi for plates 1, 3, 19, and the portrait
of Thomas Morgan Thomas; the London Missionary Society for the portrait of Robert
Moffat and Mr J. P. Viljoen for the portrait of
Jan Viljoen.

Plates 21, 22, 24, 25, and 26 are from photo-
graphs by the author. The remaining plates are
reproduced from the original sketches by
Charles Bell and are reproduced by kind permission of the University of the Witwatersrand.

LIST OF PLATES

attacked by a lioness. The head, tail and paws of the lioness have been presented to Mzilikazi.

15. Matabele men dosing an ailing ox.
16. Robert Moffat in his declining years.
17. Jan Viljoen, famous Boer hunter and close friend of Mzilikazi.
18. Thomas Morgan Thomas, missionary of Inyati, who attended Mzilikazi during his last illness.
19. Inyati, the mission founded by Robert Moffat in Matabeleland (*circa* 1862).
20. Kuruman, Robert Moffat's mission station founded in 1820.
21. Robert Moffat's original home at the Kuruman mission station as it is today.
22. The church built by Moffat at Kuruman. In 1835 Mzilikazi helped the missionary to select rafters for the roof.
23. Nyamazana, the Antelope, in 1922. Originally a Swazi queen, she became one of Mzilikazi's wives.
24. The grave of uLoziba, Mzilikazi's favourite wife. Photograph taken by the author in 1960.
25. The main pass leading to the summit of Moshesh's mountain stronghold, Thaba Bosiu.
26. The author's guide at enTumbane, Mzilikazi's sepulchre in the Motopos, Rhodesia. Note how the mouth of the sacred cave has been sealed with stones.

PREFACE

WHILE writing this book I travelled, from time to time, to the territories of the tribes who, during the last century, were subjected to the cruel, despotic rule of Mzilikazi King of the Matabele. I also followed the trail blazed by Mzilikazi through Southern Africa, setting out from the tyrant's birthplace in Zululand and reaching my journey's end at the place of his entombment in the Matopo ranges of what was then Southern Rhodesia.

It was my privilege to conduct research among the Nguni tribes of the east coast of South Africa, the Southern Sotho of the Orange Free State and the then Basutoland Protectorate (now Lesotho), the Northern Sotho of the Northern and Eastern Transvaal, the Tswana tribes of the then British Bechuanaland (now Botswana) and the Western Transvaal, and the Makalanga, Mashona and Matabele (amaNdebele) tribal groups of Southern Rhodesia. In all parts of the sub-continent I received cordial assistance from tribal chieftains, their headmen and subjects, and also from white traders, missionaries, recruiters, farmers and Government officials.

In thanking the scores of people, both black and white, whose cooperation and encouragement greatly assisted my investigations into the life of Mzilikazi, I should like to record especially the names of Paramount Chiefs Nyangayezizwe Cyprian Bhekuzulu, direct descendant of Shaka and Dingane of the Zulu; Bathoen II, C.B.E., of the Bangwaketsi tribe; Kgari Sechele II, O.B.E., of the Bakwena; Kebalipile Montshioa of the Barolong; Chieftainess Mantsebo Seeiso (who was the Regent of the Basuto); and also Chiefs Letsie of Thaba Bosiu, Kuini M. Mopeli of Butha-Buthe, and Wilson K. Mosielele of the Bakgatla of Moshupha. These rulers appointed expert guides to conduct me to historic sites, royal kraals and important landmarks, and they all contributed

17

directly towards the happiness I experienced in their territories.

I am most grateful to my old friend Gatsha Mangosuthu kaMathole, Chief of the Buthelezi, for the constant interest he took in the progress of this book, and also to his mother, Princess Magogo uZulu kaDinizulu, for the titbits of information concerning Mzilikazi's early life she sent me from time to time.

I am deeply indebted to many white inhabitants of Southern Africa, both English- and Afrikaans-speaking, for guidance, advice and hospitality received during my research excursions. My special thanks go to Mr and Mrs Cormack-Thomson of Zeerust, Hubo Going of Kanye, D'Arcy Henry of Palapye, Ron and Mabel Guest of Bulawayo and Piet Coetsee of Enselsberg (Marico district).

I am thankful for the Open Sesame given me by the Rev. Humphrey Thompson to Robert Moffat's original homestead and church at Kuruman. I received similar cooperation from the missionaries resident at Inyati, Southern Rhodesia, the mission station established in 1859 in the vicinity of the barracks of Mzilikazi's Buffalo regiment.

I paid several rewarding visits to Commandant Carl Gronum, whose farm, Sendelingspos – Missionaries' Post – is situated in the Mosega valley, erstwhile headquarters of Mzilikazi's army. 'Oom' Carl guided me through the Marico district to the sites of Mzilikazi's former royal kraals and regimental barracks, and to the battlefields where once the conqueror waged the most bloody wars of his turbulent career. I greatly appreciate the time Commandant Gronum devoted to assisting me during my visit to Mosega, and I also appreciate the opportunity given me to read his unpublished records of the exploits of pioneer Boer hunters in Mzilikazi's domains.

Finally, my thanks are due to Lionel Kaplan for scrutinizing my manuscripts, to Moira Farmer and Joan Biddles of the Witwatersrand University Library for the unflagging attention given me from the moment I started searching for references, and to Connie, my wife, and Harold and Peter, my little boys, for the patience they exercised while the midnight oil was burning.

P.B.

Johannesburg

PART ONE

CHAPTER I

UNREST IN ZULULAND

*Zululand — Mzilikazi: birth and childhood
Dingiswayo's rise to power — Shaka usurps the Zulu throne
Ntombazi, collector of royal skulls*

IN all South Africa few territories compare in beauty with the land of the Zulu. It is a country of alluring contrasts, where in the mornings the valleys are draped in blankets of mist and the sun blazes down on smooth, moist mountain slopes. As the heat of the day mounts, the mists lift and the deep hollows become sultry. A miscellany of insect-chirping and bird-song vibrates in the foliage of every bush and in the dense growth of reeds fringing the mountain streams. During dry, austere winter months the great rivers of Zululand, flanked by sun-scorched boulders, flow tardily to the Indian Ocean, but when the summer storms explode over the hills they swell rapidly to become fierce torrents. In this lovely land are wooded gorges into the remotest depths of which the sun seldom penetrates. Cascades of fountain water tumble crazily from the sides of cliffs to the rocks hundreds of feet below.

Not all Zululand is undulating. There are vast, open expanses of lush pastures and stretches of bushveld where the umbrella tree, the thorny mimosa, the leathery candelabra euphorbia and the tree-aloe thrive. Towards the sea the heat is intense. It is along this coastal belt that the subtropical beauty of Zululand unfolds, for this is the region of fern, moss, exotic flowering shrub and tree.

The inhabitants of this great country are virile, dark-skinned Africans, descendants of the warlike Zulu who during the last century took the lives of many hundreds of British officers and men, and of the Boer Trekkers who ventured into the territory in search of grazing for cattle and sheep.

In the vicinity of Eshowe, Zululand's present-day capital, is a small, picturesque settlement named Emtonjaneni – the Place of the Fountain. Almost a century ago, at this very place, Lord Chelmsford, a famous British general, mustered his forces and prepared to crush the Zulu armies nestled in their Ulundi stronghold to the north. Stand at the old British fort at Emtonjaneni and face the setting sun; your eyes will fall upon a long, shallow valley bounded by a chain of rugged hills. This was the realm of the ancestral Zulu kings and also of Shaka the tyrant. This is the valley where, until the turn of the last century, 2,000 descendants of Chief Zulu, father of the tribe, lived peacefully with their herds of long-horned cattle.

Imagine this valley, and the rest of the surrounding country, that is the Zululand of today, inhabited by scores of independent clans, all pursuing the same mode of life and all talking a similar language. Each clan was ruled by an hereditary chief, a patriarch who enjoyed great privileges and whose authority was beyond question. Imagine Zululand as a land of plenty, where at regular intervals clusters of beehive huts were to be found straddled against mountain slopes, snuggled in the depths of fertile hollows and perched on the banks of streams. Zululand in olden times flowed with proverbial milk and honey. There was an abundance of game – elephant, lion and antelope – and skilful hunters seldom failed to keep cooking-pots replenished with the choicest of meat. And never did a day pass but guinea-fowl, pheasants and partridges were caught in the traps concealed in the vicinity of the cultivated fields.

This was a land of freedom with groups of talkative men who strolled leisurely along meandering cattle-tracks or narrow, eroded footpaths. In the fields beside the huts the women sang in chorus as with their hoes they cleared the crops of weeds. With the approach of twilight the heavy aroma of cowdung fires floated over huts and cattle-folds, and from out of the valleys arose a confusion of echoes: the elated conversation of women bearing faggots of firewood on their heads, the frantic lowing of milch cows, the chatter of birds preparing to roost and the eccentric chuckle of the hyena.

*

In 1790 a clan known as the Khumalo inhabited the section of Zululand that lies between the esiKwebezi and umKuze rivers and embraces the forest-clad mountains of Ngome. This clan was divided into three small groups: Chief Donda governed the Southern Khumalo; Beje, his cousin, the Central; and Mashobane, his uncle, the Northern. Like all peoples of the east coast of South Africa, the Khumalo were tillers, pastoralists and hunters, but so insignificant a clan were they in the vastness of Zululand that it is doubtful whether they were known beyond the territories of their immediate neighbours.

Along the eastern borders of the Khumalo lived the Ndwandwe, the people of Zwide, the most powerful of the chiefs north of the Black Umfolozi river. It was from among the daughters of Zwide that Mashobane of the Northern Khumalo chose Nompethu – the Maggot – as his first bride. This was to prove a most historic union, for out of it a famous child was born, a boy who would grow to become a formidable warrior, a tyrant who would conquer half a million square miles of Southern Africa and carry death and desolation to the homes of hundreds of thousands of freedom-loving people. His parents named him Mzilikazi – the Great Road.[1]

In 1790 not a soul in Zululand suspected the birth of Mzilikazi to be an ominous event, but the day would dawn when the very mention of his name would strike terror into the breasts of black men, and when his bloodthirsty regiments would wreak havoc among white men who dared approach his conquered domains.

It was the custom among the peoples of Zululand to send the heir to the throne into exile, lest he be killed by conspirators. Therefore, soon after Mzilikazi's birth, Mashobane called his councillors together and instructed them to conduct the baby boy and his mother safely to the royal kraal of Zwide, chief of the Ndwandwe. Here, in the country of his illustrious grandfather, Mzilikazi was to enjoy an instructive education, and indeed the magnificence of nature was his classroom.

1. Mzilikazi, the colloquial form of *umzilakazi*, is derived from the Zulu noun *umzila* – a 'broad track' and the augmentative suffix *'kazi*. Mzilikazi therefore means 'a great broad track' or simply, 'the Great Road'.

Like all other children in Zululand, Mzilikazi spent the first few years of his life in the company of his mother and the young girls of the kraal. At the age of five he received his first lessons in herding calves, and at twelve he became apprenticed to older boys, whose duty it was to tend the royal cattle. Not only did the herdboys learn to know the habits of their charges, but they also acquired the ability to identify them according to colour, markings, deformities, shape of horns, size and age. And in the course of their herding they learned to distinguish between edible and poisonous plants, bulbs and berries, and between dangerous and harmless reptiles, insects and animals. Experience taught them the colours, habits, calls and nesting-grounds of a great variety of birds, and also acquainted them with the names of the indigenous trees, shrubs and grasses that adorned their beautiful land.

Throughout the country in which Mzilikazi was reared huddles of beehive huts punctuated the hill-slopes and valleys. In each of these settlements, or kraals, the cattle-fold was situated, and within its stout palisades the cows were milked by herdboys and the oxen inspected by the men for disease and injury. Encircling the kraals were tall reed hedges that served to protect the inhabitants and their stock from wild beasts and thieves. As a member of the royal kraal, Mzilikazi would have looked upon these scattered groups of huts as the homes of the clan's proletariat who venerated his grandfather and obeyed his every command.

By the time Mzilikazi reached adolescence he was mindful of the duties he would perform one day as chief of the Northern Khumalo. He saw Zwide in the role of the ruler, supreme judge and priest of the Ndwandwe and he realized that the chief of a clan was the symbol of national unity. Almost daily he was reminded by his elders of the importance of adhering to the customs and traditions of the ancestors, and in religious matters he received first-hand experience.

On occasions of both rejoicing and sorrow the peoples of Zululand worshipped their ancestral spirits. To Nkulunkulu, their Supreme Being, they attributed the creation of their country, all creatures that inhabited it and the trees, flowers, hills and rivers that ornamented it. Mzilikazi learned that the spirits of the departed held sway over the lives of all peoples, and if misfortune was to be avoided it was imperative that regular prayers and sacrifices be offered to the shades of the clan.

The survival not only of Chief Zwide's Ndwandwe, but also of all the peoples of Zululand depended on the abundance of their crops and the health of their cattle. Clansmen lived in constant dread of the wrath of their ancestral spirits and the intrigues of witches. Before Mzilikazi grew into manhood he must undoubtedly have taken part in rituals dedicated to the spirit world, and he would have played a leading role in the *Umkhosi* – the First-Fruits ceremony – that commenced in December when the moon waxed full. On this auspicious occasion the medicine-men prepared sacred decoctions from a variety of ingredients: sea water, samples of the ripening crops, herbs and the flesh of the powerful and deadly lion, the elephant and the mamba. Mzilikazi must have taken a special interest in the role played in the *Umkhosi* by his grandfather. He would have noticed that the chief was kept in isolation and drank 'black medicines' which were reputed to be lethal to anyone else. During the First-Fruits ceremony, Zwide became fierce and terrifying, and over his face, body and limbs powders of various colours were daubed. While he was kept in seclusion Zwide was being purified, for, in due course, he would lead his subjects in the worship of the ancestral spirits.

Mzilikazi would have seen that the climax of the ceremony came with the strengthening of the warriors of the clan. On an appointed day a black bull, wild and unaccustomed to people, was brought into the cattle-fold of the royal kraal. It was provoked into fury, for it was the custom that it should be slain in combat with selected members of the chief's fighting forces. The men who took part in the killing of the black bull were allowed no weapons – indeed, they were to prove their valour before their ruler and the hordes of spectators by pummelling the beast to death with their bare hands. When, after a frenzied battle, the bull was beaten into submission by a myriad of clenched fists it was stabbed to death and its carcass cut into strips. The beef was cooked and medicines were added for the purpose of strengthening the warriors.

Many solemn rites accompanied the close of the First-Fruits

ceremony. In a near-by river the warriors bathed, while the chief washed in the calf-enclosure of the royal cattle-fold. A great feast followed. The ripening crops, hitherto taboo, were eaten with relish, and the people, now ritually cleansed, looked forward to a season of abundance. All that remained was for Zwide to watch the manoeuvres of his army, and to join his subjects in dancing and in singing the hymns of the First-Fruits ceremony.

Mzilikazi's boyhood training developed in him an avid love for cattle, one that would prevail throughout his turbulent career as a conqueror. Year after year Zwide and his subjects swelled the Ndwandwe herds by undertaking raids into the territories of neighbouring clans. This was an important feature in the way of life of all the peoples of Zululand, for the status of the chiefs and the wealth of their followers were determined by the number of cattle they owned. Cattle were only slaughtered for ritual purposes; beef was a delicacy eaten only when a beast had died in the veld and its carcass was brought to the kraal for skinning and dismembering. Cattle provided the settlements with milk, curdled milk, butter, hides for clothing and dung for plastering hut floors and for lining and sealing grain-pits. Their health and safety were the stock-breeders' daily concern.

Whenever diseases affected their beasts the Ndwandwe believed they had been bewitched by a sorcerer. Immediately precautions were taken. The animals were sprinkled with medicines prepared by the witch-doctors, and specially 'doctored' sticks were planted in the cattle-fold to ward off evil spirits. Never were menstruating women allowed among the cattle lest their indisposition affect the fertility of the cows.

When Mzilikazi approached his majority he and other Ndwandwe youths of his age-group were summoned by the elders of the clan to an initiation lodge, where after being circumcised by a medicine-man, they were subjected to a rigid disciplinary training in preparation for the responsibilities that lay ahead in adulthood. Their guardians impressed upon them the fact that the carefree days of youth were over, and advised them that when the lodge closed they should marry, rear families and set about accumulating cattle.

Mzilikazi and his companions graduated to manhood at the most crucial stage in the history of Zululand, for already in several sections of the territory ominous changes in the way of life of the people were afoot. Soon patriarchal rule would make way for despotism, and clansmen would no longer be free to roam the valleys and mountain slopes, or cultivate their fields and reap their harvests undisturbed. Where once herds of long-horned cattle had grazed languidly among the thorn-trees, now there would be times when they would stampede through the bush, in a dementia of terror, before the surge of fighting-men. The days when the menfolk had gossiped in the shade of a spreading tree and exchanged anecdotes over a communal pot of beer would vanish, and where plumes of smoke had risen from the open hearths at the huts now entire settlements would be consumed in conflagrations. The mountain streams would become tinged with blood and the rivers choked with the corpses of warriors.

The unrest that was to sweep Zululand began to the south of the Black Umfolozi among the Mthethwa clan, who inhabited the highlands between the Ntseleni river and the Indian Ocean. The Mthethwa were ruled by Dingiswayo, a young chief who, before ascending the throne, had undertaken a journey into the Cape Colony, where he had traversed the territories of several foreign tribes and had also come into contact with white men. So inspired was Dingiswayo by the diversity of experiences he had gained during his wanderings, and especially by the lessons he had learned in regard to the white man's military systems, that on returning to his homeland he could not but be displeased with the simple sedentary mode of life his own subjects pursued. He contrived to introduce some of the ideas he had gleaned from the customs of the peoples he visited, and to uplift the Mthethwa and convert them into the most powerful clan in Zululand.

During the first year of his reign Dingiswayo entered into regular trade with the Portuguese settlement at Delagoa Bay, and, in exchange for the oxen, elephant tusks, carved utensils, karosses and ornaments he had sent, he received blankets, beads, furniture and other European articles. Then he turned his attention to build-

ing a Mthethwa army. His first step was to discard the ancient
practice of circumcision, and to turn the traditional initiation
guilds into military barracks. He called up the men of the clan for
military service and grouped them according to their ages under
the supervision of commanders. Regiments were formed, each with
its own name, its own war-cries and songs, each dressed in distinctive regalia. There was not a regiment whose ox-hide shields
resembled exactly those of another, for each had its own colour
scheme – black, red, white or pied, or a combination of colours
and designs.

The Mthethwa warriors were drilled, taken on short manoeuvres, and trained in the most effective methods of attack and
defence. With pride Dingiswayo watched what was once a disorderly assemblage of cattle-raiders grow into a formidable army,
and as the other clans of Zululand had little or no knowledge
of organized warfare, he decided to invade their territories and
subjugate them.

One by one the peace-loving clans yielded to Dingiswayo's
army, for never in their history had they been attacked in so
brutal a fashion. But Dingiswayo was not intent on the wanton
destruction of the peoples he conquered; indeed, he commanded
his regiments to rout those who resisted the Mthethwa invasion,
but to spare those who submitted readily. Many chiefs surrendered to the aggressors without hesitation, and pledged their
allegiance to Dingiswayo. They and their subjects were left unharmed on condition that henceforth they recognized the chief of
the Mthethwa as their potentate.

Dingiswayo's dominions increased rapidly, his subjects multiplied, and his regiments became increasingly powerful. Within a
few years his supremacy was acknowledged even as far south as
the Tugela river. It proved popular among the subjugated clans,
for the paramount chief became known as a wise and sympathetic
ruler, one who was firm, yet exceedingly just, in matters concerning law and custom.

At about the time when Dingiswayo's army was embarking on
its invasion of Southern Zululand, Shaka the Zulu was conscrip-

ted into the Mthethwa regiment known as the iziCwe. Shaka, the illegitimate son of Senzangakhona, chief of the small Zulu clan, had been living among Dingiswayo's people since his early childhood, having been banished from his homeland because of the embarrassment that the circumstances of his birth were causing his father.

As a recruit in the iziCwe regiment Shaka was but one of many unknown young men of his age-group. He was tall, lean and robust, and, like his fellow-conscripts, he wore tufts of ox-tail on his arms and ankles, leather sandals, a cluster of furry tails about his waist, and a headdress of plumes. Secured to his left arm by leather loops was an oval ox-hide shield, and in his left hand he carried three long-shafted assegais. Shaka was not to remain unknown for long. He revelled in the training he and his comrades were receiving and the excitement that military life had to offer. In the field of battle both the Mthethwa commanders and their men marvelled at his extraordinary bravery, for Shaka refused to hurl his assegais into the ranks of his enemies – as was the practice among Dingiswayo's regiments – but rushed instead into the midst of his adversaries, engaging them in hand-to-hand combat and retiring swiftly before harm could befall him.

Shaka's capabilities soon earned him promotion within the iziCwe regiment, for as Dingiswayo's expeditions into neighbouring territories proved successful, and the Mthethwa empire started to expand, the Chief became aware that this young Zulu was receiving constant praise. He inquired about him, and learned of his utter disregard for his personal safety and his insatiable lust for killing. He sent for Shaka, and was surprised to discover that he was the son of Senzangakhona, one of the subjugated chiefs of the Mthethwa. He promoted him to a position within the iziCwe regiment where his qualities of leadership might be afforded full scope.

The wars of annexation continued in Southern Zululand, and Shaka was hailed as the hero of Dingiswayo's army. In return for his many achievements on the battlefield the Chief bestowed generous gifts of cattle upon him. Now the veteran commander of the iziCwe regiment retired. Dingiswayo ordered the regiments to

assemble, and announced that he had appointed Shaka, the dauntless fighter, whose exploits all present had had occasion to extol,
as the new leader of the iziCwe regiment. On that eventful day
none could have been prouder of this promotion than the unwanted son of the Chief of the Zulu.

In 1816, when Shaka was in his late twenties, Senzangakhona
died, and the Zulu were plunged into mourning. It had been Dingiswayo's wish that Shaka should become the new Chief, despite
the fact that Shaka realized that his illegitimate birth would dis-
qualify his claim to the throne. Before Dingiswayo could act in
the matter on Shaka's behalf, Sigujana, the heir-apparent, was
proclaimed Chief of the Zulu. Dingiswayo was gravely concerned,
but unnecessarily so, for already Shaka was conspiring to overthrow the Zulu royal house.

Shaka dispatched Ngwadi, a half-brother who had lived with
him in Mthethwa country, into the valley in which the kraal of
the new Zulu Chief was situated. On reaching his destination
Ngwadi begged to be given asylum, for, he explained, Dingiswayo
had executed Shaka and sought to kill him as well. His request
was granted. He assassinated the Chief at his earliest opportunity.

By the time the bewildered Zulu clan had observed its second
spell of mourning, Ngwadi had slipped over the Mthethwa border. Shaka was elated by the success of his mission, and Dingiswayo called out the iziCwe regiment and instructed it to accompany its Zulu commander to the west. Shaka bade his mentor
farewell and departed.

The sudden appearance of the regiment, led by Shaka, so terrified the grief-stricken Zulu that none of them was prepared to
oppose its surge into the valley. Shaka had himself installed as
Chief, and selected a site for his new kraal.

Before long, at regular intervals, groups of workers were planting flexible poles in a circle, and were bending them towards the
centre to form a ring of dome-shaped frames. Talented fingers were
entwining pliable sticks with the poles and binding them firmly at
the joints. Bundle upon bundle of thatching-grass was being lifted

on to each of the structures, and the beehive huts of the royal kraal that Shaka was to name Bulawayo – the Place of Killing – were emerging in the depths of the valley. And when once they had been completed, the huts of Bulawayo formed a great ring, in the centre of which Shaka's rambling stockade was situated.

Having settled in his new kraal, Shaka concentrated on organizing a Zulu army. He mustered the menfolk of the clan and sorted them into age-groups. Those who were too old or feeble for military service he sent back to their kraals, but decreed that henceforth able-bodied men would be warriors, and as such they must banish all thought of marriage from their minds. Having formed all his available manpower into regiments, Shaka removed the youths from the circumcision guilds and brought them to Bulawayo, where, under his personal supervision, they became the Fasimba, the most fearsome of Zulu regiments.

In Mthethwa country Shaka's reputation as an intrepid fighter had arisen from his liking for hand-combat, but although victorious regiments had sung his praises, and Dingiswayo had lavished honours on him, few of the warriors had ever employed his tactics, and the Chief had insisted that his enemies be subjugated and not annihilated. Now at last, as the Chief of the Zulu, Shaka was able to dictate the strategy his own army would use. He abolished the throwing-assegai and equipped his regiments with long-bladed stabbing-spears he himself had designed. He trained his warriors in the art of in-fighting; inculcated into them a spirit of merciless destruction, and impressed upon them that in future when they engaged their enemies in battle they must conquer or die fighting.

The Zulu invasions soon to follow proved the most devastating the clans of the east coast had experienced. Settlements went up in flames, clansmen who took up their weapons in defence of their families were butchered, and herds of cattle, maddened by the pandemonium that enveloped the kraals, bolted from their enclosures. Shaka's tyranny was unleashed with a vengeance. Not even Dingiswayo could persuade the Zulu conqueror to staunch the flow of blood in Southern Zululand.

Shaka ceded all the territories he conquered to the Mthethwa empire, and by 1818 thirty chiefs recognized Dingiswayo as the paramount ruler of Zululand south of the Black Umfolozi.

And Dingiswayo might well have turned to incorporating the peoples north of the river within his dominion had not an unexpected change of events taken place.

In Ndwandwe country Zwide, the grandfather of Mzilikazi, was watching Dingiswayo's achievements with covetous eyes. Zwide was not a great warrior but during recent years he too had embarked on the subjugation of a few defenceless clans in the neighbourhood of his territory. Zwide relied on cunning to conquer his enemies rather than on the strength of his forces. He was a brooder, a treacherous adversary whose schemes were invariably inspired by his mother, a witch-like woman named Ntombazi. A firm bond of friendship existed between the mother and her son; indeed, there were occasions when Zwide routed a clan, decapitated its chief and returned to his kraal to present the royal head to Ntombazi. The old woman became a collector of chiefs' heads, and, in a hut specially set aside as a museum, she decorated the thatch with the trophies her son took in battle.

There was no more valuable prize Zwide could wish to win for his mother than the head of Dingiswayo. He knew his own forces could never match the powerful Mthethwa army in combat, but he believed he could weave a net in which to capture the great Dingiswayo.

Zwide set about his plan by invading the territories of clans the Mthethwa had already subjugated. Not only did he wreak havoc among Dingiswayo's vassals, but he also decapitated their chiefs and absconded with their heads. When reports of these atrocities reached Dingiswayo he immediately led his army towards Zwide's country, and sent word to Shaka to muster his Zulu regiments and join him in the hills of present-day Nongoma.

On reaching this appointed place the Mthethwa forces bivouacked, feasted and whetted their assegais while they waited for Shaka to arrive. Dingiswayo, in the company of a few of his retainers, decided to stroll unescorted on to the hill-slopes to spy out the positions of the enemy. He was captured by Ndwandwe scouts, who hustled him off to their headquarters, and handed him over to Zwide. Dingiswayo was put to death. His head was removed and sent to Ntombazi's hut to join the old woman's collection of grinning exhibits. Medicine-men scraped the grease from Dingiswayo's head-ring and helped themselves to portions of his corpse with which to prepare decoctions for their medicine-horns. What remained of the body was hurriedly buried.

Zwide called his forces into action, and sent them careering across the veld to the hill on which the Mthethwa were encamped. By this time the invaders had received the news of Dingiswayo's capture and were retreating homewards. Their ranks were flung into confusion as the Ndwandwe fell upon them and drove them towards the Black Umfolozi. For the first time in almost ten years Dingiswayo's army was routed.

The Mthethwa mourned the death of their chief, and feared that, as they had been denied the right to bury his corpse and perform the rites so essential to assuring his soul safe passage to the world of the ancestral spirits, they were doomed to eventual destruction. The close of the reign of Dingiswayo, the chief who had instigated the fashion of internecine warfare in Zululand, could not have been less dignified.

CHAPTER 2

MZILIKAZI'S TREACHERY

Mzilikazi's father decapitated
Mzilikazi becomes Chief of the Northern Khumalo
He flees to Shaka — Zwide routed
Birth of the Shakan dynasty

WHEN Shaka received Dingiswayo's call to arms he set out at once towards Zwide's country with a strong Zulu contingent, but on reaching the Ndwandwe–Khumalo frontier he was intercepted by Chief Donda, Mzilikazi's cousin, and warned of the tragedy that had befallen the Mthethwa. Fearing that if he were to fall into Zwide's hands he would suffer the same fate as Dingiswayo, Shaka turned his men about, and led them back to Bulawayo.

Zwide was furious when he learned of this incident, and decided Donda and his clanlet should be destroyed. The Ndwandwe regiments advanced westwards, decimated the Southern Khumalo and beheaded both Donda and his heir. Then they struck due north to the Central Khumalo clan, only to find that Beje the Chief, another of Mzilikazi's cousins, had already heard of their approach and had fled with his subjects into the depths of the Ngome Forest. Zwide's warriors moved on into the territory of the Northern Khumalo, massacred the defenceless inhabitants, besieged the royal kraal, murdered Chief Mashobane, Mzilikazi's father, and collected his head. They returned home, bringing with them a large haul of booty-cattle and also three new trophies for Ntombazi's hut.

Mzilikazi hated Zwide from the moment he learned of the Ndwandwe atrocities in Khumalo country, but he was careful not to betray his feelings for fear that, like Donda and Mashobane, he might be put to death. He might have fled the country had not Zwide sent for him and told him to return to his homeland and occupy the throne Mashobane had been forced to vacate.

Mzilikazi collected his possessions, took leave of his grandfather and his boyhood friends and strode out to the west. Now a strapping man of twenty-seven, he was welcomed home by his father's subjects and installed amidst great celebration as the chief of the Northern Khumalo clan.

During the early winter of 1818 Mzilikazi was informed by his subjects who lived close to the Ndwandwe border that Zwide had sent a punitive expedition against Shaka and had been driven back with heavy losses at Qokli, a prominent hill to the immediate south of the White Umfolozi. At one stage of the battle, the Ndwandwe had faced extermination, Mzilikazi was told, for Shaka's forces had advanced in crescent formation and had almost encircled them. And although the bulk of the invading army had managed to escape across the White Umfolozi, hundreds of corpses, including those of five of Zwide's sons, were left on the blood-soaked slopes of Qokli hill.

Mzilikazi became ill at ease. Since the murder of Mashobane he had lived in dread of an attack from the Ndwandwe, and now that Shaka was emerging as the most powerful chief in Zululand, he feared the time was drawing near when the Khumalo would be subjected to Zulu rule. He collected his people and cattle and took them across the White Umfolozi to Bulawayo, where he surrendered them to Shaka. Mzilikazi begged Shaka for protection, promised to serve him, and declared the Khumalo people would welcome the opportunity to join the ranks of the Zulu regiments. Shaka was happy to incorporate the Khumalo with his clan. He and Mzilikazi became friends from the moment of their meeting.

In 1818, more than in any previous year, intrigues and enmities disrupted the traditional mode of life of the clans of Zululand. Rumours of Zwide's vendettas against the Khumalo peoples and also of Shaka's destruction of defenceless clans swept through the east-coast territories. Chiefs fled from their kraals and offered their allegiance either to Zwide or Shaka. The day was approaching fast when the armies of the Zulu and the Ndwandwe would meet again on the battlefield.

Shaka continued to train his forces. He also formed the auxiliaries received from his vassal clans into regiments and appointed Mzilikazi as one of his group captains. He attended to the affairs of the Mthethwa, among whom there had been political confusion ever since Dingiswayo's death: the heir-apparent was a minor so, according to custom, could not be proclaimed chief until his coming of age; several prominent men were aspiring to the regency of the clan, but each of their nominations was being challenged by the councillors. Shaka intervened. He selected Mlandela, a close relative of Dingiswayo and former member of the Zulu army, as the new regent of the Mthethwa, whilst he himself became the commander-in-chief of Dingiswayo's forces. Shaka's claim to the paramountcy over the clans of Southern Zululand was now consolidated, and the foundation on which he would build his Zulu empire was laid.

Barely a year had passed since the Zulu–Ndwandwe encounter at Qokli hill when Shaka received word from one of his spies that Zwide was preparing to advance over the Black Umfolozi into Zulu territory. Shaka ordered all the non-combatants of the tribe to collect their stores from the grain-pits, to round up their cattle, to clear the fields of corn, and to proceed into the rugged chain of hills in the region of the great Nkandla forest.

The Ndwandwe army set out for the south. It was twice the size of the one that had fared so ingloriously at Qokli hill, and its warriors were equipped with a new type of assegai designed to match, in close combat, the Zulu stabbing-spear. The commander-in-chief was Soshangane, a brilliant tactician, who in years to come would rise to fame as an African conqueror. Zwide preferred not to take part in the invasion and encamped not far north of the Zulu border.

The Ndwandwe crossed the Black and White Umfolozi rivers, skirted Qokli hill, and pressed on to Bulawayo. They found the Zulu kraals deserted, the cattle-folds empty and the fields stripped of corn. And Soshangane might well have halted to consider the question of rations for his men – for armies always foraged in the countries they invaded – but he learned that the Zulu were close by, and decided to overtake them and destroy them. Little did he know that the regiments he was pursuing were decoys deployed by Shaka to lure the Ndwandwe southwards.

Three days passed and the Ndwandwe failed to make contact with the enemy. They were compelled to conserve the rations they had brought and dared not risk sending hunting-parties in search of game lest they be captured by Shaka's elusive regiments. On reaching the Tugela river Soshangane abandoned his pursuit of the Zulu and retraced his steps along the eastern slopes of the Nkandla ranges. By this time his warriors were becoming footsore, fatigued and hungry, and were being harassed by groups of Zulu who would rush on them suddenly from the shadows of the woods.

The Ndwandwe retired to a coppice and bivouacked, and when darkness fell and they lay down to sleep one of Shaka's regiments of veteran warriors set upon them with stabbing-spears and then vanished swiftly into the night. Next day the Ndwandwe retreated into the Umhlatuze valley. Shaka hurled his entire army into the valley and brought about what is referred to in Zulu history as the Ndwandwe Fiasco.

So sudden and devastating was the Zulu attack that Soshangane started withdrawing his army across the Umhlatuze river. In a desperate effort to avoid destruction the Ndwandwe fought bravely, but they were hewn down in the tardy flow of the Umhlatuze until the waters ran red with blood and the banks were strewn with corpses and wounded men writhing in agony. Night saved the Ndwandwe from annihilation, and Soshangane and his depleted columns struggled homeward while the Zulu waited for the dawn.

With his aggressors in full flight Shaka sent two fleet-footed regiments ahead of them to capture Zwide. On reaching the Chief's kraal the Zulu warriors discovered that Zwide had already escaped across the Pongolo river in the north. They fired the royal kraal, took old Ntombazi – the collector of heads – captive, and set out to pillage and sack the remaining settlements in Ndwandwe territory.

Meanwhile, Soshangane's routed warriors struggled back to

their homeland only to find their huts razed to the ground, their womenfolk and children butchered or missing, and their Chief's kraal in ruins. They dispersed in various directions in a bid to save their lives from the Zulu regiments that continued to hound them through the country. In the company of a small group of men Soshangane managed to reach the coast, but on finding that there were Zulu looters in the area he turned northwards. He was not heard of again until years later when he emerged as the conqueror of the tribes of Portuguese East Africa and the potentate of the Shangana empire.[1]

Of Zwide little more need be told other than after crossing the Pongolo he roamed the domains of chiefs who regarded him with suspicion and were therefore hostile towards him. Eventually he settled in the present-day Barberton district. It is said that although he had not yet turned sixty Zwide was transformed by the ravages of malaria into a decrepit, wizened and feeble-minded old man. Five years after his flight from Shaka he died, and his body was laid to rest at Evande.

With the destruction of the Ndwandwe Shaka became the Paramount Chief of all the clans on both sides of the Black Umfolozi. His great empire, now to become known as kwaZulu – Zululand – extended from the Pongolo in the north to the Tugela in the south, from the Nyati or Buffalo river in the west to the Indian Ocean in the east. When mopping up operations were completed in Zwide's dominions, Shaka saw personally to the execution of Ntombazi, and other Ndwandwe celebrities, and then he returned in triumph with his regiments to Bulawayo.

Details of the actual part played by Mzilikazi in the Zulu–Ndwandwe campaign are obscure, but today in Zululand and other parts of Southern Africa, when greybeards discuss the exploits of their forefathers, they claim it was in this battle that

1. After the 'Ndwandwe Fiasco' yet another of Zwide's fugitive commanders proceeded to the north, where eventually he conquered the tribes of Nyasaland and founded the powerful aNgoni tribe of East Africa. He was Zwangendaba, originally of the Jele clanlet of Zululand.

Mzilikazi proved so dauntless a warrior that he won Shaka's admiration and became his favourite. Shaka was undoubtedly impressed by Mzilikazi's capabilities, for it is known he rewarded him with cattle and took him as one of his advisers.

In 1819 Mzilikazi and his small following were domiciled at Bulawayo. The long, troubled winter passed, and with the arrival of the spring rains in October the Zulu tilled their fields and planted their crops. A period of comparative peace set in while Shaka took stock of his newly won territories.

Suddenly Shaka decided to move his capital from the valley where for centuries his ancestors had ruled over the small Zulu clan. In search of a new site he journeyed towards the sea, and on a bushy ridge overlooking the serene Umhlatuze valley, seventeen miles from where Eshowe stands today, he ordered his people to start building a new Bulawayo, the royal kraal later to be known as Gibixhegu.[1]

Gibixhegu was to grow into a mammoth settlement. It was described by Nathaniel Isaacs, an English Jew who arrived at Port Natal in 1825 and visited Shaka soon after, as follows: 'The circumference of the imperial kraal I should think would exceed three miles, and it includes within its space about 1,400 huts.' Referring to Shaka's seraglio, Isaacs added: 'The King's palace, which is situated at the head of the kraal, on the eminence, comprises about 100 huts, in which none but girls live, as men are not allowed to enter the palace.'[2]

It was in this royal kraal that Mzilikazi was to enjoy two more years of Shaka's friendship, and where he would dream of the day when he would be an independent ruler and as great a conqueror as his Zulu overlord.

Since the murder of his father events had moved rapidly in Mzilikazi's life, but they had provided him only with short-lived

1. Meaning 'Take out the old man', this was the name given to the second Bulawayo kraal after Shaka had sorted out the greybeards among his subjects and executed them because they were no longer fit for military service.

2. Nathaniel Isaacs, *Travels and Adventures in Eastern Africa*, vol. 1, p. 73.

periods of happiness and contentment. He had been installed as Chief of the Northern Khumalo sooner than he had expected, only to have been compelled thereafter to abandon his royal kraal, his homeland and his right to rule over his clan; he had had no option but to seek sanctuary in the domain of a chief not many years his senior, a man who once had been regarded by his people as an outcast, but had eventually succeeded Senzangakhona of the Zulu, not by right of birth, but by force of arms; he could not deny that Shaka had treated him kindly, accepted him as a companion, and granted him positions of status both in Court circles and in the Zulu army; and yet he was dissatisfied, for he believed he was destined not to a life of subservience, but to one where he would enjoy supreme authority. He brooded. He contrived to snatch the first opportunity to free himself, and his people, from Shaka's influence.

In June 1822 Shaka announced that he intended expanding his southern dominions beyond the Tugela, and would also send some of his regiments over the north-western borders of Zululand on cattle-raiding excursions. He suggested that the Sotho clan of Chief Ranisi be attacked; and such was his faith in Mzilikazi's qualities of leadership and his loyalty to the Zulu cause that Shaka appointed him commander-in-chief of the expedition. Ranisi's people were considered 'foreigners' by the Zulu. They belonged to the great family of Sotho tribes of South Africa, and although, like the clans of the east coast, they were tillers, pastoralists and hunters, they spoke a language completely unintelligible to the Zulu. Mzilikazi accepted his first independent command with gratitude, and agreed to invade Ranisi's territory. Thereupon Shaka declared he had also decided the time had come for the Khumalo to return to their homeland and for Mzilikazi to be reinstated as their Chief. He would expect Mzilikazi first to lead his subjects back to their kraals and then to set out, with the regiments under his command, against Ranisi's clan.

Mzilikazi saw Shaka for the last time on the parade ground of Gibixhegu. Standing at the head of two regiments, made up mainly of Khumalo warriors and other Zulu vassals, he led his people in shouting *'Bayete!'* the royal salute. He greeted Shaka and moved away at a trot to the gates of the kraal. He struck out for the valley where the first Bulawayo had stood; he guided his followers across the White Umfolozi, traversed with them the undulating regions below the Ngome forest, and reached the kraal whence he had fled three years ago.

After resting a day Mzilikazi and his regiments continued to the Zulu border and pounced on Ranisi's clan. They met with little opposition; indeed, no sooner had they scattered the Chief's defenceless hordes than they collected their cattle and drove them back to Mzilikazi's kraal. Now with a valuable haul of cattle in his possession, it riled Mzilikazi to think that, because he was a vassal of Shaka, he would be obliged to deliver the spoils of battle to Gibixhegu, and that if he refused to do so he would be arrested and executed. He wondered whether it would not be worth the risk to defy Shaka by keeping all of Ranisi's cattle for himself.

Mzilikazi's return from the border was followed by victory celebrations which included feasting, dancing and the chanting of praise-songs. When eventually the excitement died down, and the routine of tribal life was resumed, it occurred to Shaka's representatives, who had accompanied the marauding expedition, that the booty-cattle should have already been dispatched to Gibixhegu. Respectfully, they reminded Mzilikazi of the oversight and added that Shaka had been informed of Ranisi's defeat. Day after day Mzilikazi procrastinated and the representatives became suspicious. At length, when they were told that Mzilikazi had no intention of surrendering the herds, they were taken aback.

They predicted that, like many other upstarts who had dared to incur Shaka's wrath, Mzilikazi was doomed to face a cruel death.

CHAPTER 3

FLIGHT FROM ZULULAND

Mzilikazi defies Shaka — Boulder bombardment
Mzilikazi betrayed — Battle on enTubeni
Mzilikazi escapes — He destroys Nyoka

ONE morning as Mzilikazi sauntered towards his cattlefold, his attention was drawn to the kraal-gates, where a small party of Zulu dignitaries stood talking to an *induna*[1] of the Khumalo regiments. He beckoned them to enter, and scrutinized them as they swaggered towards him. They were Zulu noblemen from Gibixhegu. Dressed in full battle attire they carried shields and assegais, and on their heads they wore clusters of *sakabuli*[2] tail plumes. Mzilikazi greeted them with calculated frigidity, and asked them what their business was in Khumalo country.

The men explained they were envoys sent by the great Shaka to inquire of Mzilikazi when the booty-cattle might be expected to arrive at Gibixhegu. Shaka was growing impatient, for many days had already passed since the news of Ranisi's defeat had been reported to him.

Mzilikazi smiled derisively. There would be no delivery of cattle to Gibixhegu, he assured his visitors, but if Shaka insisted that the herds the Khumalo had won in battle belonged to him, he should consider fetching them himself.

The envoys were thunderstruck and glared at each other incredulously. Then one of them spoke up: he advised Mzilikazi that, for his own sake, he should take heed of the law which demanded that the spoils of war be presented, without delay, to the potentate of Zululand. If Mzilikazi chose to defy the royal

1. An officer.   2. The widow-bird.

decree he must prepare himself and his subjects for Shaka's vengeance. Mzilikazi became angry at the Zulu's impudence and ordered the arrest of the whole party.

Now, with a stabbing-spear in his hand, Mzilikazi approached the envoys and sliced the *sakabuli* plumes from their heads. He told them to hurry back to their master and report what had befallen them in the kraal of Mzilikazi, Chief of the Khumalo.

Mzilikazi called his people together and sent them, with their belongings and stock, into the esiKwebezi valley, and across the river to an afforested hill called enTubeni – the Pass. The two Khumalo regiments followed close behind, conducted the women and children into the depths of the forest and then climbed to the crest of the hill, where they entrenched themselves. Mzilikazi considered enTubeni an impregnable stronghold, for, apart from the fact that it was embraced by precipices, there was only one trail that led to its summit, and the Khumalo alone knew where to find it.

During the next few days Mzilikazi set his men packing mounds of boulders along the edges of the krantzes or walls of rock, for he had planned to repulse Shaka's punitive forces with weapons other than stabbing-spears. The sentinels looked out over the mountain ranges, the valleys, the streams and parklands that lay beneath them. In due course they detected Shaka's iziMpohlo – Bachelor – regiment streaming into the esiKwebezi valley. The Zulu followed the tracks of the Khumalo cattle towards the river and losing them at the water's edge, crossed over to the opposite bank and moved slowly along the base of enTubeni. Then they started to climb the slopes of the hill. They crawled along an eroded cattle-track, hacked their way through an entanglement of undergrowth, reached the first of the precipices and paused to consider whether they should attempt to scale its jagged face.

A section of the van of the regiment moved on to inspect the gradient of the slopes ahead. Suddenly, to their dismay, the Zulu heard the krantzes explode above them, and saw a multitude of boulders descending from the sky like a flight of mountain vultures. Panic-stricken, they turned to flee, but so treacherous was the terrain that, for a moment, they stood as if rooted to the ground. The boulders burst into their midst, crushing some of them and bowling others over into the surrounding crevices and trees. Another deluge of boulders came flying and bouncing towards them, and soon not a member of the small group of warriors was alive.

The rearguard of the Bachelor regiment was out of range of the boulders, and it retreated in confusion down the side of enTubeni. The Zulu regrouped in the valley, and waited while their commanders conferred about the tactics they should employ in order to oust Mzilikazi from his fortress.

Next day the iziMpohlo approached enTubeni from a different angle, but no sooner had they reached the krantzes than they were driven back by another of Mzilikazi's bombardments. The officers conferred a second time, and for the following reason they decided to call off the assault on enTubeni: they had agreed that the izi-Mpohlo regiment could not expect to defeat the Khumalo unless it could come to grips with them; there was no pass that they knew of which would lead them to Mzilikazi's fortress, and the forest was so dense it often concealed the krantzes from which the boulders were being thrown. They called their men to order, and set out to Gibixhegu to report the failure of their mission to Shaka.

It was a rule in the Zulu army that if the warriors displayed cowardice on the battlefield they would be put to death with the executioner's club, the impalement stick or by being fed to the hyenas or crocodiles. For a regiment to return to headquarters without having defeated the enemy was regarded by Shaka as tantamount to cowardice; indeed, from time to time, groups of so-called cowards were clubbed to death at the isiHlahla Samagwala – the Coward's Bush.[1] When the iziMpohlo regiment returned

1. The original isiHlahla Samagwala, a *kei*-apple bush where Shaka once executed the cowards of his army, may be found today along the Empangeni-Eshowe road. It is conspicuously situated about half a mile from the small monument that marks the site of Shaka's Gibixhegu kraal.

from its ill-fated expedition into Mzilikazi's country there were whispers at Gibixhegu that Shaka would order its destruction. The officers explained to their king that the enTubeni stronghold was impregnable and that as long as Mzilikazi and his people chose to occupy it the Khumalo would never be conquered. Instead of condemning the warriors to death Shaka scoffed at them, and he seemed almost happy that Mzilikazi had managed to drive them back. The councillors of Gibixhegu were astounded. They could see that Shaka's love for Mzilikazi had not changed, albeit of late he had been defied and insulted by him.

As months passed and it became apparent to the councillors that Shaka had no intention of sending a second expedition against the Khumalo, they criticized him and reminded him that when a bull-calf challenged the bull of the herd it was always punished. It was only when public opinion at the royal kraal became so inflamed at Mzilikazi's persistent flouting of Zulu authority that Shaka agreed reluctantly to invade Khumalo country. The Belebele, or Endless Worry, brigade was instructed to go out and disperse the Khumalo, but to capture Mzilikazi and bring him unharmed to Gibixhegu.

Meanwhile, Mzilikazi was still on the enTubeni hill, for he knew the Zulu would return. Having succeeded in avoiding defeat in his first encounter with Shaka's forces, he was confident his regiments would never be defeated in the krantzes. But he made one important change in his strategy: he split the non-combatants into two groups, keeping one on enTubeni and sending the other into the Ngome forest.

Towards the close of 1822 the Belebele brigade set out and reached the esiKwebezi valley early in the New Year. On arriving at the foot of enTubeni, it encamped among the trees while scouts stole into the slopes in order to ascertain the whereabouts of Mzilikazi's men. When the officers were informed that the Khumalo had been sighted in the krantzes they sent more scouts to search for the secret pass, for they were reluctant to expose their warriors to the onslaught of Mzilikazi's boulders. But the pass was not found, and the Zulu believed there was no hope of capturing Mzilikazi on the hill.

It was then that Nzeni, Mzilikazi's half-brother, walked into the camp to surrender himself to the Zulu and to offer to lead them to the Khumalo by way of the secret pass. Nzeni was an ambitious young warrior who resented the fact that Mzilikazi, and not he, had become the chief of the clan after Mashobane's murder. He had quarrelled frequently with Mzilikazi over trivial matters and during the past few months, when the defences on enTubeni were being prepared in anticipation of the second encounter with the Zulu, he had planned to betray his half-brother and claim the chieftaincy of the Khumalo for himself.

Although at first the leaders of the Belebele brigade were suspicious of Nzeni, they were eventually convinced that he was as keen as they were to oust Mzilikazi from enTubeni. They accepted his services as their guide, and then convened a council of war to discuss tactics. It was decided that a section of the brigade should stage a series of manoeuvres and feints in the vicinity of the krantzes and while it was occupying the attention of the Khumalo the rest of the warriors would follow Nzeni along the pass and attack Mzilikazi from the rear.

Therefore, in full view of the Khumalo, the Zulu rose and started to climb the hill-slopes; but no sooner were they engulfed by the trees than they split up as arranged, one section proceeding towards the krantzes, and the other, by way of a circuitous route, towards that part of the forest where the pass would be found.

Mzilikazi's forces watched the enemy as it approached. They found it odd, however, that in the course of the next few hours the Zulu crept in and out of the trees and rocks beneath them, yet never ventured close enough to be bombarded with boulders. It was some time later, when the forest resounded to the piercing screams of women and children, that the Khumalo guessed they had been deceived.

enTubeni was thrown into confusion. The Zulu, led by Nzeni, streamed on to the summit, where they were attacked by a group of Khumalo warriors. A fierce tussle took place. It ended when the Zulu surrounded the Khumalo group, closed in on it, and wiped it out. Meanwhile, a rabble of women, children, greybeards and their livestock had scrambled a short way down the pass, and were moving deep into the forest. Mzilikazi and the majority of his forces had scattered pell-mell and had gone into hiding in the undergrowth, the chasms and rocky outcrops. The Zulu dared not follow them, fearing if they were to get lost in the forest they would not find their way back to the esiKwebezi valley. They retraced their steps along the pass, and linked up with the remainder of the Belebele brigade that awaited them at the base of enTubeni.

When darkness fell the Khumalo stole from their hide-outs and looked down on the fires that blinked at them from the enemy camp, and, until well into the night, they listened to the singing of the Belebele warriors. Next morning, at daybreak, Mzilikazi's sentinels climbed to the highest points of enTubeni, and as the sun lit up the countryside they beheld the Zulu retiring slowly out of the esiKwebezi valley. Fearing the enemy might be withdrawing merely as a hoax to lure the Khumalo from their hiding-places, Mzilikazi dispatched spies to follow them. Towards evening, when these men returned, they reported the Zulu had progressed far to the south and were homeward bound.

During the next few days messengers moved through the forest to inform the Khumalo that they must proceed with their cattle to a meeting-place, where Mzilikazi would await them. In this way Mzilikazi rallied his warriors and effected a juncture with the refugees from enTubeni hill and the Ngome forest. He led his reunited clan – women, children and three hundred warriors – to the north-west through the present Vryheid district.

On reaching the territory of the emaNgweni clan of Northern Zululand, Mzilikazi visited the Chief, Nyoka – the Snake – to tell him of the Khumalo's arrival on the border, and also to beg him for hospitality. But when Nyoka learned Mzilikazi was fleeing from Shaka he would offer no assistance. He explained that the emaNgweni were vassals of the Zulu, and therefore if they harboured Shaka's enemies they would be destroyed. Mzilikazi understood, for he himself had until recently been one of Shaka's vassal chiefs.

Then Mzilikazi asked that he be allowed to lead the Khumalo

47

through Nyoka's country to the west. The Snake wavered. It struck him that if he did not resist Mzilikazi's advance it would not be long before Shaka summoned him to Gibixhegu to stand trial as a traitor. He answered Mzilikazi obliquely, and then ignored him completely.

Mzilikazi grew impatient. Had he not wanted to avoid exposing his women and children to unnecessary danger, he would have dropped the formalities of etiquette and called his regiments to attack the timid chief and his clan. He reflected that, for the time being at least, it would suit him to be discreet.

Towards evening, on hearing Nyoka had sent word to Shaka that the Khumalo were encamped on the emaNgweni border, Mzilikazi took action. He informed his followers they must be ready to continue the journey northwards at a moment's notice. During the night, whilst the Khumalo slept, Mzilikazi schemed, and in the early hours of the morning he roused the camp, commanded one of his regiments to proceed with the women, children and cattle, and the other to take up its shields and stabbing-spears and to follow him.

Mzilikazi and his warriors advanced to the outskirts of Nyoka's kraal, encircled it, squatted in the grass, and waited. When the chirping of the birds rose from the trees, and the first pale light of dawn appeared in the east, the men moved cautiously forward and padded into the settlement. They crawled into the inky shadows of the beehive huts, and plunged their spears into the bodies of the sleepers who lay snuggled in their skin-blankets. Death-groans shook the inhabitants from their slumbers. Wails of agony mounted to shrieks of terror. Within moments, those who had not yet received a Khumalo blade rushed to the narrow doorways, and vied with one another to escape into the morning air. The few people who did manage to force their way out of the huts were plucked off by warriors who stood waiting for them outside.

By mid-morning Mzilikazi had wiped out Nyoka and his people, had rounded up their cattle, looted their grain-pits and set their kraal alight. The regiment struck out to the north, meeting no opposition along the way, and overtook the rest of the clan in the course of the afternoon.

Flight from Zululand

A long, arduous trek lay ahead for the Khumalo. Soon they would be crossing the border of Zululand into a vast country populated by a mosaic of foreign clans and tribes.

CHAPTER 4

THE PEOPLES OF THE INTERIOR

West of the Drakensberg – Land of foreign tribes

So far, our story has been confined to the territories east of the
Drakensberg mountains, to events that led to an era of internecine warfare and brought about the birth of conquerors of
clans. Now we must move to the west of the great barrier, into the
interior of South Africa, and consider briefly some of the peoples
who would soon be playing leading roles in the life-drama of
Mzilikazi.

The east-coast regions of South Africa, inhabited by African
peoples classified as the Nguni,[1] comprise mountains, forests,
bushveld and plains; the valleys are watered with wild rivers, the
ravines with springs, and the gorges with waterfalls. The fertile soil,
soaked throughout the summer months by a generous rainfall,
yields not only the most luscious of green pasturage, but also the
richest of harvests.

In the country west of the Drakensberg the scenery and climatic conditions vary considerably. As one advances from the east
the land rises gradually in a succession of steps, until eventually a
vast plateau is reached, in the centre of which is a basin. This part
of South Africa is drained by the Vaal and Upper Orange rivers.
The highveld, although undulating in places, is predominantly
flat, and as one proceeds either to the distant west or the north,
regions densely wooded with indigenous bush unfold. To the ex-

1. Nguni is the generic name of the peoples who, since about A.D.
1600, have inhabited the east coast of South Africa from Swaziland in
the north to the Great Fish river in the south. The 200 clans that Shaka
eventually moulded into his Zulu dynasty, together with the Swazi
and Xhosa tribes, constitute the three main Nguni groups of South
Africa.

treme west lies the Kalahari desert, a picturesque wasteland of scattered bush and a large expanse of veld and sand-dunes.

Apart from a few minor exceptions, the people who inhabit the interior of South Africa, as far afield as the Kalahari, the Limpopo in the north, and the Orange in the south, are of Sotho stock.[1] In 1823, hen Mzilikazi fled from Zululand and crossed the Drakensberg, he was to find that the Sotho peoples spoke a strange language and that, whereas Khumalo, Zulu, Ndwandwe, Mthethwa and other Nguni clans lived in small scattered kraals, these foreign tribes congregated in their hundreds, in tremendous villages.

When once he was domiciled in Sotho territory Mzilikazi became acquainted with names of clans and tribes such as Batlokoa – the Wild Cat People; Bakwena – the Crocodile People; Batlhaping – the Fish People; and Bakgatla – the Baboon People. It was the custom among the Sotho for a young chief, separated from the parent tribe in order to form his own independent clan, to name his followers after some animal, event, or important person. To this day the people of the Rhinoceros (Bahaole), Rain (Bapula), Buffalo (Banyati), Python (Batlaru), Lion (Bataung), Mist (Bafokeng), and a host of others, are to be found living in the interior of South Africa.

The Sotho clans and tribes lived independently of each other, under the rule of hereditary chieftains, and yet their way of life followed a similar pattern. Like the Nguni, they were tillers of the soil, planters of crops, cattle-breeders, hunters and collectors of edible berries, herbs and roots.

The Sothos commenced cultivation of crops two moons after the harvest had been collected. Each morning after the village boys had milked their father's cows and had driven them to the com-

1. The tribes of South Africa are divided ethnically into the Nguni, Sotho, Venda, Lemba and Shangana-Tsonga. The Nguni and Sotho are the largest of these groups. The Sotho peoples are subdivided into three distinct groups: the Southern Sotho of Lesotho (formerly Basutoland and the Orange Free State, the Western Sotho of Botswana (formerly the Bechuanaland Protectorate) and adjacent territories, and the Northern Sotho of the Northern Transvaal. They all speak a related language.

munal grazing grounds, the womenfolk set out for the fields with handmade hoes. There, to the accompaniment of singing, they toiled until mid-afternoon. The Sotho employed the most elementary of farming methods.

According to Arbousset and Daumas, who, during the early years of the last century, travelled by ox-wagon through the domains of the Sotho, the tribes took little trouble to form their fields into any regular shape. They dug here and there, making the most confused patchwork imaginable. Nevertheless, these two missionaries marvelled at the harvests of Indian millet, beans, watermelon, pumpkin, gourds, calabashes and sugar-cane that were reaped.[1]

With their crops the Sotho prepared plain, yet wholesome vegetable dishes – porridge made of meal, boiled with milk or water, and also tasty millet bread. They relished the roasted flesh of animals killed in the hunt and although they regarded beef as a delicacy they ate it on rare occasions only, for their cattle were too valuable to be slaughtered. One of their chief items of diet was curdled milk, large quantities of which always hung in skin bags, in the trees about the huts. The inhabitants of the villages, irrespective of age, drank milk, but by far the most sought-after drink among mature men was sorghum beer.

Over vast stretches of South Africa the rainfall is poor. It is true that in the time of Mzilikazi many of the Sotho tribes inhabited well-watered regions and were prosperous, but there were equally as many who were constantly subjected to the rigors of drought and were often almost exterminated by recurring famines. A tribe known as the Bakgalagadi – the Kalahari People – presents a striking example.

Centuries ago the Kalahari People were among the first of the migratory Sotho tribes to settle in what is today Botswana. On arriving in this subtropical country, they found it inhabited by the Bushmen, a race of diminutive hunter-folk, whom they either dispersed into the desert or enslaved. Then waves of the Bechuana

1. Arbousset and Daumas, *Narrative of the Exploratory Tour to the North-east of the Colony of the Cape of Good Hope*, p. 64.

tribes, also of Sotho stock, started streaming into the country, and the Kalahari People in turn were attacked and driven from the arable soil into the parched desert wastelands. One of these tribes, the Bakwena or Crocodile People, waged a relentless war against the Kalahari People and, after having routed them, subjected them to serfdom.

The Kalahari People, who incidentally inhabit parts of the desert to this day, were skilful hunters. With spears, bows and arrows and dogs, they tracked down game. They delivered the pelts and hides they collected to their overlords, and received small portions of the Bakwena crops in return. In times of drought both the Crocodile and the Kalahari People were faced with starvation and famine. The cattle died, the crops became stunted and withered, and the large herds of antelope moved away in search of water. The impoverished tribes turned to eating insects, rats and mice, the bark of shrubs and even dung. They also learned to prepare a palatable dish from roots of trees. In Botswana there is a bush called the *motlopi*. The people dug out pieces of its roots, which they crushed in a mortar and then spread out in the sun to dry. Later they pounded the fibrous substance into a flour, and by adding what milk was available and leaving it to ferment in the heat of the sun they prepared a nourishing substitute for millet porridge and bread.

So important has rain always been to the survival of the tribes of South Africa that one cannot but notice how frequently it is mentioned in the course of conversation. The people delight in either describing the phenomenal growth of their crops or the excellent condition of their cattle since the recent showers. On the other hand, when drought invades the land their first words of greeting are invariably followed by *'Pula ha lieo* – There is no rain.' *Pula* – rain. This must surely be one of the first words the Sotho infant learns. On important tribal occasions, when the men gather before their chief, they salute him with *'Pula! Pula!'*

In the time of Mzilikazi, in the dry areas of central South Africa tribal rain-makers were in constant demand. When summoned to a village for the purpose of driving drought from the

country, they selected ingredients for their decoctions and prepared the villagers both for the rain-making rituals and also for
the prayers that were to be offered to the spirits of the dead. If
these efforts failed to attract storm-clouds the rain-makers sacrificed a beast and set out at dawn, together with the inhabitants
and their cattle, in order to display their discontent by destroying
shrubs, killing game that crossed their path and flinging stones,
in an act of defiance, into the dried-up pools. Towards noon they
would return homewards, and as they drove their cattle before
them the women wailed bitterly, chanted prayers and beseeched
the ancestral spirits to send *pula* – rain.

The longer the drought persisted and the more stubborn the
spirits appeared to be, the more dejected and confused the people
became. Invocations were conducted more frequently and in the
course of new rituals even the simple porridge-spoon came to
play the part of a magic wand. The urgency with which the
Bamangwato of Northern Bechuanaland (now part of Botswana)
regarded drought was illustrated by the Rev. W. C. Willoughby.
He wrote of their striving to solicit the approval of the spirits by
sacrificing a black ox at the tomb of Chief Mathibe, a famous
ancestor. The entrails of the beast were buried in the grave, and
then the carcass was consumed by the members of the tribe who
had gathered to take part in the sacrificial rites. As the Bamangwato stood in the sacred burial grounds, they raised their voices
in mournful prayer.

'We come to beg rain by means of this ox,' they quavered in
unison, 'here it is, O Chief, our father! *Pula! Pula! Pula!* Chief,
we are dead who are your people.'[1]

And in the broiling Bechuanaland sun the Bamangwato sang
rainsongs, and danced beside the grave.

The lives the Sotho people led were dominated by the ancestor
cult, superstition, the evil intrigues of sorcerers, tribal laws and
justice, and the supernatural powers of witch-doctors, medicine-
men and diviners. Adolescents of the tribes could only be admitted

1. W. C. Willoughby, *The Soul of the Bantu*, p. 209.

to adulthood after having been subjected to a prolonged and gruel-ling period of initiation.

When boys became eligible for manhood they were ushered by their fathers to an initiation lodge, where a witch-doctor circum-cised them with a sharp flint. Although during this operation they were allowed no opiates to relieve them of pain, they showed no signs of emotion lest they became known to the tribe as cowards.

Immediately after circumcision the initiates received the per-sonal attention of the witch-doctor, who dressed their wounds with indigenous medicines to prevent septicaemia from setting in. Whilst their wounds were healing, the boys were whipped, cuffed and often injured, but they dared not complain. Most of the food-stuffs they relished in their parents' villages were now taboo, and they were fed on porridge 'in which, it is sometimes said, a little human flesh was boiled in order to render them bold and courageous'.[1]

In the course of the four to five months of their isolation even this dish was denied them. They were driven to the veld to fend for themselves. The boys were expected to steal food from villages in the neighbourhood, but if they were caught in the act they were thrashed. They were also trained in the art of fighting, and, in order to assure that one day they would be invincible in battle, they were dosed with powders from the witch-doctor's medicine-horn.

The Sotho believed that by subjecting their young boys to the rigid discipline of the initiation lodges they would turn them into adults capable of enduring hunger, thirst, cold, heat, pain and even death without complaint. This endurance would soon be put to the test, for Mzilikazi was already on the threshold of Sotho territory.[2]

1. D. F. Ellenberger, *History of the Basuto*, p. 282.
2. The ritual of circumcision and graduation to manhood is still practised among some of the South African tribes. In Zululand, however, circumcision was on the wane before Shaka's time, and to this day the Zulu look upon it with scorn. Circumcision has almost

Apart from the time' they devoted to cultivating their fields, tending their cattle, attending rituals and hunting for the pot, the Sotho tribes also took part in a host of other activities. The men brayed and tanned skins, from which they made clothes and sandals for themselves and their families; they carved milk-pails, food-bowls, spoons, porringers and ornaments, and extracted metals from ore for the manufacture of adzes, battle-axes, hunting-spears, knives and assegais. With clay the women fashioned cooking utensils; also pots of many shapes and sizes for storing milk, water, beer and grain. From reeds they wove sleeping-mats, baskets and huge, spherical granaries.

At the *kgotla*, the gathering-place of men, the patriarchs spent their leisure in gossiping and drinking from a communal beer-pot, while, in the shade of the trees or the overhanging roofs of their rondavel-huts, the women played with their babies. There were occasions, however, when differences arose between clans and ended in skirmishes.

During certain months of the year the villagers sent their herds to cattle-posts where grazing and water were plentiful. Situated some considerable distance from the main settlements, these cattle-posts were raided from time to time by rustlers from neighbouring clans across the borders. Organized stock-theft was a popular pastime, especially during the winter when the crops had already

---

disappeared among the Sotho tribes, and is practised only in very remote areas.

Circumcision lodges in isolated sections of Botswana have been revived recently. Among the Xhosa tribes of the Cape Province circumcision ceremonies are conducted annually. They commence in March when the crops have ripened, and close in September when the spring rains fall. The ages of the initiates range between twenty and twenty-five.

In 1956 the author was granted permission to conduct research in the circumcision lodges of the Bomvana tribe, known as the 'Little Red People'. The Bomvana inhabit the territory south of the Xora river in the Transkei. See *Sandy Tracks*, by Peter Becker, chapter XXIII.

been harvested, but invariably it involved the clans concerned in bloodshed.

In 1820 the Rev. John Campbell of the London Missionary Society journeyed by ox-wagon into the territories of the Sotho tribes inhabiting the western regions of South Africa. In the records he kept he referred to the unrest, due to cattle-raiding, that prevailed among the Sotho peoples. He concluded that the clans became 'formidable enemies' whenever the rustlers raided their territories. As an example he mentioned the Bakwena, the Crocodile People of the Transvaal and Bechuanaland, who had become a 'warlike' tribe as a result of the raids that were being conducted on its cattle-folds 'by covetous nations around'.[1]

An entry in Campbell's diary dated 6 May describes an 'uproar' in the capital of the Bahurutsi, a great tribe that lived in the plains around the present town of Zeerust, in the WesternTransvaal. Apparently news had spread from village to village that a Bakwena raiding-party was approaching. There was panic and confusion in the Bahurutsi capital as 'numbers of whistles sounded in every direction', men shouted and 'about five hundred cows and oxen that stood in an enclosure near [Campbell's] wagons bellowed with all their might...'[2]

The Bahurutsi prepared to defend their capital against the raiders who 'had been seen skulking in the neighbourhood'. A commando set out to engage them in battle and to drive them back over the border. The clash that was to take place between the two clans did not amount to more than the usual inter-tribal skirmish, for at sunset on the same day the frenzied Bahurutsi bolted back into the capital. With their battle-axes and spears held aloft and oxhide shields drawn close to their bodies they presented an impressive sight.

Their faces were daubed with white clay, wrote Campbell, every face marked differently, and 'their legs were painted with the same clay up to the knees, resembling stockings. On halting they went through all the different manoeuvres used in attacking the enemy with their spears, etc. Sometimes they leaped to a great

1. J. Campbell, *Travels in South Africa*, p. 291.
2. ibid., p. 233.

height as if to escape an arrow or assegai. Their movements in advancing and retreating were in a zig-zag direction, as if to prevent the enemy taking aim at them.'[1]

Campbell marvelled at the military power of the Bahurutsi, the Bakwena and other tribes with which he came into contact, but the events of the next decade were to prove that, on the whole, the Sotho were not a warlike people. In 1820 the fashion of internecine war, instigated in Zululand by Dingiswayo and adopted and perfected by Shaka, had not yet spread to the west of the Drakensberg, where the Sotho still lived in comparative peace. Soon Campbell would be learning of Mzilikazi, and he would know that among the dark-skinned races of South Africa there were none more fearsome in battle than those who were of Zulu stock.

Before telling of Mzilikazi's arrival in the interior of South Africa, it is necessary to devote a few final words to other aspects of the military systems of Sotho tribes.

It will be recalled that the various Sotho tribes followed a similar way of life, dressed in like fashion, and spoke dialects that revealed only minor differences in vocabulary. Therefore, in times of strife, the warriors of the different groups decorated themselves in distinctive war regalia, and smeared their bodies with designs in coloured clay, lest, in the course of battle, they became confused and slew their own comrades. Apart from their warpaints the Bahurutsi wore white turbans made from the skin of the wild hog. Leopard-skins and fur tippets hung from the shoulders of most warriors.

The Batlhaping, or Fish People, who inhabited the Northern Cape, prepared their warpaints from red clay. The Batlokoa, or Wild Cat People, who lived along the Wilge river in the Orange Free State, could be recognized at a glance by their black shields, black ostrich-feather headdresses and black mantles and capes. Even their bodies were daubed with a black substance prepared from a mixture of soot and animal fat.

Sotho armies were well armed. The tribes of the western limits

1. ibid., pp. 237–8.

of South Africa, among whom the most noteworthy were the Batlhaping, Bakgalagadi, Bahurutsi and Barolong, were armed with bows and arrows, battle-axes, clubs and assegais. In contrast with the massive Zulu shield, those of the Sotho tribes were small, light and rectangular. The Bamangwato of Northern Bechuanaland manufactured a large range of weapons: long, heavy, broadbladed javelins, a variety of assegais both plain and barbed, doublebarbed arrows and formidable battle-axes. Many of the tribes smelted iron and copper ore in simple clay furnaces, but in the art of working metals into weapons, the Bamangwato were unrivalled. The Batlokoa army carried large shields, similar to those of the Zulu, clubs, javelins, and also a curious weapon that resembled a scimitar. This sickle-shaped weapon was razor-sharp; it was used as a missile and also for hacking the enemy in close combat.

Although in the early 1820s the armies of the smaller Sotho groups could not have exceeded a thousand warriors, those of the large tribes were known to number many thousands. The population of the Bataung – the Lion People – was in the region of twenty-five thousand, and that of the Batlokoa forty thousand.

These estimates are undoubtedly inaccurate, but they establish the fact that when Mzilikazi entered Sotho country his forces would be overwhelmingly outnumbered. One cannot but be baffled by the thought that, although he had only three hundred warriors at his disposal, Mzilikazi managed to usher his clanlet into the interior of South Africa. A far greater achievement was his ability to establish his people as an independent group in a country so densely populated by foreign tribes.

CHAPTER 5

EKUPUMULENI–THE PLACE OF REST

Mzilikazi crosses the Drakensberg – Massacre of Sotho clans
He builds ekuPumuleni – Steelpoort campaign
Stampede of cattle – Impalement of Mokotoko

AFTER the murder of Nyoka – the Snake – and the destruction of his kraal, Mzilikazi and his Khumalo moved slowly north-wards, driving their herds before them and halting periodically to bivouac. Eventually they entered the present-day Piet Retief district, turned to the west and then crossed the Drakensberg probably in the vicinity of the source of the Compies river. Having left Zululand for ever and having reached the country of foreign tribes, Mzilikazi became apprehensive: no matter how alluring the countryside might have been to him, he dared not settle with his people, nor even loiter, for, apart from the fact that he was trespassing in the domains of Sotho chiefs who might seek to destroy him, it was also essential that he proceed far out of reach of Shaka's regiments.

Mzilikazi veered north and led his clan into the Transvaal. He was soon to find that, rather than become involved in battle, the Sotho villagers he encountered shrank from before his regiments and fled to the hills. He regarded their cowardice as strange, but then he learned that in recent months bands of Zulu had crossed the Drakensberg, had hurried southwards and had wrought havoc among the Sotho clans of the Orange Free State. It was small wonder that the villagers fled from the Khumalo: they identified them by their robust, naked bodies, their oval shields and their stabbing-spears as the same aggressors who had caused so much misery in the south.

From thenceforth the Sotho spoke of Mzilikazi's clan as the

abakwaZulu – the People of Zululand. And whenever the cry
went up that the abakwaZulu were approaching, the peace-loving
cattle-breeders whose villages punctuated the southern reaches of
the Transvaal took to their heels and went into hiding.

Mzilikazi reached the Ermelo district, where he was confronted
with two urgent problems: first, as unwanted nomads in a vast,
densely populated country the Khumalo were finding food increasingly difficult to come by, and then, as they had always been
accustomed to Zululand's subtropical climate with its hot summers and mild winters, they were discovering to their dismay that
the highveld regions of the Transvaal were bitterly cold. Indeed,
spring had not yet arrived when Mzilikazi reached the high alti-
tudes of the Ermelo district, a corner of South Africa notorious for
its cruel, piercing winds, heavy frosts and freezing, metallic night
air. Whereas before the scantily clad Khumalo had been able to
find shelter at night among the thorn-trees, now they were faced
with the danger of perishing from exposure. As was his habit at
times of crisis, Mzilikazi schemed.

He decided to dispatch groups of scouts to reconnoitre the surroundings in order to establish the exact positions of the most
prominent Sotho villages. This done, Khumalo fighting-men stole
out at nights, surrounded the sleeping habitations, set fire to the
thatch of the hut-roofs and butchered the men, women and children as they careered panic-stricken into the darkness. Village
after village was besieged, razed to the ground and looted, and in
due course Mzilikazi succeeded in clearing the Sotho from a substantial area where he established himself as a temporary yet un-
disputed chieftain.

With these victories Mzilikazi's herds increased and his food-
supply became plentiful. Then he instructed his womenfolk to cut
thatching-grass and collected flexible poles for constructing huts.
Mzilikazi had not the slightest intention of remaining long in the
Ermelo district, but his people needed shelter and he believed that
if his plans for the immediate future were to succeed he must
establish provisional headquarters.

His kraal completed, Mzilikazi embarked on the first of his
organized daylight raids on Sotho villages. At the head of his regi-

ments he advanced cautiously, and on receiving reports from his scouts on the movements of the inhabitants and the size of their herds he charged with his warriors and attacked swiftly. Huts went up in flames, and the villagers who were brave enough to attempt to defend their families were disembowelled. The Khumalo were careful to spare the lives of young maidens and youths, for Mzilikazi had decreed that in future he would increase the size of his clan by collecting concubines for his warriors and recruits for his fighting forces. Often it happened that the old women and men of the villages, escaping death at the hands of the Khumalo, were left among the smouldering ruins, eventually to die of thirst, hunger or exposure, or to be dragged away by beasts of prey that roamed the highveld plains. Infants whose parents lay dead about the huts were ignored by Mzilikazi. Like the aged, they too suffered slow deaths or were devoured.

The tactics adopted for each attack on a Sotho village always followed the same pattern: first, Khumalo scouts skulked in the neighbourhood of settlements, soon to be followed by Mzilikazi and his regiments; then huts were fired, the inhabitants massacred, young men and women taken prisoner, babies and old people left uncared for, cattle driven off, huts cleared of karosses, utensils and weapons and finally every morsel of food stolen from the granaries.

The bewildered Sotho clans, whose main experience in warfare had been confined to the skirmishes that usually followed on cattle-raids, were no match for Mzilikazi's superbly trained Khumalo regiments. So great was their consternation on finding their villages besieged that they often became paralysed with terror, for 'they had never before seen discipline so perfect as that of the naked braves, or a weapon so deadly as the Zulu stabbing-spear'.[1]

Not only did Mzilikazi's possessions increase rapidly, but also his power. Such was his strength of personality, his extraordinary gift for leading men, his experience as a warrior and his cunning, that he was able to 'triumph over the minds of his men, and make his trembling captives soon adore him as an invincible sovereign. Those who resisted and would not stoop to be his dogs, he but-

1. G. M. Theal, *South Africa*, p. 169.

chered'.[2] He trained the Sotho youths whom he had recruited in his own tactics, and in the course of time the foreigners in his growing army outnumbered the original nucleus of Khumalo warriors.

Mzilikazi's first important battle since his flight from Zululand occurred when his regiments fell upon a Sotho clan known as the Maphuthing. Bewildered by the sudden appearance of the marauders, the Maphuthing fled to the neighbouring Nyawo clan, whose chief Sembane commanded a powerful fighting force intended for the destruction of the Khumalo if ever they trespassed in his domain. With the arrival of the fugitive Maphuthing at his royal village Sembane assembled not only his own warriors, but also those of the neighbouring clans.

Sembane and his army located the Khumalo in Maphuthing country and swooped down on them. A bitter struggle ensued. Although hopelessly outnumbered, the Khumalo, with their young chief in the front line of battle, gradually drove the allied force back and set upon it with their stabbing-spears.

Startled by the ferocity with which their athletic adversaries attacked them, Sembane's hordes bolted and, in the confusion of their retreat, careered over a precipice to fall to gory deaths in the rocky bed of a ravine. The few who managed to escape into the surroundings would remember to their dying day the fierce, half-naked Khumalo warriors fighting behind cover of their oxhide shields, and Mzilikazi, their chief, a white ostrich feather reaching up from his forehead, leading them on to the attack.

How long Mzilikazi remained in the Ermelo district can only be guessed, but in all probability, with Shaka's punitive regiments constantly in mind, he moved off during the spring when the warm weather set in and entered the Middleburg district to the north.

Wherever he journeyed in those highveld regions Mzilikazi continued to attack the Sotho clans he encountered. Villages went up in smoke. Huts were looted, cattle-folds robbed, granaries

2. Robert Moffat, *Missionary Labours and Scenes in Southern Africa*, p. 545.

emptied, crops destroyed and corpses left strewn in every place where people once had lived in peace.

Many a petty chieftain who had heard of Mzilikazi's heinous killings, but had not been able to flee in time, sought to be spared by offering the Khumalo hospitality, generous gifts of cattle and provisions for their journey to the north. Mzilikazi accepted these kindnesses with feigned gratitude, and then murdered his hosts, appropriated their possessions, fired their kraals, selected the cream of their subjects for his own clan, and proceeded nonchalantly on his way.

Throughout the following year the Khumalo continued their nomadic way of life. Theirs was a routine existence of brigandage and grim slaughter. Every village within reach was laid waste. By the winter of 1824 Mzilikazi, known as the Great Road, had carved a bloody 200-mile trail through the eastern regions of the Transvaal. In a single year the strip of country he had traversed 'was covered with skeletons, and literally no human beings were left in it'.[1]

Mzilikazi led his people into the northern, subtropical regions of the Middelburg district, the wooded hills and sultry valleys of which resembled the land of his origin. After his turbulent exodus from Zululand and the discomforts his clan had suffered west of the Drakensberg, Mzilikazi must have believed that here, at last, his wanderings were at an end. In the serene surroundings of the Upper Olifants river the Khumalo pastured their stock and set about building a royal kraal for their chief; a vast settlement of beehive huts which Mzilikazi named ekuPumuleni – the Place of Rest.

But at ekuPumuleni there was to be no rest for Mzilikazi and his clan. The spring of 1824 was approaching, and with it the first storm-clouds that drift from the east during the afternoons. The men set to work clearing large expanses of bush for fields and when in late September or early October the rains came, the daily routine of tilling and planting began. With the passing of the months the women took over the agricultural activities, and day

1. G. M. Theal, *History of South Africa*, vol. 1, p. 456.

after day, from dawn to dusk, they cleared weeds from the crops that would provide Mzilikazi's settlement with rations. Relieved of their responsibilities in the lands, the men went out hunting. The Middelburg district teemed with game: a variety of antelope, both large and small, lion and elephant. Like Zululand, it was an ideal country for the wild sports in which virile men enjoyed taking part.

Meanwhile, in his royal kraal Mzilikazi's reveries were turning to ambitions other than hunting. He was growing weary of the quiet life he was leading as chief of a clan and commander-in-chief of an inactive army. He decided to erect military kraals in the vicinity of ekuPumuleni and to organize his warriors into regiments according to the Shakan pattern. This marked the beginning of a new and vital era in Mzilikazi's career. Had he chosen, in 1824, to live peacefully in his Place of Rest rather than continue as a conqueror, his name, like several other chiefs of his time, would barely have deserved mention in the history of Southern Africa.

In that fateful year he planned a series of short military expeditions into the Middelburg bushveld. All his available regiments were dispatched in different directions for the purpose of destroying clans they came upon, pillaging villages, capturing young women and commandeering able-bodied Sotho men for the Khumalo army. The Sotho clans whose settlements dotted the immediate vicinity of Mzilikazi's newly established domain were wiped out. Most of them had offered little resistance, for in living memory, never had so powerful and brutal an enemy crossed their boundaries.

Not thirty miles to the east of ekuPumuleni the Steelpoort river meanders through the bush to join the waters of the Olifant in the north. Several decades before the intrusion of Mzilikazi in those parts Sotho chiefs and their subjects occupied the valleys traversed by the river, built their villages and planted their crops.

The Steelpoort flows through a country of uncommon beauty: thorn-bush and indigenous trees follow its course, spread out into the plains and climb the slopes of the surrounding kopjes. Weather-scarred faces of krantzes gaze on an orchestration of

colour: the scarlet plumes of the giant aloe, the tarnished green
of the euphorbia, the gold of the acacia clusters, the lustrous verdure of the rank elephant grass and a myriad of tints and hues of
the great canopy of bushveld foliage. Here and there musical
rivulets hasten down the hillside from springs almost obscured by
ferns, arum lilies and rushes. In the damp shadows of the cliffs,
nodular roots twist, like serpents, in and out of the jumbles of
granite. This is the country of the wild apricot, fig and pear, of
rock-rabbits, baboons, blue-apes, vultures, mambas, pythons,
cobras, lizards, spiders, scorpions, and a large variety of small
birds.

In the days of Mzilikazi the lands flanking the Steelpoort river
yielded rich harvests; cattle grew fat, and in the vicinity of the
Sotho villages game abounded. And yet the clans were not always
entirely happy, for each year in January their settlements were
stricken by a mysterious disease that claimed the lives of hundreds. They were unaware that the swampy banks of the Steelpoort were the breeding grounds for the malaria mosquito.

In 1824 the ravages of fever were to appear trivial by compari-
son with the danger that loomed up to the immediate west of the
Steelpoort. Rumours of the atrocities committed by Mzilikazi
filtered through the bush into the valley; the people lived on
tenterhooks.

Foremost among the petty chieftains of those fever-stricken
parts was Mokotoko, whose clan inhabited the country north of
the present-day town of Roos-Senekal. His people, the Maphuthing, were a branch of the clan Mzilikazi had driven over a precipice in the course of his advance through the Transvaal highveld.
Mokotoko was a newcomer to the Middelburg district. Endless
feuds among the leaders of the parent Maphuthing tribe had induced him to move with his subjects and seek a new country in
the north. Experience had taught Mokotoko the importance of
vigilance, and while other Sotho clans about him were being wiped
out by Mzilikazi he and his people had collected their belongings
and fled to a neighbouring chief named Sibindi – the Brave. Mokotoko and Sibindi became allies, and with the Khumalo invasion

threatening their clans, they wasted no time in preparing their armies for battle.

In the Steelpoort valley the Sotho clans crumbled beneath the advance of the Khumalo. Mzilikazi struck out for Maphuthing country, but on finding the villages deserted he pressed on until he reached Sibindi's clan, where he learned that a great army had been mustered by the two chiefs to meet him in battle.

The Khumalo moved slowly through the bush until at length they entered a clearing on the opposite side of which Sibindi's royal kraal was situated. Barely had Mzilikazi and his regiments traversed half the breadth of this flat, treeless gap in the bushveld than the quietude of the surroundings was disrupted by the shouts of hundreds of throats, the rumble of a multitude of cloven hoofs on the hard earth and the bellowing of cattle.

For a brief moment the Khumalo stood in stolid silence and turned their startled ears in the direction whence the noise had risen. They might have started retracing their steps had not the bush ahead burst open as a great herd of white cattle came surging towards them. Heads lowered, tails on high, nostrils snorting, the beasts stampeded in a swirling cloud of dust. Behind them ran the warriors of Mokotoko and Sibindi's armies.

The two chiefs had hoped that on seeing the cattle Mzilikazi and his men would turn tail. They visualized the Khumalo being crushed by the weight of the herd, and any survivors being plucked off by the allied forces that followed. Instead, the Khumalo rushed forward to meet the strange foe that came rolling towards them. They, in turn, set up a tremendous din. The clatter of spear-shafts, one upon the other, mingled with the beating of ox-hide shields, the stamping of feet and a pandemonium of shouting and whistling.

Bewildered by the sudden charge of the frenzied warriors and their hullabaloo, the cattle swerved to the left and right and careered towards the bush. But the Khumalo, preventing this escape, drove the cattle back until the entire herd wheeled and bore down on the warriors of Mokotoko and Sibindi.

The allies turned and bolted helter-skelter across the clearing and into the bush. The Khumalo followed in hot pursuit, and with the cattle dispersed and the confusion ended, they spread out to stalk the enemy through the undergrowth. Mokotoko and Sibindi, together with the majority of their women and children, managed to escape, but those of the Sotho clansmen captured by Khumalo were run through with stabbing-spears.

During the days that followed, Mzilikazi's regiments ransacked every hut and granary they came upon. Great herds of cattle and flocks of sheep and goats were collected and driven back to eku-Pumuleni – the Place of Rest. In the course of their pillage the Khumalo searched in the krantzes, chasms, caves, dongas, and ravines for the two chiefs who had planned their destruction. They surrounded isolated groups of fugitives who, on finding themselves at the mercy of their enemy, begged that their lives be spared in exchange for their allegiance to Mzilikazi.

Hordes of suppliants poured in, and gradually Mzilikazi succeeded in rounding up most of the followers of Mokotoko and Sibindi. He had the aged killed and also those whom he considered to be of no use to his clan. He had compassion on the young women and adolescent girls, for they were to become concubines and servants at the Place of Rest. He herded the able-bodied men and youths into companies, for in the near future they would be escorted back to the Khumalo headquarters to be trained and then drafted into the regiments.

Mzilikazi returned to ekuPumuleni, but in the Steelpoort region a section of the Khumalo regiment remained to continue mopping-up operations, looting and the search for Mokotoko and Sibindi.

This small force marched to the north until it reached the Steelpoort's confluence with the Olifant. The Khumalo came upon a Sotho tribe known as the Bapedi, whose chief, Sekwata, was a ruler of great wisdom and ability. They stormed two mountain fortresses on which the Bapedi were entrenched, but were almost routed. Indeed, the Bapedi defences were impregnable, and so expert were these mountain-dwellers in concealing themselves behind rocks and trees, and in moving swiftly over the most treacherous of rugged slopes, that they confused their aggressors and even succeeded in repulsing them.

The Khumalo withdrew and as they trotted away the victorious Bapedi flung jeers, insults and taunts at them. For several years after this embarrassing incident Mzilikazi's warriors spoke of the Bapedi as the people who fought not like men, but like rock-rabbits. They vowed they would return one day to destroy the mountain villages of Chief Sekwata.

When all his forces had returned from the Steelpoort valley Mzilikazi dispatched two powerful regiments to find Mokotoko. On this occasion Mokotoko's lair was located without difficulty, for it had become a simple matter for the Khumalo to persuade their captives to disclose the likely hiding-places of their chief. Mokotoko was captured. The search for Sibindi continued, but as no record of his eventual fate exists it can be assumed he was never found.

With Mokotoko taken alive, the Khumalo regiments retraced their steps past the ruins of the Maphuthing villages, over the Steelpoort river and through the bush to ekuPumuleni. At victory celebrations they recounted the invasion of the Steelpoort valley. They had brought back a great haul of grain, stock, concubines, servants and recruits – a feat worthy of commemoration. They sacrificed to the spirits, feasted, rejoiced and sang praises to Mzilikazi. Since the stronghold at the Place of Rest had been established, the destruction of Mokotoko and Sibindi's clan had been Mzilikazi's crowning achievement.

Mzilikazi sent for Mokotoko. Already he had decided that the Chief should die, but none could guess by what method. When Mokotoko was dragged into his presence Mzilikazi glared at him with contempt. He reminded his royal captive of the plan that had been devised to crush the Khumalo regiments beneath the hoofs of the herd of white cattle. When it became clear that Mokotoko was unimpressed by his words Mzilikazi grew impatient Turning to the executioners he instructed them to remove the Chief and conduct him to the spot where he would spend the last hours of his life.

Not far from the main entrance of ekuPumuleni stood a pole, a sharp stake that Mzilikazi had caused to be erected specially for Mokotoko's impalement. The executioners lifted the ill-fated

Chief, dropped him in a sitting position on to the spike, and left him to writhe in agony in the presence of a circle of inquisitive spectators.

It is said the Chief of the Maphuthing died slowly but bravely.

CHAPTER 6

TRIBAL TURMOIL

Mzilikazi escapes destruction – Mantatisi: the woman
conqueror
Lifaqane – Surge of the Wild Cat People
Fish People saved by Robert Moffat – Cannibalism

WHEN in the early winter of 1823 Mzilikazi crossed the Drakensberg into Sotho country, he chanced to move northwards into the Ermelo district of the Transvaal. What fate would have awaited him had he chosen to lead the Khumalo southwards into the Orange Free State?

The previous year, 1822, when Mzilikazi was awaiting Shaka's second attack on enTubeni, the Khumalo stronghold, a chief named Matiwane was living with his clan, the emaNgwaneni, along the Nyati (Buffalo) river. A section of the Zulu army, sent by Shaka to invade Natal, approached the Nyati and put Matiwane and his people to flight.

In direct line of Matiwane's flight was the Hlubi clan, occupying a strip of territory between the Nyati and the Tugela rivers. Matiwane took the Hlubi by surprise, drove them from their kraals, butchered them, took possession of their cattle and stores of grain and then murdered their chief and his heir. Some of the Hlubi fled to the south, but Mpangazita, second eldest son of the deceased ruler of the clan, raced off with his followers to the west and took refuge in the heights of the Drakensberg.

He then led his people through the folds of the mountains, struggled with them among the peaks, and on effecting a crossing, descended into the foothills along the western slopes. The Hlubi pressed on and entered the Harrismith district of the Orange Free

State, a vast, flat, highveld country, inhabited by a Sotho tribe known as the Batlokoa – the Wild Cat People.

Mpangazita encountered the Wild Cat People in a valley through which the Wilge river flows, and on the banks of streams flowing into the Upper Vaal. The ruler of this Sotho tribe was Mantatisi, a woman endowed with fabulous qualities of leadership, and whose notoriety as an exterminator of Sotho tribes was to be surpassed only by Mzilikazi in the years to come.

Mantatisi was a woman of outstanding intelligence. Tall, straight and lean, she was lighter in complexion than most of her subjects, and 'her expression of countenance was sweet and agreeable'.[1] Mantatisi was described by the early missionaries as astute and vigilant, and as being of dignified deportment. In 1823, when Mzilikazi was approaching the Drakensberg from Zululand, she was already known far and wide in the central plateau of South Africa as a ruthless conqueror, 'utterly callous to human suffering'.[2]

Ever since her husband's death in 1813 Mantatisi's reign had been turbulent. She was the daughter of the chief of the neighbouring Basia clan and, as a foreigner, members of the royal house of the Wild Cat People sought to kill her and also to prevent her minor son, Sikonyela, from becoming the new chief of the clan. During all the years before the arrival of the invaders from Zululand Mantatisi's reign had been punctuated with incessant quarrels, strife and even civil war, but so steadfast had she been to see her son on the throne of the Wild Cat People that she overcame all opposition and ruled as regent with supreme authority. In the course of time not only did Mantatisi gain tremendous prestige, but she came to be venerated by the very people who had plotted to kill her.

But then Mpangazita and his Hlubi flocked into the Harrismith district and fell upon the villages of the Wild Cat People. Mantatisi was taken unawares, and abandoning her royal kraal, she fled with her subjects to the country of her kinsmen, the neighbouring Basia. Mantatisi did not remain long with the Basia, for not only

1. Arbousset and Daumas, op. cit., p. 58.
2. G. M. Theal, op. cit., vol. II, p. 442.

did she realize there would be insufficient food for the two clans, but she also predicted that it would not be long before the invaders from Zululand arrived. She turned to the west with her hordes and attacked the Bafokeng – the Mist People. Nor was her departure premature, for Mpangazita invaded the Basia, having been driven from the Harrismith district by a newcomer to Sotho country – Matiwane, his old enemy, who also had decided to flee from Shaka's tyranny.

The movements of these three chiefs created a fashion in intertribal warfare that was to become unique in Sotho history: a ghastly series of massacres which produced few tangible results and reduced the peace-loving peoples of the Central Plateau to a state of abject misery.

Known as *lifaqane*,[1] these wars began when Mantatisi drove the Mist People from their country and then moved on to the west, either to destroy other clans or to disperse them. In this way a congestion involving hundreds of thousands of people developed. Sotho groups both large and small turned westwards, each trespassing on the domains of another. Powerful armies annihilated their weaker neighbours, confiscated their possessions and moved on, knowing full well that if they loitered they too would be attacked by wave upon wave of people advancing from the east. *Lifaqane* hurled the Sotho peoples into a maëlstrom of destruction, until eventually an estimated twenty-eight distinct clans disappeared, leaving not a trace of their former existence.

The horrifying effects of *lifaqane* on the way of life of the Southern Sotho peoples of the early 1820s will be better understood if we follow the career of the most fascinating female African conqueror of all time – Mantatisi, Queen of the Wild Cat People.

With her eighteen-year-old son at her side Mantatisi led her hordes into the Caledon valley, a great fertile country interspersed with sandstone hills which, by virtue of their precipitous slopes,

1. Pronounced *di-fa-qa-ne*. The *q* is a palato-alveolar 'click', formed by pressing the upper part of the tongue-tip against the division between the teeth-ridge and the hard palate and drawing the tongue sharply downwards.

were to become the fortresses of many a fugitive Sotho clan. Mantatisi crossed the torrid sands through which the Caledon river flows, and advanced on Butha-Buthe – the Place of Lying-down – a mountain on which lived Moshesh, a young, unknown sub-chief, and his handful of followers.[1]

From the heights of Butha-Buthe, Moshesh and his subjects gazed down on the surge of Mantatisi's warriors. Had they not retreated earlier to this well-watered tableland forming the summit of the mountain, they would have been wiped out. But now they were safe, for their stronghold was encompassed by lofty, overhanging cliffs, carved by nature out of solid sandstone.

Skirmishes took place, but Mantatisi was more concerned in destroying the huts at the base of the mountain and collecting booty than in struggling up the tortuous passes leading to Moshesh's small group. The Wild Cat People camped on the banks of the stream flanking Butha-Buthe and, on consuming Moshesh's stores, departed for the west to embark on an orgy of devastation.

Clan after clan perished beneath Mantatisi's advance. Thousands of people, on learning of her approach, fled into the highlands, to regions few other than the dwarf-like Bushmen had ever considered fit for habitation. Waves of refugees rolled forward like animals before a band of hunters. Sotho groups that for many generations had lived side by side in comparative harmony became bitter enemies. A general scramble for cattle took place. Battles broke out. Bands of brigands zigzagged across the Caledon valley in search of unharvested fields to strip and granaries to raid. And ever on the eastern horizon, stalking the refugees, was Mantatisi's

---

1. A few years later, when the *lifaqane* wars came to an end, Moshesh (Moshoeshoe) emerged as a hero, the gatherer of wanderers and starving refugees, and the founder of the Basuto nation of present-day Lesotho. Moshesh was destined to become one of the greatest chiefs of all time. Within a decade of his having been attacked by Mantatisi's hordes he came to grips with Mzilikazi. The astounding consequences of their meeting will be related in a later chapter.

Wild Cat hordes, and the two Zulu conquerors from across the Drakensberg.

The course Mantatisi followed ran parallel with the Caledon river. Unknown to her, Mpangazita's Hlubi were proceeding in the same direction, but to the immediate north, and it was only when she reached Peka, not many miles from where Maseru, the capital of Lesotho, is situated today, that she came upon this, her most dreaded enemy. A struggle for the supremacy of the Caledon valley followed between Mantatisi and Mpangazita. The Wild Cat People fared badly. In fact, had it not been for Mantatisi's ingenuity their marauding adventures might have ceased then and there.

Undaunted by their setback at the hands of the Hlubi, the Wild Cat People struck out northwards through the Orange Free State, attacking and subjugating clans, rounding up cattle, pillaging and leaving only desolation in their wake. They seem to have adhered to no planned route, for soon they were retracing their steps and were entering the plains between the Caledon and Orange rivers. They decimated all the clans they came upon, but left the many Bushman bands in the area unharmed.

On finding the Orange in flood, the Wild Cat People turned back to the Caledon, crossed it and returned to the Orange Free State, where some months earlier they had butchered the Sotho inhabitants. They then moved off to the north-west towards Bechuanaland.

Meanwhile, frightening rumours had been sweeping across the interior of South Africa and had even reached the remotest villages of the Bechuanaland tribes. Stationed at the Kuruman mission, on the fringe of the Kalahari desert, was a young evangelist, the Rev. Robert Moffat, who wrote as follows of the disturbing news he had received of Mantatisi's exploits:

For more than a year, numerous and strange reports had at intervals reached us, some indeed of such a character as induced us to treat them as the reveries of a madman. It was said that a mighty woman, of the name of Mantatee [Mantatisi], was at the head of an invincible army, numerous as locusts, marching onward among the interior nations, carrying devastation and ruin wherever she went;

that she nourished the army with her own milk, sent out hornets before it, and, in one word, was laying the world desolate.

Moffat scoffed at these rumours, being convinced they had risen as a result of the wars that were raging beyond the Drakensberg in Shaka's country.

Meanwhile Mantatisi was approaching Bechuanaland with forty thousand men, women and children. It was January 1823, the time of the year when crops were ripening and food was usually plentiful. But the Wild Cat People were compelled to live frugally, for so great had been the chaos brought about by *lifaqane* in general and the plunderings of Mantatisi, Mpangazita and Matiwane in particular that entire tribes had vanished from their settlements even before they had tilled their fields in preparation for planting. Indeed, the Central Plateau swarmed with hunger-stricken stragglers and small, detached parties of bandits. Apart from roots, bulbs, and berries, there was little food to be found in the veld, certainly not enough to feed so large a horde as that of Mantatisi.

What little food was available Mantatisi rationed among her fighting-men, but she insisted that the rank and file of her followers should forage in the surrounding veld. Many of the Wild Cat People started dropping out along the route. Women and children, and especially the aged and ailing, became stragglers who invariably died of exhaustion, exposure or hunger, or were devoured by beasts of prey that always followed at a distance.

Weeks of marching brought the Wild Cat People to the land of the Bechuana tribes, an immense belt of the Kalahari desert. They entered the domains of the most prosperous of Bechuana chiefs, Makaba of the Bangwaketsi.[1] Lured by fields of ripening corn and the herds that roamed the countryside, the Wild Cat People besieged the nearest outstations, dispersed the terrified inhabitants, collected booty and advanced towards a cluster of hillocks among which Makaba's royal village was situated.

1. The present Paramount Chief of the Bangwaketsi of Botswana is Bathoen II, C.B.E. He lives in Kanye, the capital village, with thirty thousand of his subjects.

Meanwhile, the old Chief had decided not to surrender to Mantatisi without a fight. He called up every available warrior, garrisoned every pass leading to his capital, and with the guile for which he was famous, prepared traps into which he planned to lead his aggressors.

Since her flight from the Harrismith district Mantatisi had managed to brush aside all opposition in the territories she traversed, but now in the stifling bushveld of Bechuanaland she was to come face to face with a foe whose fighting forces were as numerous and also better fed than those of the Wild Cat People. The vanguard of Mantatisi's army strode into ambuscades; large groups of men toppled headlong into concealed pitfalls and met their death beneath volleys of barbed javelins. A battle broke out, in the course of which hundreds of the invaders were massacred. Before the situation could develop into a rout Mantatisi suddenly disengaged her armies and retreated with her hordes to the east. Thus Makaba became the first Sotho chief to repulse the formidable Wild Cat army, and to this day he is spoken of as the 'Man of Conquest'.

The Wild Cat People flowed into the adjoining territory of the Bahurutsi, a tribe almost as vast in numbers as the Bangwaketsi, but not nearly as powerful. Mantatisi grew cautious. Her subjects were ravenous, and the Bahurutsi crops, now heavy in ear, were too valuable a prize to miss. Furthermore, she saw what must have seemed a multitude of warriors, their bodies daubed with war paints, traversing the veld in the vicinity of Tshwenyane, the capital village. Mantatisi took Tshwenyane by storm, reduced it to ashes and butchered its inhabitants. And while she supervised looting operations, the Bahurutsi refugees streamed westwards to become wanderers in the waterless wastelands of the Kalahari.

The invaders hastened away to the south, fell upon the Barolong tribe, carried chaos and death into the villages, and sent thousands of fugitives on a witless journey to the desert. Then they moved on to the Batlhaping, the Fish People, among whom Robert Moffat and his colleagues of the London Missionary Society laboured.

*

Robert Moffat hurried to Lithako – the Ruins – the village of the Chief of the Fish People, and in the *kgotla*, the gathering-place of men, he related the stories he had heard of the atrocities committed by Mantatisi among the people of the Central Plateau and Bechuanaland. He urged his audience to have faith in God and to face with fortitude the dangers that threatened the Fish People. The Chief called a council of war to discuss what steps might be taken to save the tribe from annihilation. Some of the councillors proposed trekking to the desert, but Moffat objected. He believed that if the Fish People could solicit the support of the Griqua, a race of half-caste Hottentots, living a hundred miles to the south at Griquatown, they would defeat Mantatisi's hordes. He volunteered to visit Nicholas Waterboer, the Griqua Chief, and persuade him to lead his own men and the Fish People against Mantatisi.

Moffat set out immediately by ox-wagon and reached Griquatown several days later. There he met John Melville, a surveyor, and George Thompson, a Government official from Cape Town. These men conducted him to the home of old Nicholas Waterboer. On learning of Mantatisi's approach the Griqua Chief summoned his captains to a council of war, and instructed them to prepare their forces to destroy the Wild Cat People.

Having accomplished his mission in Griquatown, Moffat left for home, taking Melville and Thompson with him. The three white men found the villages of the Fish People in chaos, and Moffat observed that 'the minds of the primitive Batlhaping had become completely unhinged'.[1]

The Griqua, upon whose military aid the survival not only of the Fish People, but also the missionaries, their wives and children, now completely depended, were an offshoot of the original dwarf-like Hottentots of the Cape Colony. They were a hybrid race through whose veins flowed the blood of the early Dutch settlers, Negro slaves and Bushmen. Having lived for generations in the Cape, prior to migrating to Griquatown in 1803, they spoke Dutch, dressed in the fashion of the white settlers, and hunted and waged war on horseback. Armed with muskets, they were to

1. Robert Moffat, op. cit., p. 347.

become the dreaded enemy of the Bushmen and Sotho tribes, and in the near future they were to be involved in a desperate struggle with Mzilikazi.

Eleven days after Moffat's departure from Griquatown a commando of a hundred or more Griqua horsemen trotted into the mission station at Kuruman. After a brief sojourn it set out with Moffat and Melville for Lithako, whence it was hoped negotiations with the armies of the Wild Cat People might be opened. At Lithako, Moffat was astounded to find that the village had already been occupied by the invaders and that a second division had bivouacked close by.

The missionary and old Nicholas Waterboer 'advanced to within two musket shots of the enemy'[1] and, with a view to discussing with them the futility of waging war against the defenceless Fish People, they attempted to attract the attention of the commanders. At great personal risk Moffat dismounted and approached the Wild Cat hordes unarmed. Barely had he left his saddle than the warriors rose and bore down on him. Moffat remounted, dug his heels into his horse's flanks and galloped away through a shower of assegais.

At sunrise the next morning the Griqua set out across the plains of Lithako and advanced on Mantatisi's army. The enemy, at the unfamiliar sight of mounted men, remained strangely calm. Indeed, Moffat could not but wonder at their apparent unconcern. The Griqua contingent ventured to within 150 yards of the Wild Cat People, hoping it would so intimidate them that they would surrender or flee without raising an assegai.

For several long minutes the atmosphere was charged with evil foreboding. Suddenly the hordes rose, lifted their voices in a terrifying war-whoop, spread out fan-wise and converged on the horsemen. Waterboer's commando galloped out of range, turned and fired into the foremost lines of their frenzied pursuers. Never having encountered so mysterious a weapon as a musket, the Wild Cat People were momentarily taken aback. But then they continued the charge, loping over the corpses of their comrades and wrenching javelins and clubs from the hands of their wounded. As

1. ibid., p. 356.

row upon row of warriors careered into the Griqua bullets and tumbled to its death, a host of Fish People, armed with bows and arrows and poisonous barbed assegais, swarmed down the slopes of a coppice near by, but so terrified did they become on seeing a handful of Mantatisi's men turn to face them that they turned tail. For almost three hours the Griqua pounded their enemy, pausing only to reload or retire beyond range of the assegais.

The Wild Cat People halted. They had flung every available man into the inferno, but had not succeeded in dislodging a single Griqua from his saddle. They bolted, and although their rearguard turned on occasions to harass the riders who pursued them there was no doubt whatsoever that Mantatisi's people had had enough of war. Forsaking their cattle and the grain they had looted, they struggled eastwards.

For about four months the Wild Cat People hung about Mafeking, licking their wounds, foraging in the neighbourhood and conducting half-hearted raids into the villages of the Barolong tribe. Then they moved on, crossed the Vaal and wandered into the denuded plains of the Orange Free State. Starvation threatened them; desperate bandits, the victims of the *lifaqane* wars, plucked off their stragglers.

Then Matiwane appeared, the renegade chief from Zululand, whose bands of brigands had been picking the bones of almost every Sotho tribe that had been involved in the turmoil of *lifaqane*. He intercepted Mantatisi's war-scarred hordes and sent them fleeing, terror-stricken, in the direction of the Caledon valley.

Mzilikazi's progress northwards through Zululand, his crossing of the Drakensberg into the Ermelo highveld, his campaign against the Sotho of the Steelpoort valley, his building of ekuPumuleni – the Place of Rest – and his rise to power as a conqueror all coincided with the turbulent era of *lifaqane* that was raging in the south. Mzilikazi was enjoying a period of peace and prosperity in his new country, while the peoples of the central plateau of South Africa were being haunted by the dreadful carnage that threatened their existence from day to day.

As famine swept the country, hunger pangs afflicted thousands
of refugees. No longer did Sotho warriors regard the corpses of
their enemies as visible signs of success in battle, but as their
only source of meat-supply. Indeed, whilst Mzilikazi's Khumalo
were planting their crops in the vicinity of the Place of Rest, and
eating freely of grain and beef, the wretched victims of *lifaqane*
were turning to cannibalism.

At first the Sotho of the south fed only on the bodies of enemy
dead, but it was not long before starvation drove them to devouring their fallen comrades and even the wives, husbands and children who succumbed to the vicissitudes of endless trekking. Having once acquired the taste for human flesh, the cannibals formed
themselves into hunting bands and set out daily to capture refugees.[1]

Many a cannibalistic band fled from the Basutoland lowlands
into the mountains. Almost every overhanging ledge, cave and
cranny, the former haunts of Bushmen, became the hide-out of
hunger-tormented man-eaters. Remnants of the Bafokeng, the
original peace-loving Mist People, settled with their chief in the
Leribe district, and so vicious a group did they become that even
today their descendants are often referred to as Mariwa – the
Cannibals.

At Mamathes – the Place of Spitting – not thirty miles west of
Leribe, the greatest caves in Lesotho are situated. Once the home
of the dreaded cannibal chief Rakotswane, they form gigantic
mouths in a gaunt faces of sandstone cliffs rising 500 feet above
a wooded gorge.

Ten years after *lifaqane* had ceased, Arbousset of the Paris
Evangelical Missionary Society visited the area and was astounded
to discover that, although in possession of cattle and sheep and
large supplies of grain, the people were still living as cannibals.

During *lifaqane*, the 'Dark Age' in Sotho history, not one of the
tribes managed to gain supremacy over the peoples of the central
plateau of South Africa. The chiefs who had been obliged to forsake the comfort of tribal life for the hazards of prolonged inter-

1. During this time, Peete, the grandfather of Moshesh, was captured and eaten by cannibals in the vicinity of present-day Leribe.

necine warfare were either destroyed or reduced to abject poverty. Mpangazita, first of the chiefs of Zululand to invade the Orange Free State, was eventually slain by his rival Matiwane and in later years, as Matiwane continued to plunder in the Central Plateau, he was to clash with Mzilikazi, who drove him to the south. Growing weary of the precarious existence he and his people were leading, Matiwane returned to Zululand in quest of peace. There this conqueror who had played a leading role in *lifaqane* was arrested and tortured to death on a knoll, not three miles from Shaka's original Bulawayo kraal.

Mantatisi and her son returned to the Caledon valley, but the great assemblage that she had once led through the interior on marauding expeditions disintegrated. Groups of Wild Cat People roamed the country in bands until eventually they were wiped out or absorbed into the ranks of superior foes. Years after *lifaqane* had ended, Arbousset and Daumas found Mantatisi living in Merabing – the Place of the Puff-adder. She and her son were enjoying sanctuary in the domains of Moshesh, the founder of the Basuto nation, the petty chief whom they once had sought to dislodge from his mountain stronghold at Butha-Buthe.

How fortunate was Mzilikazi that in 1823 he chose to journey into the Transvaal, for had he turned southwards into the Orange Free State, he, his three hundred warriors and his clanlet would have been consumed in the holocaust of *lifaqane*! Not only was Mzilikazi spared the horror of these internecine wars, but Mantatisi was prevented from penetrating far beyond the Vaal. For, had Mantatisi not been repulsed by the Man of Conquest, Makaba, Chief of the Bangwaketsi, and driven towards the muskets of the Griqua, she would have continued to the neighbouring country of the Bakwena, the Crocodile People, who owned large herds and tremendous stores of grain.

Sooner or later, therefore, the Wild Cat People would have located Mzilikazi, and it is doubtful whether, at that stage of his career, the young Khumalo chief could have survived an attack from so formidable a foe. It was only in the years to come that Mzilikazi would clash with some of the characters who played leading roles in the tragedy of *lifaqane*.

CHAPTER 7

EXPANSION WESTWARDS

Mzilikazi abandons Middelburg district
Slaughter of the Crocodile People
Mzilikazi's followers become the Matabele
Huge military kraals — Plight of the Bapedi slaves

MIDSUMMER at ekuPumuleni – the Place of Rest – was unbearably hot. Since the last planting of the crops hardly a drop of rain had fallen despite the bombardments of lightning and thunder which often rocked the royal kraal, and the heavy yokes of cloud that hung almost daily over the bushveld. The fields were parched. Acre upon acre of stunted crops fretted in the vicious glow of a subtropical sun, springs dried up, streams dwindled into precarious trickles and the herds became skinny and disease-ridden.

Although at first Mzilikazi did not regard with undue concern the misfortune that threatened his newly won domain, when weeks passed into months and there seemed no hope that the drought would break he became desperate and sent word to all his rain-doctors to appear before him. Mzilikazi commanded them to produce rain immediately and warned them that if they failed he would hold them responsible for the drought. The rain-makers selected ingredients for their decoctions, slaughtered beasts, sacrificed them to the spirits and prayed for the clouds to gather and the rain to fall. But nothing happened. The only storm they succeeded in producing was the roar of abuse that Mzilikazi showered upon them. They tried again and again, but the sun merely blazed down and not a single rain-cloud was seen approaching.

The rain-makers trembled with fear, for such was Mzilikazi's wrath that they knew they would be sentenced to death. In due

course they were seized by the Chief's executioners, bundled off
to the river and fed to the crocodiles.

And still the drought persisted.

Although during recent months his plundering excursions had
yielded copious stores of grain, the fact that his crops were doomed
to failure, and a long, dry winter lay ahead caused Mzilikazi grave
concern. He reflected that his royal kraal had been prematurely
named the Place of Rest, and wondered if he should move farther
afield, to regions where climatic conditions would be more favourable for both the agricultural and pastoral activities of his people.
It is doubtful whether Mzilikazi would have remained in the
Middelburg district much longer anyway, for it was his constant
dread that Shaka would send an expeditionary force to capture
him.

To the immediate west of the Middelburg district lay the vast
territories of the Bakwena – the Crocodile People, one of the
largest and most prosperous of Sotho tribes. For months past recon-
naissances into Bakwena country had taken Mzilikazi's spies
through the Pretoria and Rustenburg districts as far as the Limpopo. These men had returned to their Chief with stories of the
colossal villages in which the Crocodile People lived, of the im-
mensity of their cornfields, and the innumerable herds roaming
the bush. Mzilikazi was intrigued. He decided to waste no time in
preparing the exodus of his clan from ekuPumuleni.

In the autumn of 1825 Mzilikazi commanded his subjects to
collect their things and proceed with the regiments to the west.
Before he himself took leave of his royal kraal he dispatched some
of his courtiers to prepare torches to fire the great circle of huts,
the palisades and the cattle-folds. He insisted that not a single
item of value be left, lest it be found by enemies who might
chance to pass that way.

On the previous day Mzilikazi had found three men guilty of
treachery and, to the consternation of the councillors who had
attended their trial, he had refused to pass judgement, saying he
would decide their fate on the morrow. During the hours they
were held in captivity the condemned men must have wondered
what dreadful punishment lay in store for them. It was only when

ekuPumuleni went up in flames that they knew: they were bound and led into a beehive hut, there to wait the onslaught of the fire and a death that, hitherto, only the lowliest of Mzilikazi's enemies had suffered. Before the blaze had spread half-way across the Place of Rest, Mzilikazi had left it to join his people on their westward journey.

Within the next two months the Khumalo reached the Rustenburg district, that part of Bakwena territory situated between the Magaliesberg (Kashan) mountains and the Limpopo. This was rugged country. The ranges, varying from the jagged and precipitous to the smooth and round, threaded a course through bushy lowlands. Conical-shaped hillocks were dotted haphazardly in every part, and knolls, crested with twisted brushwood, tree-aloes and prickly-pear, peeped over a roof of thorn-bush foliage extending for hundreds of miles beyond the Limpopo. Rivers, vivid with vegetation, glided northwards, and spruits curled like dust-clad serpents into the hollows.

Scattered over Bakwena country were villages encircled by stone walls. The huts of the Crocodile People, built in the rondavel-style, were among the most beautiful of all the tribes of South Africa. Their huge overlapping roofs were supported on stout wooden pillars, the walls were plastered with a mixture of cowdung and clay, polished smooth with river stones and decorated with artistic and geometric floral and animal designs. Around each family residence was a *lapa* – a mud wall – within the confines of which the mothers attended to their domestic chores, passed their leisure moments in gossip and romped with their children. Within the villages the cattle-folds were situated. It was here the cows were milked and the sacred tribal rituals were conducted. And, in the vicinity of the settlements, the lands were cultivated and the cattle pastured.

On reaching the Magaliesberg, Mzilikazi entered the bushveld to the north, and established temporary settlements for his subjects. Then he considered plans for the subjugation of the Crocodile People. He believed that, despite its great numbers, this Sotho tribe had little knowledge of organized warfare. He had noticed that, although armed with heavy barbed assegais, the Bakwena had made no effort to drive the Khumalo from their territory. Mzilikazi decided to wait for the new moon before launching the Bakwena campaign. He informed his regiments that, for a while at least, attacks on villages would be conducted only after sunset.

The Crocodile People had barely begun their reaping when Mzilikazi's regiments moved into action. Villages were surrounded and fired, old people and children were butchered, young women and girls captured, and men and youths bound and sent back to headquarters, to be prepared as warriors for the Khumalo army.

Accounts of the strategy employed by Mzilikazi in the series of conquests to follow present a horrifying picture, but if the character of the African conqueror is to be portrayed without bias they must not be omitted.

More often than not, when a village had been surrounded, Mzilikazi commanded his warriors to herd large sections of the terrified inhabitants to a spot not far from the outer row of huts and to club them to death. If any of the Bakwena males were so foolhardy as to resist capture, or to attempt to defend their homes, they were dragged away with their wives and children to a 'ferocious, horrid and cruel punishment'.[1] Mzilikazi could not have sentenced them to a more dreadful death. These unfortunate people were bound and flung to the ground; grass saturated with animal fat was packed about their bodies and set alight, and they were left to roast.

In remote villages little notice was taken of infants. Usually, after having pillaged and destroyed the Bakwena huts, granaries and cattle-folds, the Khumalo hurried away leaving the babies to perish from starvation and thirst, or to be dragged into the bush by lions, leopards or hyenas. However, there came a time when Mzilikazi decreed that all infants be destroyed, for fear they might be rescued by a clan who, as yet, had not been wiped out. He was afraid, if ever these infants reached manhood, they would become

---

1. Robert Moffat, op. cit., p. 554.

the most dangerous of his enemies, for without doubt they would seek to avenge the death of their parents.

Mzilikazi turned the Bakwena cattle-folds into incinerators. Babies were fetched from the huts, wrenched from their mothers' bosoms or backs and then cast into the cattle-folds. By raising a great pile of brushwood over their struggling bodies and setting it ablaze, Mzilikazi reduced the future tribesmen of the Crocodile People to ashes.

Already in 1825 Mzilikazi's people were being spoken of as the Matabele, the fearsome aggressors, who carried immense ox-hide shields behind which they 'sank out of sight' (*-tebele*) when challenged with an assegai. Wherever Mzilikazi journeyed on his mission of death his approach was heralded by hysterical exclamations of 'Matabele!' and when columns of black smoke rose in some distant part of the bushveld the Crocodile People knew that yet another village had been laid waste by these fiendish intruders – the Matabele. Indeed, in the language of the inhabitants of the luxuriant Rustenburg district, no word described impending death more lucidly than 'Matabele'.

Day by day Mzilikazi's Matabele grew stronger and more hostile. They became a motley group, consisting of the original Khumalo nucleus and several thousands of the sons and daughters of the Sotho-speaking tribes Mzilikazi had routed during three years of conquest.

Within a few months of their invasion of Bakwena country the Matabele destroyed almost every settlement. They reduced the Crocodile People east of the Limpopo to a rabble of wanderers. Long streams of captives, the cream of the Bakwena, were used as beasts of burden to carry booty from the plundered villages to the Matabele kraals. Multitudes of cattle were driven to Mzilikazi's stronghold, and the very people from whom they had been stolen were compelled to herd them.

As Mzilikazi's invasion of Bakwena country continued it became the fashion among the Matabele for 'foreign' recruits to accompany them on their marauding expeditions. Not only were the Bakwena youths loaded with their masters' heavy accoutrements, but they were also expected to keep pace with the main regiments. As Mzilikazi's forces were trained to travel at a trot, it happened that groups of their carriers became too exhausted to continue without periods of rest. They were put to death, for Mzilikazi believed a conquering army dared not have encumbrances in its ranks, especially Bakwena weaklings.

In the course of time Mzilikazi spared the lives of an ever-increasing number of Crocodile People. Eventually he commanded that not only men and women, but also children must be selected for the roles they would have to play as the future mothers, fathers and warriors of the Matabele tribe.

Many of the children were orphans whose parents had been slain by the invaders. They feared their captors. Observing this, Mzilikazi instructed his subjects to tie the children's hands behind their backs, and to nourish them with milk and special mixtures which he believed would wean them from fretting for their mothers.

Mzilikazi was scrupulous in selecting Bakwena children for his tribe, and if he regarded them as unlikely to develop into robust adults he had portions of their ears cut off and abandoned them in the smouldering villages. In the future, if ever he came upon men with cropped ears, he would know them as the enemies of the Matabele.

When spring arrived, no crops were planted in the Rustenburg district. Bakwena tribesmen who by some strange fortune had managed to flee before the Matabele besieged their villages became tormented by starvation, and like the Sotho clans which Mantatisi and other conquerors had decimated south of the Vaal, they were driven to foraging in the bush. Hundreds of families inhabiting the most westerly limits of Bakwena country escaped through Bechuanaland into the Kalahari desert, but finding neither food nor water in those barren flats they perished before they could retrace their steps towards their homelands. There were remnants of the Crocodile People who scattered to the north and south, a few to receive hospitality from other Bechuana tribes, a few to become cave-dwellers and to be forced by circumstances to resort to cannibalism.

In certain respects the plight of the Crocodile People resembled that of the clans to the south, the Sotho who, at that very time, were still being ravaged by *lifaqane*. Nevertheless, it would be false to imply that *lifaqane* in its true sense ever existed in the territories invaded by Mzilikazi.

By early 1826 Mzilikazi had completed the Bakwena campaign between the Magaliesberg and Limpopo, and the Matabele had become a prosperous and powerful tribe. The tempo of events during the past three years had moulded Mzilikazi into an experienced military tactician and an astute ruler. The stringent training he had received in Zululand, the part he had played in the struggle for supremacy between Shaka and Zwide and his subsequent advance through the Transvaal, had taught him that if a chief became complacent sooner or later he would be destroyed. Mzilikazi's life became dominated by an urgent desire for even greater power, an ambition to rule supreme over countless subjects, to lead armies even mightier than those of Shaka and to accumulate multitudes of cattle. He dreamed of boundless Matabele dominions, studded with great royal kraals and regimental barracks, a realm the might of which even the Zulu, whom he feared so intensely, would hesitate to challenge. Mzilikazi threw himself with ardour into planning several ambitious projects. He occupied his mind with little else.

In April the Matabele were still housed in temporary kraals somewhere to the north of the Magaliesberg range. A year of siege had left the country scarred with the ruins of the Bakwena villages. The fields, where once crops of millet, pumpkins, gourds and beans had grown, were matted with weeds, and about the deserted huts the skeletons of the hapless Crocodile People lay strewn.

Mzilikazi commanded his people to select suitable sites for the erection of permanent kraals, and also to collect material for huts, cattle enclosures and fortifications. Large circles of hemispherical huts were soon being built around rambling cattle-folds; loads of heavy branches, studded with menacing thorns, were being packed, one on the other, to form tall, compact kraal hedges. Military kraals sprang up, colossal strongholds in which the Matabele regiments would be barracked and trained for the conquests their potentate was contemplating.

Within the course of a year three of Mzilikazi's principal military kraals, built according to the style of Shaka's Gibixhegu, rose along the Aapies and Crocodile rivers; enKungwini – the Place of Mist – was situated on the right bank of the Aapies, in the vicinity of the present suburb of Pretoria North, while enDinaneni lay farther down the course of the same river. emHlahlandlela – Cutting a Path – was to be the largest of the new military kraals. As this was to be the Matabele capital, Mzilikazi decided it should guard the most northerly borders of the country. He chose a site for its erection on the Crocodile, not far from this river's confluence with the Limpopo.

Hundreds of workers were involved in the building of emHlahlandlela: hewers, artisans and thatchers. Day after day, from dawn to dusk, captive men and women toiled in all conditions of weather. There was no time for rest, for Mzilikazi was impatient to complete his headquarters. The Matabele overseers he had assigned to the responsibility of supervising the workers were to prove the cruellest of taskmasters.

It was while these building operations were in progress that a most important development in the social and political organization of the young Matabele tribe took place. From the Eastern Transvaal groups of Ndwandwe warriors arrived to plead that they be allowed to join the Matabele regiments. These were the vanquished followers of Zwide, Shaka's erstwhile enemy. They were kinsmen of Mzilikazi, tried fighters who, after having been dispersed in 1819 by the Zulu, had led an existence of perpetual unrest. And, having heard eventually of Mzilikazi's rise to power, they believed that he, the grandson of the illustrious Zwide, would accept them as members of the Matabele tribe. They were heartily welcomed by Mzilikazi.

Over the years, as the Matabele tribe had filled with Sotho-speaking subjects, the original nucleus of Nguni clansmen had grown proportionately smaller. Therefore, with the arrival of these Ndwandwe warriors, Mzilikazi realized that the strain of Nguni blood would be strengthened, and also that the Matabele army would benefit by the inclusion of experienced warriors. It was his firm belief that a warrior of Nguni stock equalled fifty Bakwena men in the line of battle.

There were similar pleasant surprises in store for Mzilikazi: beyond the Vaal, Mpangazita and Matiwane, two of the foremost of the *lifaqane* conquerors, had crossed paths, and become involved in a fierce struggle. For almost three years Matiwane had hounded the Hlubi chief over the Free State plains and through the Caledon and Orange River valleys. But somehow, Matiwane had failed to overtake Mpangazita until late in 1825. Matiwane's foraging parties had swooped down on the Hlubi, had slain their chief and decimated what was left of the regiments. Immediately, a section of the survivors had transferred their allegiance to Matiwane, but Mahlomaholo, the second eldest son of the vanquished Mpangazita, had escaped to the north with a substantial following, and had arrived at emHlahlandlela to offer his services to Mzilikazi. Mzilikazi was happy to receive them.

The endless strife that existed in Zululand also played a part in increasing the manpower of the Matabele army. So cruel had Shaka's tyrannical reign become, so unbearable his series of mass executions, that Nguni clansmen were continually fleeing into the interior. From time to time groups of fugitives found their way across the Magaliesberg and begged Mzilikazi for protection. Two distinct social classes formed within the Matabele tribe: a relatively small, yet privileged Zulu-speaking *élite*, and a vast proletariat made up of Sotho-speaking captives.[1]

The year wore on, and the building of the military kraals continued. emHlahlandlela, Mzilikazi's proudest project, proved so tremendous an undertaking that it progressed slowly.

Mzilikazi decided to send five of his young regiments on a long

1. The Matabele now included members of the following Nguni clans: Khumalo, Ndwandwe, Mthethwa, Mkwanazi, Koza, Ndlovu, emaNcwageni, Gumedi and Hlubi (A. T. Bryant, *Olden Times in Zululand*, p. 425).

and arduous expedition. He instructed the commanders to lead their men to the Limpopo and to reconnoitre the country beyond the river, where Chief Mgibe ruled over a great section of the Mashona, a tribe of cattle-breeders. As will be seen, this was not the main purpose of the expedition, but, as Mzilikazi planned to attack the Mashona in the near future, he was keen to learn about their size, wealth and fighting potential.

He instructed his regiments to proceed from Mgibe's country to the Upper Olifant and Steelpoort regions and to attack the Bapedi, who since 1824 had continued to boast that theirs was the only Sotho army ever to have defeated the fearsome Matabele. The words of the Bapedi national songs referred to Mzilikazi as a 'wicked brute' who had grown so fatigued that it slept most of the time. No longer were the brave Bapedi warriors troubled by its 'bellowings'.[1]

Arrogance such as this prodded Mzilikazi's pride; his mind also harked back to the insults his regiments had been obliged to endure several years ago before the Bapedi defences. But the grudge he bore the Bapedi was not his only reason for sending a Matabele force into their country. There was an urgent need for extra hands to help complete the great emHlahlandlela kraal, and by defeating the Bapedi Mzilikazi reasoned that he could round up their men and compel them to work as his slaves.

The five regiments set off towards the end of 1826. After completing a brief reconnaissance of the Mashona territory, they turned towards the Olifant river. A gruelling march over hundreds of miles of rugged terrain brought them, in 1827, to the borders of Bapediland.

In preparing their attack, the Matabele commanders decided to advance on Makhwarane, the capital village of the tribe, rather than beseige the mountain strongholds where they had suffered a defeat in the past. Here the Bapedi defences were inadequate; in fact, so little opposition did the Matabele encounter that they sacked the royal kraal, exterminated most of its inhabitants and collected their herds without the loss of a warrior. The Matabele

1. Arbousset and Daumas, op. cit., p. 268.

loaded their backs with plunder, and returned to emHlahlandlela, together with a group of slaves.

Six months later Mzilikazi sent a battalion of his most redoubt-able warriors, under the command of an experienced captain named Kutsane, to drive the Bapedi 'rock rabbits' from Matamoga and Morema, the mountain strongholds. On this occasion the Bapedi failed to repulse the Matabele. Neither their fortresses nor their skill in traversing the rocky slopes could save them from the ruthless onslaught of Mzilikazi regiments. Now they believed that the 'wicked brute' about which so much had been sung in recent years had awakened; furthermore its 'bellowings' struck terror into their breasts.

During this battle no great slaughter took place. Instead, the Bapedi were taken prisoner, were herded together and escorted in batches through the bush to Matabele country where Mzilikazi awaited them at his emHlahlandlela kraal.

Although during the past five years most of Mzilikazi's atten-tion had been devoted to waging wars, expanding his territories, gathering subjects and consolidating his supremacy as a con-queror, he had also found time to keep a seraglio in which he housed a bevy of his royal women.

When the Bapedi captives arrived, forty-four huts had already been built in the royal seraglio of emHlahlandlela, but the pali-sades that would isolate them from the rest of the community had not yet been started. This task was assigned to the Bapedi slaves.

Mzilikazi planned a gigantic wooden enclosure for emHlah-landlela – six feet deep, six in height, and half a mile in circum-ference. He sent the Bapedi to chop mimosa logs in the distant forests. While slaves felled the trees and carried the heavy green stumps back to emHlahlandlela, they were constantly being thrashed by their impatient Matabele overseers. They were allowed little food and almost no rest, and many of them col-lapsed from fatigue. Those who managed to continue the journey sighed a lament known to this day among the Bapedi of the Northern Transvaal:

Mosegare Maahlo a rena a tletse dikeledi,
(By day our eyes are in tears,)
Re robala ka tlala.
(By night we sleep in hunger.)[1]

In the course of constructing emHlahlandlela's enclosure the Bapedi slaves grew so frail that even their fearsome masters could not compel them to carry on. They became known as *amahole* – encumbrances – and were bundled off to recuperate in their homeland. Fresh labour gangs were fetched from Bapedi country, and so streams of slaves flowed to and from emHlahlandlela until eventually Mzilikazi's enclosure was complete.

At the close of 1827 the kraals of Mzilikazi's subjects spread from the vicinity of Pretoria to the Magaliesberg and the Limpopo river. It would be impossible to estimate the Matabele population of that time, or even to guess how many regiments Mzilikazi had at his disposal. However, there can be no doubt the tribe had increased even beyond the wildest expectations of the young conqueror himself. Surrounded by his courtiers, his warriors, harem women and servants, Mzilikazi relaxed in emHlahlandlela. But as the months passed, he became restless, plagued by an inflexible resolve to extend his boundaries beyond the Magaliesberg and the Limpopo, and to include all the wealthy tribes of Bechuanaland within his growing empire.

During the day he would climb on to the great enclosure the Bapedi slaves had built round emHlahlandlela, for not only did he 'take a singular delight in walking on the top of this terrace, whence he could command the whole town',[2] but he could also gaze into the distant limits of the country over which he ruled.

1. ibid., p. 269.   2. ibid., p. 268.

PART TWO

CHAPTER 8

WHITE MEN AND FIRE-ARMS

White settlers and explorers – First news of Mzilikazi
Andrew Geddes Bain's expedition
Mzilikazi learns of fire-arms – He defeats Matiwane
Robert Schoon trades and hunts along the Matabele border

THE destruction of the Transvaal Bakwena and the occupation of
their country by the Matabele marked the close of an important
era in Mzilikazi's life, and heralded the approach of another, far
more turbulent. So far, Mzilikazi's conquests had been confined
to the unwarlike Sotho tribes, but in the next decade his supremacy would be challenged by many enemies, the most formidable
of whom would be half-breeds and white men mounted and armed
with muzzle-loaders.

In 1825, when the Matabele surged into the territory between
the Magaliesberg and the Limpopo, almost two centuries had
passed since the occupation of the Cape by the Dutch. Fifty thousand colonists, mainly of Dutch, French and German descent,
and also a small group of British officials, inhabited the Colony,
whose northern frontiers extended as far as the Orange river.
Apart from the Cape and a few scattered mission stations, Euro-
peans were settled in two other parts of South Africa: at Port
Natal, where Francis Farewell, James King and other Englishmen
were trading and hunting in a vast area bought from Shaka, and
at Delagoa Bay, where Portuguese settlements manned by white,
half-caste and black soldiers studded a belt of fever-stricken coast-
line and the lower reaches of the Zambezi.

The interior of South Africa was still relatively unexplored territory. Dr Burchell, a naturalist and traveller of repute had pene-

trated Bechuanaland as far as Chue Lake, and John Campbell of the London Missionary Society had undertaken a journey to the Bahurutsi tribe in the Western Transvaal. But beyond these points the subcontinent was unknown to the white men of the Cape Colony.

Mzilikazi's arrival among the Crocodile People coincided with the white man's infiltration into the interior, for in this year the Cape Government approved a scheme for fostering trade between the colony and the non-white peoples. It issued licences and offered special facilities to traders and hunters who wished to travel to any part of the subcontinent, however remote.

Among the first to take out a trading licence was Andrew Geddes Bain, a Scot who, since 1822, had been living in Graaff-Reinet. In May 1826 he, John Biddulph an 1820 settler, Benjamin Kift a Colonial, their wives and children, a few Hottentot servants and a Bushman interpreter set out from Graaff-Reinet. With wagons laden with food, luggage, arms and ammunition, and a variety of barter goods, they proceeded through the Colony, crossed the Orange, and on reaching the Vaal, hugged its banks until eventually they came upon the tents of two Wesleyan missionaries, Hodgson and Archbell.

Like Bain and his party Hodgson and Archbell were heading north, but the purpose of their trek was to establish a mission station among the Barolong tribe, in the vicinity of Warrenton. The two groups of travellers spent a few days together, discussing, among other things, the misery brought about among the Sotho tribes by the war of *lifaqane*, and it was here, for the first time, that Bain learned of the Matabele and of Mzilikazi, their chief.

Hodgson was telling the traders how, two months before, he had undertaken a journey to the Vet river, where the settlements of Bataung, or Lion People, were situated. He explained that the Bataung had been Mantatisi's vassals but, after the disintegration of the Wild Cat People, they had broken away, had wrought havoc among the Barolong, and destroyed the Wesleyan mission station at Makwassie. The purpose of Hodgson's visit to the Lion People had been to implore Moletsane, the Chief, to lay down his weapons and spare the defenceless Barolong. To his surprise, on reaching the Vet, he had found the kraals deserted. A few days later, with the help of a band of Bushmen, he had located the Lion People beyond the Vaal.

Never having met a white man, Chief Moletsane had treated Hodgson with reserve, but before long he grew friendly and related the reason for the flight of Lion People. Recently news had reached him that an army of naked warriors, armed with shields and deadly stabbing-spears, and led by a cruel conqueror named Mzilikazi, had wiped out the tribes to the north, and had also embarked on pillaging excursions to the villages of tribesmen inhabiting the approaches to the Vaal. It had been reported to Moletsane that this army was approaching the Vet river and, fearing for the safety of his subjects, he had ordered them to flee.

The visit to the Lion People augured well for the future of the Wesleyan mission, Hodgson assured his listeners, for Moletsane had promised not to attack the Barolong, provided that they in turn never molested his tribe or encouraged the Griqua to attack them.

And, while the missionaries and traders camped on the banks of the Vaal, exchanged anecdotes, reminisced and discussed plans for the future, there was not one among them who guessed that soon Bain, Biddulph, Archbell and Chief Moletsane would be coming face to face with the tyranny of the conqueror of the unexplored interior – Mzilikazi, Chief of the Matabele.

Bain and his party took leave of the missionaries and proceeded westwards to Boetsap, the shabby village of Barend Barends, captain of one of the Griqua clans. There was nothing about this settlement that pleased Bain, and he regarded its impoverished huts as matching the 'lazy and imbecile' half-breeds who occupied them.

Barend Barends was as wily and picturesque a character as Bain had ever met in South Africa. He welcomed the traders to Boetsap and, learning of their intention to journey to the north, insisted that he become their guide. As Bain knew the Griqua hunted regularly beyond the Molopo river and were acquainted with every square mile of the country, he accepted Barend's offer. A day or two later the convoy and its escort of mounted Griqua threaded a way through Boetsap and followed a sandy trail to the north-west. On 18 July 1826 they reached Kuruman, the mission outpost of Robert Moffat.

It was here that Bain met Mothibe, who in later years would be the only Bechuana chief to avoid being subjugated by Mzilikazi. Mothibe was living at New Lithako, not a mile from the mission station, having moved the Fish People from the original Lithako, the scene of the battle between Mantatisi and the Griqua. Bain found Mothibe an unpleasant personality, describing him as a deceitful, avaricious, hypocritical, grovelling, louse-infested creature whose shaggy beard, 'clogged with filth', and hair plastered with clay and fat, hardly concealed his 'phlegmatic dullness'.[1] He was revolted by the assortment of grimy bones, sheep's trotters, horns and intestines that ornamented Mothibe's neck, and also the greasy kaross that hung about his shoulders.[2]

From Kuruman the expedition moved due north, along the route taken by Burchell thirteen years earlier. Learning that the white men intended trading in Bangwaketsi country, old Barends threatened to return to Boetsap. He warned Bain that recently the royal village of the Bangwaketsi had been sacked, and Makaba, the famous 'Man of Conquest', slain by the Makololo clan led by Chief Sebitoane, one of Mantatisi's former henchmen. Bain refused to alter his plans, and by supplying Barends with a generous quota of alcohol pursuaded him to continue the journey.

Ten days' laborious trekking brought the expedition to Chue Lake, the most northerly part of Bechuanaland reached by Burchell. Then the traders crossed the Molopo river and, as they moved into Bangwaketsi country, they noticed the tribe was still smarting from the horrors of Sebitoane's invasion. In the vicinity of what is today Kanye, the royal village, they descended into a valley, vast areas of which were carpeted with the skeletons of the Bangwaketsi who had opposed Sebitoane's advance. A depressing

1. H. M. Lister (ed.), *Journals of Andrew Geddes Bain*, p. 13.
2. Bain omitted to mention that Mothibe and his people inhabited a desert region where there was barely water for drinking purposes, far less for washing.

stench of death hung in the air, and Bain could not but wonder whether, in the near future, the bones of his own party might also be bleaching in the sun-drenched valley.

Chief Sebego, successor to 'the Man of Conquest', was delighted to meet the traders, for he was about to attack Sebitoane, and needed guns to support the Bangwaketsi army. He fêted his white guests and presented them with elephant tusks. He also succeeded in persuading Bain to help him drive Sebitoane from Lithubaruba, capital village of the Crocodile People of Bechuanaland.

Towards the end of 1826 Bain, mounted on a horse, Biddulph, on a war-ox, and three Hottentot musketeers followed the Bangwaketsi to Lithubaruba, and while Sebego's army besieged the capital village they 'kept up a brisk fire'[1] until the Makololo were fleeing panic-stricken to the north. After the engagement Bain confessed he and his companions had merely fired over the rooftops of the village, but so great an impression had the din of musket-fire made on all present that news soon spread far and wide. Sebitoane's Makololo had been routed by the mysterious thundering weapons of a handful of strangers.

Indeed, Matabele spies, lurking in the neighbourhood, careered across the Limpopo, and reported to Mzilikazi the part played by white and yellow-skinned men in dispersing the Makololo tribe. Mzilikazi dispatched his regiments to harass Sebitoane's hoardes as they struggled northwards. Twice the Matabele scattered the Makololo and robbed them of their herds, but on each occasion Sebitoane managed to rally his forces and retrieve his cattle. Mzilikazi acknowledged Sebitoane as a great warrior, and he reflected that had the Bangwaketsi not been assisted by the strangers, whose weapons belched thunder and fire, they would never have defeated the Makololo.[2]

Mzilikazi pondered on these strangers who, he learned, inhabited the regions in the south. He realized that if ever they

1. ibid., p. 69.
2. In quest of a new land, Sebitoane led the Makololo though the desert regions of Northern Bechuanaland, and settled along the Upper Zambezi, where he and Mzilikazi were to meet twice in battle. David Livingstone visited the Makololo in 1851.

found cause to attack the Matabele they would prove a dreadful foe.

Late in 1827 there was an uproar in emHlahlandlela, the Matabele capital, when Mahlomaholo, son of Mpangazita, the *lifaqane* conqueror, revolted against Mzilikazi's authority, collected his followers and fled. It will be recalled that this young warrior had joined the Matabele in 1825, when Matiwane crushed the Hlubi marauders in the south. He never really acknowledged Mzilikazi as his superior and, had he not deserted emHlahlandlela, his execution would have been inevitable. Mzilikazi was infuriated by this Hlubi cockerel's impudence. He sent a strong force to capture him so that his tail feathers might be plucked.

Meanwhile, Matiwane was informed of the approach of the fugitives and their pursuers and, as for some time it had been his intention to attack the Matebele marauding parties along the banks of the Vaal, he ignored Mahlomaholo and went out with three of his regiments to engage Mzilikazi's forces in battle. By interfering in the quarrel between the renegade Hlubi commander and the Matabele potentate, Matiwane was to bring about his own downfall.

For his regiments fared badly against the Matabele. The years of campaigning against Sotho people, who had offered little resistance, so softened them that they faded before the vicious onslaught of Mzilikazi's well-fed and superbly trained warriors. Matiwane fled. He led his people hither and thither across the Caledon valley, eventually to be driven out by Moshesh, who by now had succeeded in gathering the victims of *lifaqane* and converting them into a united tribe known as the Basuto. Matiwane struggled across the Orange, wandered aimlessly for two years in the territories of hostile tribes, and then returned in desperation to Zululand, whence he had fled in 1822.[1]

Despite this important victory in the South Mzilikazi had reason to feel ill at ease. On the return of his regiments he learned of the presence in those parts of a yellow-skinned race who tra-

1. In Zululand Matiwane, one of the three most powerful *lifaqane* conquerors, was arrested and sentenced to a gory death. His execu-

versed the plains in groups, mounted on hornless animals. He listened intently to the stories he was told of the magic of their weapons, the thunder and invisible fire that burned through ox-hide shields and sent the best of warriors reeling to his death. Mzilikazi became plagued by moody reveries. From the description of these weapons he knew they were the same as those that had been used in the dispersal of Sebitoane from Bakwena country. Mzilikazi decided that at all costs the secret of these weapons must be discovered. In the future, he wanted his own army to be as well armed as the yellow-skinned men of the South.

Unbeknown to Mzilikazi, a Scot named Robert Schoon was travelling by ox-wagon through the beautiful Marico district, in the Western Transvaal, to the Bahurutsi country. Schoon was a trader from Grahamstown, an open-air fellow who, like Andrew Geddes Bain, preferred the quietude of the bushveld, the company of a camp fire and the rustic comfort of a tented wagon to the comparative luxury of a town house. Recently he had procured a licence for trading and hunting north of the Orange, and had chosen to follow John Campbell's route into the interior rather than the routes taken by Burchell and Bain through Bechuanaland. He was never to regret this choice, for the Bahurutsi were keen to barter what goods they had for beads, tobacco, cloth-lengths and trinkets. Robert Schoon journeyed as far as the Marico river, then turned back with some of his wagons laden with skins and ostrich feathers and others with the tusks he had received from the inhabitants of the country or the elephants he had shot in the bush. So lucrative was his first expedition into Bahurutsi country that no sooner had he returned to Grahamstown than he commenced preparations for a second trip.

From the Bahurutsi, Matabele spies learned of Schoon's visit to the Marico district. Mzilikazi was filled with happy expectation,

---

tioners gouged out his eyes, forced wooden pegs up his nostrils into his brain, took him to a rocky knoll situated not three miles from Shaka's first Bulawayo kraal, and twisted his neck. To this day this place of execution is known throughout Zululand as kwaMatiwane.

especially when he was assured that this white man was of a friendly nature, that he sought only to trade and hunt, and that he had promised the Bahurutsi he would return during the next harvest time. Mzilikazi believed that at last he would find a person to teach him the secrets of the weapons of thunder. He resolved to do everything possible to have Robert Schoon brought to the land of the Matabele.

CHAPTER 9

THE VICTORIOUS BULL ELEPHANT

Yellow-skinned desperadoes
Jan Bloem's army invades Matabele territory
Mzilikazi obtains fire-arms

MZILIKAZI was to possess fire-arms sooner than he had anticipated, even before the return of Robert Schoon to the Marico district, and he would get them from the yellow-skinned horsemen
who haunted the regions in the South.

These people were the Bergenaars, or Mountain Men, a nomadic
horde of cut-throats. Originally they had emerged as a distinctive
group from among the criminal elements of Nicholas Waterboer's
Griqua tribe. They had scorned the teachings of the missionaries,
ignored the laws of the Cape Colony, and challenged the authority first of their captains and then of old Waterboer. They had
broken away from the Griqua and embarked on careers of brigandage in the territories of the Bechuana tribes, in the plains of the
Orange Free State and in Basutoland.

At the beginning of the *lifaqane* period the Bergenaars were
joined by the most turbulent sections of the Koranna, a kindred
tribe of half-breeds, and soon they moulded themselves into the
most fearsome of desperadoes ever to ride the interior of South
Africa.

The Bergenaars spoke Dutch and dressed in European style;
they bought and stole horses in the Cape, and along the Colony's
northern frontiers they traded cattle for contraband arms and
ammunition. They possessed enormous herds, the great majority
of which had been stolen from the villages of the tribes they
attacked. This motley horde of *banditti* waged a relentless war
against the black peoples of the South. They even attacked their

kinsmen, the Griqua, and terrified the missionaries who lived unarmed at Griquatown and Kuruman in isolated mission stations.

The most unruly members of the Bergenaar bands were the
Koranna. They were similar to the Griqua both in their appearance and habits, but their lives were more frequently plagued by
the jealousies and quarrels that crept up among their captains and
the vendettas and blood-vengeances that occurred all too often
between rival clans.

At Taung – the Place of the Lion – the Great Koranna tribe was
ruled by Jan Taaibosch – the Sticky Bush – while the Rats, Scorpions, Sea-cows, Springbok, and other petty clans lived with their
own captains along the lower reaches of the Vaal.

Had it not been for Mzilikazi's sudden rise to power the Bergenaars might well have succeeded in causing incalculable damage
among the tribes of the South. So accustomed were these *banditti*
to decimating the armies of the Sotho peoples, and so lucrative
were their endless cattle-raids, that when once they learned of
Mzilikazi's arrival and his destruction of the Crocodile People
they could not resist casting their eyes in the direction of the
Magaliesberg, where the Matabele pastured their multitudinous
herds.

They started raiding Mzilikazi's most exposed cattle-posts,
always keeping well out of sight before swooping down on the
herdsmen who watched over the royal herds. And before the news
of their depredations could reach the Matabele military kraals
they would vanish into the bush and hurry towards the Vaal.
Their plundering excursions to the Magaliesberg remained clothed
in mystery. Although time and again reports reached Mzilikazi
that cattle-folds had been looted and herdsmen murdered, no one
could explain how the culprits had managed to disappear so
swiftly.

After one of these successful cattle-raids the Bergenaars were
almost overtaken by the Matabele and, had it not been for the
wisdom of their captain, they would have been engaged in battle
by regiments the like of which they had never encountered. They
were absconding to the south with one of Mzilikazi's herds when
their scouts reported a great column of Matabele warriors advanc-

ing towards them. Realizing that it would be impossible to out-pace the Matabele and hoping at all costs to avoid betraying their identity, the Bergenaars presented their haul of cattle to a rabble of homeless Sotho tribesmen and then galloped away to safety. The unsuspecting Sotho were *lifaqane* victims, wretched nomads who for months on end had eked out a precarious existence by foraging in the veld. When they were discovered by the Matabele, they were rejoicing beside the fires they had kindled in prepara-tion for a feast of beef. Mzilikazi's forces encircled them and wiped them out to a man. The Matabele cattle were collected and driven back to the Magaliesberg.

At the end of 1827 the stage was set for the first serious clash between the Matabele and the Bergenaars by Moletsane, Chief of the Bataung, or Lion People. Ever since Hodgson had visited him on the Vaal, Moletsane had honoured the promise he made not to attack the Barolong tribe. He had even befriended the Barolong and persuaded the Chief to join the Lion People in the invasion of Matabele territory. Moletsane was so determined to rid the Transvaal of the notorious Mzilikazi that he also visited a section of the Bergenaars and invited Jan Bloem, captain of the Springbok band, to lead the allied army beyond the Magaliesberg to the Matabele kraals.

Jan Bloem, a Koranna by birth, was a seasoned campaigner, a hunter of elephant, rhinoceros, lion and antelope, and his was one of the most ruthless groups of *banditti* that ever rode the flats either to the north or south of the Vaal. The son of a Hottentot mother and a German father, whose criminal record was at one time legendary throughout South Africa, Jan Bloem was the one man who, so Moletsane believed, could crush the Matabele army and break Mzilikazi's power for ever.

Bloem was never a man to shirk a battle, particularly if his allies were as powerful as the Lion People and, moreover, when the stakes were herds of cattle as large as those of Mzilikazi. He agreed to command the expeditionary forces and prepared his commandos for the trip whilst Moletsane hurried home to muster his Bataung and Barolong army.

But if Jan Bloem at any stage of his negotiations with the Chief of the Lion People had imagined that the defeat of the Matabele would be a simple matter, he was soon to learn that even the javelins and battle-axes of the Bataung and Barolong, together with the muskets of the Springbok Bergenaars, would prove futile against the guile of the Matabele Bull Elephant – as Mzilikazi had already become known.

At the head of his huge allied army, Jan Bloem set out across the Transvaal and moved into Matabele territory. Experience had taught him that at the sound of gun-fire the tribesmen of the interior became terror-stricken, and he guessed that the Matabele would be no exception.

Indeed, now for the first time since he had fled from Shaka, Mzilikazi was faced by a foe he could never hope to repulse. When the news was received in the regimental barracks that the Matabele kraals along the fringe of the country were being sacked, and that a mighty Bataung and Barolong army, headed by a group of mounted yellow-skinned men carrying weapons of thunder and fire, was approaching, Mzilikazi ordered his forces to withdraw rapidly into the depths of the bushveld, and to take the women and children of the tribe with them. In their flight the Matabele were obliged to abandon most of their cattle. Nothing could have distressed Mzilikazi more than the thought of his coveted herds falling into the hands of the aggressors.

The invasion turned out to be a half-hearted affair. Jan Bloem decided not to pursue the Matabele into the bushveld, but to collect cattle and send them back to his settlement on the Vaal. To the layman Bloem's sudden decision may seem strange, but bearing in mind that the Griqua and Koranna, and especially those of their brethren who had joined the ranks of the Bergenaars, were primarily interested in hunting and stealing cattle, it becomes clear that Jan Bloem had undertaken this important excursion into Matabele territory mainly for the purpose of collecting stock for his Springbok band.

Jan Bloem's greed for cattle knew no bounds, and if it could be satisfied without the risk of bloodshed so much the better. Chief Moletsane could hardly have expected his Bergenaar friend to devote his attention to waging war with Mzilikazi when the deserted Matabele kraals and the surrounding plains swarmed with untended cattle.

During the first day of their arrival in Mzilikazi's country, Jan Bloem's people started looting the Matabele kraals. Bands of rustlers, supervised by Bloem's men, rounded up Mzilikazi's herds and drove them towards the Magaliesberg. Dust clouds rose into the mountain slopes as a rolling mass of cattle started surging southwards. Bloem was jubilant. Next day he withdrew his forces from enemy territory and headed for the Vaal.

Two days and two nights passed and Bloem had progressed, without incident, far into the lower reaches of the Transvaal. After sunset on the third day the army halted and prepared to bivouac in the open veld. Jan Bloem and his comrades kindled camp fires and settled down to a meal of grilled beef and a quiet pipe of tobacco. Later in the evening, when they lay down to sleep to a lullaby of the lowing and snorting from Mzilikazi's herds, they were inspired to dream of wealth and happiness, and of the trips they would undertake in the future to the land of the Matabele.

Bloem's army took no precautions against a surprise attack by the Matabele. Not even Chief Moletsane believed that Mzilikazi would attempt to retrieve his cattle, despite the fact that during the past year the Lion People had heard many an awe-inspiring story about the cunning of the Matabele Bull Elephant. Apparently nobody present knew Mzilikazi well enough to realize that he struck hardest when his foes least expected an attack, and when the shadows of night concealed the manoeuvres of his regiments.

Whilst the Bataung, Barolong and Bergenaars lay snoring in their karosses, a few cattle herdsmen sat bandying anecdotes beside a fire. From time to time they stretched their legs by visiting their charges, to make sure that none had strayed from the camp. Not for a moment did they turn their minds to the dangers that could be lurking in the veld about them.

A sudden rush of Matabele warriors, whooping and hissing, followed by the frantic yells of the herdsmen, wrenched the entire encampment from its slumbers. The Bataung and Barolong sprang to their feet and fled into the night, and the Bergenaars raced for their horses, mounted and galloped away. The majority of Jan Bloem's army managed to escape, though many were killed and many mortally wounded.

The sun rose and the Matabele regiments rejoiced as they beheld the corpses that lay scattered in the ashes of smouldering fires. They rejoiced at the sight of the accoutrements, the javelins, clubs and battle-axes. But even greater was their delight when on searching among the impedimenta abandoned in haste by the Bergenaars, they came across muskets, the weapons of thunder and fire their illustrious Bull Elephant so eagerly wished to possess.

The Matabele collected their cattle, sent them in the charge of herdsmen to the north and then prepared to hunt down the fleeing enemy. They travelled swiftly to the Vaal, and discovered the fugitives had crossed the river and were heading for the Orange valley. But the Matabele were unaware that the confederates had already split up and branched off in different directions.

Then the Matabele picked up a trail which they learned had been taken by the Barolong. They moved swiftly through the Orange Free State, and would undoubtedly have overtaken and exterminated the Barolong had they not run into an unexpected hazard on the banks of the Orange river.

At that moment a strong commando of Boers from the Cape happened to be patrolling the Colony's northern frontier. Having been informed of the desperate flight of the Barolong and the approach of a powerful Matabele army, the Boers had moved to the south bank of the Orange, to watch developments and prevent at all costs the crossing of Mzilikazi's forces into the Cape Colony.

When the Matabele came into sight, the Boers opened fire. Bewildered, the regiments fell back, leaving some of their warriors sprawling in the sands of the river. They advanced a second time, but, realizing they would never succeed in approaching close enough to drag the riders from their mounts and stab them to death, they turned and trotted homewards across the highveld plains.

This was the first meeting between the Matabele and the Boers of the Cape Colony, and the first clash of a series that would culminate in one of the most bloody wars ever to be waged between the black and white races of South Africa.

JOURNEY TO THE PLACE OF MIST

Shaka assassinated
Mzilikazi observes the Ceremony of First-Fruits
White traders journey to Mzilikazi's kraal
Defeat of the Lion People – Tree-dwellers

BETWEEN the Magaliesberg and the Limpopo, the Matabele emerged from their hiding-places and tribal life returned to normal. Now Mzilikazi decided that in view of the recent invasion of his country he should move his headquarters from emHlahlandlela to enKungwini, his military kraal situated on the banks of the Aapies not many miles north of the present-day city of Pretoria. He had never intended establishing the Matabele capital so far to the east, mainly because he had feared Shaka so intensely. It struck him that perhaps his fears had been unfounded, for since the day he escaped from enTubeni and left Zululand for ever Shaka had never bothered to attack him.

Mzilikazi was not entirely satisfied with the affairs of his country, for although his victory over the Bataung, Barolong and especially Jan Bloem's Bergenaars had been a magnificent achievement the reverse the Matabele regiments had suffered at the hands of the mounted white men troubled him.

In recent years it had been Mzilikazi's ambition to possess the weapons with which the yellow-skinned riders and white men of the South hunted and waged war, and although since the return of his regiments from their pursuit of the allied invaders he had become the proud owner of several of these fire-arms, not a single member of his tribe, not even his witch-doctors, knew how to manipulate them. His thoughts turned to the white friend of the Bahurutsi, the hunter-trader who had visited the Marico district during the winter of the previous year. Mzilikazi had not the slightest doubt that this friendly man would return as he had promised the Bahurutsi, and that he could be persuaded to visit enKungwini, the new Matabele capital.

The year 1828 brought no major military achievements. It is true that throughout the year Mzilikazi's regiments never ceased raiding the cattle-folds of the Sotho peoples who inhabited the Transvaal highveld, but these were routine outings which served merely to increase the royal herds.

Harvest time arrived in June. All the members of the tribe, except the warriors actively engaged in military affairs, reaped, threshed and carried sorghum corn to the grain-pits situated in the cattle-folds; they brought pumpkins, melons and gourds to the storehouses and spread their bean-crops on tall, flat-roofed structures that stood beside their huts.

Winter stole over the country, bringing with it not the gnawing cold of the Transvaal highveld, but a mellow warmth similar to that which Mzilikazi had known as a young man in Zululand. It was the season when the men drank more beer than usual at the gathering places beneath the trees, when women found more time to play with their babies, and herdboys drove the cattle from the bush and the veld to the lands where the stalks of recently harvested crops stood bleaching in the sun. Spring arrived before the rains, but soon the skies became heavy with banks of cloud and thunder-storms started beckoning the boys to drive their cattle out of the fields to the bush. The men prepared to plough and sow, and the women made ready their hoes for weeding. Summer came, and a trembling, steaming heat enveloped the Matabele kraals.

It was about this time, December 1828, when Mzilikazi received word that Shaka had been assassinated by Dingane, his half-brother, in the royal kraal of Dukuza. Perhaps at first, when his messengers delivered the news, Mzilikazi was relieved by the thought that now he need fear no black man and that he, King of the Matabele, would take Shaka's place as the greatest tribal conqueror. Nevertheless, there must have been times when Mzilikazi's mind harked back to Zululand, to the days when he had been the petty-chief of the Northern Khumalo clanlet. He must undoubtedly have ruminated upon the encouragement he had received from Shaka, the great friendship that had existed between them and Shaka's confidence in him. Mzilikazi might even have been ashamed of the way he had defied Shaka.

But if in 1828 Mzilikazi found relief in the news of Shaka's murder, he would soon learn to regret it, for Dingane, the new King of the Zulu, was to become one of the Matabele's most dreaded enemies.

In December, when the moon waxed full, Mzilikazi and his people gathered to take part in the Great Nxwala, the ceremony of First-Fruits. Like the Umkhosi, the Zulu festival that included among its rites the killing of a black bull by unarmed braves, the Nxwala was the most solemn occasion of the year, for it was then that the King became a medium for direct communication with the royal ancestors of the tribe. Potent decoctions were prepared by the medicine-men; sacrifices, accompanied by prayers, hymns, offerings and dances, were dedicated to the spirits and the important ritual of cleansing the tribe took place. The entire proceedings were devoutly observed by all who gathered about Mzilikazi, for, no matter how prosperous the Matabele might have become in 1828, each member of the tribe feared the whims of the spirit world and strove to keep the ancestors appeased. It was only at the close of the ceremony of First-Fruits that the Matabele families dared eat of their ripening crops. If the people entered half-heartedly into this religious festival, they could not look with confidence to a future of good fortune and prosperity.

The Nxwala had barely closed when rumours started floating into the country that Chief Moletsane of the Lion People was planning a second attack on the Matabele. Early in the new year Barolong messengers arrived at enKungwini to report that Moletsane had turned hostile towards the Barolong tribe and was also determined to overthrow Mzilikazi's power in the Rustenburg district. The messengers pleaded with Mzilikazi, on behalf of their chief, to forgive the Barolong for having joined Jan Bloem's army against the Matabele. They asked Mzlikazi to consider supporting the Barolong army in a war against a tribe both they and the

Matabele regarded as enemies – the Lion People of Chief Moletsane. Mzilikazi reflected that for almost three years he had striven
in vain to capture Moletsane. He agreed to support the Barolong,
and instructed the messengers to assure their chief that, as soon as
the Lion People launched their attack on the Barolong settlements,
the Matabele army would arrive to crush them.

Meanwhile, Mzilikazi was determined that nothing must prevent his meeting the white man who had promised the Bahurutsi
he would return to the Marico district during the winter. In Feb-
ruary, two moons after the ceremony of First-Fruits, he selected a
group of his most reliable *indunas* to undertake the responsibility
of finding the white man when once he reached Bahurutsi territory. Mzilikazi warned these dignitaries that if they returned to
enKungwini and reported their mission had been unsuccessful,
they could expect to be executed. He instructed them to take oxen
with them, as presents from the King of the Matabele for the
white man.

In Grahamstown Robert Schoon was preparing his wagons for
his second trading and hunting expedition into the interior of
South Africa. During his first trip through the Western Transvaal and the bushveld to the immediate west of the Marico river
he had often heard of Mzilikazi, and so frightful had been the reports of the Matabele tyrant's treachery that Schoon had not the
slightest desire to venture towards the Magaliesberg.

He was essentially a businessman, and his interests lay in trading, hunting and travelling, as these activities enabled him to
procure valuable loads of ivory, skins and ostrich feathers. As he
had been able to accomplish his ambitions among the friendly
Bahurutsi tribe, he had no intention of penetrating into the
domains of a ruthless conqueror like Mzilikazi.

By the time Mzilikazi's *indunas* set out on their journey into
Bahurutsi country Robert Schoon, with his wagons laden with
barter goods, arms, ammunition, and personal belongings, had left
Grahamstown and was travelling northwards in the region of the
Great Fish river. Accompanying him was his friend William
McLuckie, a fellow-Scot who, since 1827, had become enthralled

by what he had learnt of the riches awaiting fortune-seekers in the
territories beyond the Orange and Molopo rivers. McLuckie had
decided to turn from his tranquil existence as a Grahamstown
shopkeeper to that of an itinerant trader.

Early in June Schoon and McLuckie crossed the Orange river,
pressed on to Campbell (a modest outpost of the London Missionary Society), and after a brief sojourn with the hospitable missionaries, continued through Griqua country to the north. Their route
took them through the parched regions of Danielskuil – Daniel's
Pond – and towards the end of the month they reached Boetsap,
the impoverished village of old Barend Barends, the Griqua captain whom Andrew Geddes Bain had befriended two years earlier.

Robert Schoon's party followed the Rev. John Campbell's route
into the interior, through sandy, waterless wastes, punctuated
with patches of pallid grass, twisted shrubs, succulents and
stunted thorn-bushes. From day to day the traders struggled to
find water, for the few springs known to ooze from the scattered
outcrops of limestone had been cunningly concealed by Bushmen
hunters, and the desert rivers had ceased to flow many thousands
of years before modern man ever thought to enter the Kalahari.
On 12 July they reached a salt pan where they came upon a small
party of Bechuana who, with their hunting-dogs, were stalking
game. Eleven days later they entered Barolong country and
reached the Molopo, the rapid flow of which delighted everyone,
and especially William McLuckie, who in all his life had never
before been subjected to the pangs of thirst or the hazardous experience of travelling by ox-wagon through desert regions.

And while they were watching their oxen at the Molopo river,
a black stranger driving four oxen arrived at the wagons. By his
plumed head, his naked torso, the cluster of tails that hung about
his loins and the ox-hide shield and stabbing-spears he carried, the
traders recognized him as one of Mzilikazi's warriors. The man
informed Schoon and McLuckie that he had been sent by his King
to meet them and invite them to trade and hunt in Matabele territory. As a token of the great Mzilikazi's friendship the warrior
had brought them a present of four royal cattle.

Two days later the wagons crossed into the Marico district.

They were travelling in a north-easterly direction through the lush grasslands between Mafeking and Zeerust. Once again the traders were intercepted by a Matabele warrior, an *induna* who told them he had already waited four months for their wagons to appear. He pleaded with Schoon and McLuckie to accompany him to Mzilikazi's royal kraal, for if they refused he would be put to death. The *induna* gave them six white oxen, declaring they were a special present from the illustrious Mzilikazi, Bull Elephant of the Matabele. By this time Robert Schoon was so impressed by Mzilikazi's eagerness for the trading party to visit Matabele territory that he dispatched a messenger with large quantities of beads to tell the King the white men were grateful for the cattle they had received and that it would not be long before they presented themselves at enKungwini – the Place of Mist.

The wagons moved on. They cut a trail through well-watered vales, vast expanses of shrubs and withered grass, and an endless mass of deciduous bush. They skirted colossal Bahurutsi villages, and on 29 July, six weeks after leaving Boetsap, they drew into Tshwenyane – the Little Baboon village, the Bahurutsi capital that had been sacked by Mantatisi in 1823 and had since tumbled into ruins. Here two more Matabele *indunas* arrived to inquire whether the white men had been met by Mzilikazi's representatives in the South. They said Mzilikazi had as yet received no news of Schoon's intentions and was becoming more impatient every day.

While Schoon and McLuckie were enjoying the serenity of the rugged yet beautiful surroundings of the deserted Little Baboon village, they might have learnt from Mzilikazi's emissaries that the Matabele were waging war with the Lion People of Chief Moletsane. For, true to his word, when once Mzilikazi heard that the Lion People were attacking the Barolong, he sent about a thousand warriors to the South. The scantily clad Matabele advanced on the rearguard of the Lion People, who were chasing a disorganized Barolong horde, war-weary, timid and almost defenceless, retreating across the Vaal river into the plains beyond. The startled and enraged army of the Lion People turned to meet the Matabele and the Barolong rabble. The battle ended with the Matabele and the jubilant Barolong sitting side by side wiping their spear and javelin blades after the Lion People had been slaughtered. Some of the Matabele must have been happy to find muskets clutched in the hands of a few of Moletsane's fallen warriors.

Schoon and McLuckie, accompanied by Mzilikazi's *indunas*, left the Little Baboon village and crept slowly towards the treeless flats in the north. They arrived at a disused Bahurutsi mine, a series of deep trenches where seams of copper lay embedded in soft black clay. There were also excavations where the alluvial deposits of iron ore were so rich that only heating and limited beating was necessary to produce iron bars. Leaving the mines, the traders branched off in an easterly direction and by the end of July reached the Marico river, whose waters were clear, deep and abundant in fish, but also infested with crocodiles.

It was on the banks of this river that Robert Schoon shot one of these monsters, a sixteen-footer, whose belly was so rotund that the trader could not but wonder what strange assortment of foodstuffs lay within. Schoon cut open the massive brute and discovered it had recently feasted on one of the local tribesmen. Among the many evil-smelling items that dropped from the crocodile's stomach were a pair of sandals, a thong for tethering cattle, and a dog which had been bitten in two.

On crossing the Marico the traders moved into Matabele country. They entered wooded, undulating regions, struggled through a series of streams and then the Elands river, to find their trail blocked by the toe of the Magaliesberg range. They followed the curves of the mountains, and the farther they progressed the more impressed they were with the variety of wild animals that grazed in the surroundings. Schoon realized that at last they were entering the territory of the ill-fated Crocodile People, and were now approaching the first of Mzilikazi's outposts. Five years earlier this had been one of the most densely populated parts of the Transvaal; now there was not a living soul in sight.

From time to time Schoon and McLuckie stopped to inspect

deserted Bakwena villages, and they came upon gory evidence of the slaughter that had taken place during the Matabele invasion. Huts lay in ruins, and among the rubble and ashes, in the court-yards and beside the rotting palisades of the cattle-folds, the two Scots saw heaps of skulls and bones, the remains of the Crocodile People whom Mzilikazi's warriors had butchered. On the out-skirts of the villages and also in the veld their eyes followed long lines traced by the skeletons, the tribesmen and their families who had attempted to escape from the Matabele, but had been sur-rounded and cut down.

Several more days of travelling brought Schoon and McLuckie to the homes of the first human beings they had seen in the entire ravaged country. These people were Bakwena wretches who by some strange chance had escaped the Matabele stabbing-spears and who had been tormented by hardships and terrors ever since. For, with the extermination of the Bakwena, great changes had taken place in the country about the Magaliesberg: beasts of prey, and especially lions, had infested the settlements, fields and pastures which for many generations had been the habitat of pros-perous Bakwena cattle-breeders. So numerous and so bold were these wild animals that the survivors of the Matabele invasion were compelled to live like apes in the loftiest trees. Indeed, the few timid tribesmen discovered by the traders were tree-dwellers, whose small, hemispherical huts were built on platforms secured to the boughs of a mimosa tree.

Twenty miles farther along the Magaliesberg range were situ-ated the first of the Matabele kraals. Schoon's party drew up near a circle of beehive huts and was welcomed by the inhabitants, who apparently had received instructions from headquarters to treat the white strangers with the utmost courtesy.

Schoon noticed immediately the prosperity enjoyed by Mzili-kazis' subjects. Their cornfields were fertile, their cattle grazed in luxuriant, wooded pastures and there were streams and springs everywhere. In contrast to the Bakwena tree-dwellers, who eked out an existence by snatching up whatever food they could lay hands on, the followers of the Matabele tyrant feasted on the sorghum stored in their grain-pits, on pumpkins, melons, beans and cane, and on the fresh and curdled milk they obtained from the three thousand head in their cattle-fold.

At this kraal the traders were given a milch cow. Knowing that the Matabele never dared slaughter cattle unless instructed to do so by their ruler, Schoon shot the cow and insisted that it be dismembered and prepared for a feast. The report of the fire-arm and the sudden death of the beast so terrified the Matabele spectators that they fled. During the rest of the day they could speak of nothing else, and the prestige of Schoon and his companions became firmly established.

The traders departed next morning, and for two days journeyed through the country to the immediate west of the Crocodile river. Somewhere in that beautiful part of the Transvaal they met a large black army led by Matabele regiments, and although for a moment they feared they had been led into a trap they soon learned that these were warriors who had recently defeated Chief Moletsane's Lion People. The regiments were returning to report the details of their magnificent victory to Mzilikazi.

Schoon estimated the army at between four and five thousand strong. The great majority were of the Barolong tribe. He noticed that several of the men were footsore and fatigued and he invited them to ride on the wagons. This simple gesture, coupled with Schoon's friendly disposition, won him the immediate confidence of Mzilikazi's victorious regiments. Now the wagons were escorted eastwards by the army. They passed many of Mzilikazi's cattle-posts, some manned by a headman and not more than eight herdsmen, others by as many as forty or fifty hand-picked warriors.

On 12 July the traders arrived on the outskirts of enKungwini and were instructed by Mzilikazi's *indunas* to outspan their oxen and to proceed no farther until word had been received from the Bull Elephant of the Matabele. They obeyed. It is interesting to note that in those times, as indeed also to this day, it would be an unforgivable breach of tribal etiquette if a stranger were so presumptuous as to enter the gates of a kraal without the sanction of the *induna*-in-charge or the Chief. An experienced traveller like Robert Schoon would have been aware of this jealously guarded tradition, and would have known that, as among the black peoples, time is no object and patience is one of man's glorious virtues, and he and his friends would be obliged to wait until Mzilikazi condescended to allow them to approach and enter his royal kraal.

CHAPTER 11

THUNDER FOR THE KING

Mzilikazi meets Schoon and McLuckie
Despotism in the Place of Mist
Schoon demonstrates the workings of fire-arms

MZILIKAZI was overjoyed to hear of Schoon and McLuckie's arrival and sent a group of *indunas* to welcome the traders to enKungwini and present them with four oxen. However, observing the tribal custom of keeping visitors to royal kraals waiting, Mzilikazi did not say when he intended granting the traders an audience.

By the following morning Mzilikazi was so anxious to meet the white men that he instructed one of his chief men to go to the wagons and summon Schoon and McLuckie to the kraal. The Matabele dignitary set out, bade the traders prepare to present themselves before the King, and warned their servants not to move the wagons unless commanded to do so by the Bull Elephant. Then he and the two white men strode through the bush and reached the tall hedge that encircled enKungwini. They entered the kraal through the main gateway, proceeded between lines of beehive huts and approached the cattle-fold where Mzilikazi sat among his regimental officers, councillors, courtiers and menials.

Having heard so many awe-inspiring tales about Mzilikazi's tyranny, Schoon and McLuckie were expecting to meet a stern, unfriendly and arrogant conqueror. Great, therefore, was their surprise when they were brought before the King. Mzilikazi was jovial and dignified, young and exceedingly handsome, a man of medium height and excellent physical proportions.

From the moment they exchanged greetings with the Bull Elephant – the one black man in all South Africa whom white colonists had never dared visit – the traders felt at ease. Schoon noticed that Mzilikazi was a man of exceptional intelligence, who was engrossed in every detail of what he and McLuckie had to say. Mzilikazi's black, shining eyes seldom departed from those of Schoon, and his thick lips crooked frequently into a smile. And when once or twice Schoon jested with him, the Matabele Bull Elephant flung back his head and rocked with hearty laughter.

In honour of his visitors Mzilikazi had prepared a feast: oxen had been slaughtered, fires kindled for roasting beef and large quantities of beer brewed. The regiments were eventually summoned to dance before the King and his white visitors. When the heavy warrior feet started stamping the rhythm of a war dance on the dry earth and the voices rose in harmony, Mzilikazi ran forward and flung himself into the foremost line of men to lead the dance.

In the meantime the aroma of roasting meat drifted across the kraal. Baskets of beef were being carried by servants to an open space and laid out on a vast carpet of ox-hides. The violent war dance continued, but suddenly Mzilikazi came loping back to his guests and invited them to eat. But before the King and the white men began their meal a royal taster swallowed small portions of food from each wooden bowl, for it was the custom then (as it is in some of the great royal kraals of South Africa today) for important people never to partake of food or drink not tasted for poison.

The hubbub of singing and dancing ceased as Mzilikazi beckoned an *induna* to his side, and ordered him to call the names of seven or eight warriors whose bravery and devotion to duty in the recent Matabele victory over the Moletsane's Lion People had earned them the admiration not only of the King but also of the regiments. The heroes filed out and bowed before their ruler, who scrutinized them with obvious pride. Mzilikazi praised them and told them to retire to the ox-hides, to enjoy the privileges of selecting the choicest portions of beef. Later Mzilikazi announced that all the inhabitants of enKungwini would feast. The courtiers, warriors and commoners rushed into the open space, scrambled to reach the ox-hides and voraciously fell upon the heaped beef.

Schoon and McLuckie were to be the guests of honour at several other regimental dances, and as the days wore on they became ever more conscious of the extraordinary authority Mzilikazi exercised over his subjects. Every word the King spoke, even his slightest gesture, was regarded by the people as significant. He was hailed from morning till night with 'Bayete!' – the royal salute which implied that those who addressed the King, or as much as looked upon his magnificent person, withered like the leaves of a delicate plant in the fierce rays of the sun.

The traders noticed there were occasions when Mzilikazi chose to sit alone, steeped in thought. They observed that when he called courtiers or messengers they grovelled in the dung of the cattle-fold, or the dust of the courtyard, and approached on their knees. The influential *indunas* alone were allowed the honour of remaining on their feet while talking to their King, but even they spoke in muted tones and adopted the humblest of attitudes.

In the daily sittings of the tribal court no one dared challenge Mzilikazi's decisions. Transgressors who appeared before him were not permitted to utter a word in their own defence, and there was no one to plead their case. When sentence was passed on them they praised Mzilikazi for his wisdom and expressed gratitude for the punishment chosen for them.

Schoon and McLuckie did not remain at enKungwini long enough to learn of the variety of ghastly sentences the King in council passed on subjects found guilty of murder, witchcraft, treason, adultery, theft, cowardice, and even disobedience and negligence. Nevertheless, Schoon was told of a tribesman who attempted to rape a Matabele woman. The culprit was arrested and brought before Mzilikazi. After a brief trial he was found guilty and led away to the outskirts of the kraal, where warriors appointed by Mzilikazi sliced off his ears and genital organs. Schoon abhorred what he heard of Mzilikazi's cruel punishments. Apparently what Schoon did not then realize was that this transgressor would have been sentenced to a far more gruesome death if he had succeeded in raping the woman.

During Schoon and McLuckie's sojourn in Matabele country there were times when they found the cold atmosphere of despotism almost unbearable, and yet they could not but be impressed by the courtesy, hospitality and cooperation they received from Mzili-kazi.

Schoon noted that the King was exceptionally wealthy. Mzili-kazi enjoyed sole ownership of all the harvests reaped between the Magaliesberg and the Limpopo, all the spoils of war, and all the booty collected in the territories of neighbouring tribes. The King owned herds of cattle far larger than any Schoon had seen among the Bechuana tribes, and his seraglio housed between fifty and sixty women. Primarily concerned in trading and hunt-ing, Schoon was amazed to find huge stores of ivory in Mzilikazi's kraal. In due course he ventured to discuss trading with Mzilikazi, but was told the time was not yet ripe. The King instructed Schoon to move with his wagons to the haunts of the elephant, along the Magaliesberg range, to collect as many tusks as he liked, and then to return to enKungwini and display the goods he had brought from the Colony for barter.

The details of the events that took place during the next few weeks are obscure, for apparently neither Schoon nor McLuckie found time to keep a written record of their experiences in the Magaliesberg. Nevertheless, it is known their trip was successful, for on their return to the royal kraal they were able to boast that at least one of their wagons was laden with ivory. Mzilikazi was delighted to see them again. He had them ushered into enKung-wini, entertained them with feasts and dancing displays and lavished hospitality on them.

Now Mzilikazi insisted that the white men show him the barter goods they had brought from the South. On seeing the multi-coloured beads Schoon placed before him on a box, Mzilikazi's face lit up. He confessed that although during past years he had traded with long-haired, tawny-skinned men from the Portuguese colony to the east, the coarse beads he then received in trade com-pared neither in beauty nor in quality with Schoon's English beads. Henceforth he would have no dealings with the Portuguese traders, and would decorate his harem women, his regiments and courtiers with beads Schoon promised to bring on his next trip to Matabele country.

In return for their wares Mzilikazi traded ivory, ostrich

feathers, hides and pelts. When the transactions closed the traders estimated their visit to the Matabele had yielded a haul worth no less than £1,800 sterling.

Six weeks had passed since Schoon and his party had arrived at Mzilikazi's royal kraal and the sultry months of summer were approaching. Schoon prepared to take leave of his illustrious host, fearing the rivers would become impassable if the rains set in. Then the heavily freighted wagons would be marooned in the quagmires formed in the country north of the Little Baboon village, and his party would be stricken with fever. In previous years, when Schoon had traded among the Bahurutsi tribe, he had always arrived in the early winter, and had turned homewards before the spring. Now, as October approached, he was far to the east of his regular hunting and trading grounds, and he wondered whether he would ever reach Grahamstown, in the distant south, with his valuable cargo. He informed Mzilikazi of his intention to trek immediately towards the Marico.

At the gates of the royal kraal the traders and their servants gathered to bid Mzilikazi farewell. They found the King in the best of spirits, but it struck them as strange that he should choose this hour of departure to request that they divulge to him the secrets of their fire-arms. It became obvious to Schoon that as Mzilikazi had not accompanied his regiments on their expeditions to the South and therefore had not personally encountered the Bergenaars, the Lion People or the Boers, he had never seen a musket fired.

Schoon learned that during the past few weeks when he and McLuckie had been hunting along the Magaliesberg range, Jan Bloem and his band of Springbok cut-throats had invaded Matabele territory and pillaged some of the outlying settlements. Mzilikazi assured Schoon that many of the *banditti* had been ambushed and cut off by the Matabele regiments, and that the muskets of the slain had been collected and stored in a special hut which housed the war-shields of the regiments.

Before being called upon by Mzilikazi to demonstrate in public the magic of the fire-arms, Schoon was shown a stack of muskets which the Matabele had taken from Jan Bloem's horsemen and Moletsane's Lion People during recent years.

In the vicinity of the hedge encircling enKungwini, Mzilikazi selected a large stone as a target for Schoon. Schoon instructed one of his servants to load a musket. Mzilikazi studied each detail of the preparations intently. He was elated. For two summers and two winters he had awaited the arrival of the white trader to learn the mysteries of the sticks of thunder and fire. At last his patience was to be rewarded.

At Schoon's command, the servant raised the musket, aimed at the stone and fired. The ball, partly lead and partly pewter, splashed on the face of the target, leaving a blue mark. Mzilikazi was not unduly impressed. He examined the stone closely, and remarked with a derisive grin that had he but breathed on the stone the effect would have been similar.

A bullock that was to have been slaughtered that day for Mzilikazi's meal was led to a spot in the veld. Now more sanguine than ever for a second demonstration in the use of fire-arms, the King called upon Schoon to kill the beast. Schoon loaded and fired. The shot took the ox behind the ear. The animal collapsed, and only a momentary trembling of the forelegs followed the thud of its body on the ground.

With the crack of the explosion still drumming in his ears, Mzilikazi glared incredulously, first at Schoon and then at the weapon that smoked in his hands. No matter how he tried to conceal his bewilderment, he failed, for as if in a trance he strode backwards towards the gates of the royal kraal and then hurried moodily to his hut.

The wagons of Robert Schoon and William McLuckie rumbled laboriously westwards, through the bush flanking the Magaliesberg, to the Marico river. They churned through the sands of dried-up river-beds, creaked and clattered over rolling grasslands and pressed on across the borders of Matabele territory.

The traders looked with pride and satisfaction on the rich load of merchandise they had procured in the land of the great Bull Elephant. They chatted for hours about their many strange experiences in enKungwini – the Place of Mist. As for Mzilikazi, he was equally happy that this historic visit had taken place, for at last he had made contact with white men. He believed that as long as he could be counted among the friends of this influential and powerful white race his future as the potentate of the young and growing Matabele tribe would be secure. So ardently had Mzilikazi desired to foster good relations between his own people and the white man that he had asked two favours of Schoon and McLuckie: first, that they encourage other friendly white men to visit enKungwini, and second, that they conduct two senior Matabele *indunas* to the white settlements in the South.

It was Mzilikazi's wish for his envoys to meet the white missionaries, about whom the Bahurutsi had so often spoken, and especially those missionaries living in a place in the South called Kuruman. Mzilikazi instructed the *indunas*, before their departure with the traders, to remain a short while with the white missionaries, to gather knowledge about their customs and, above all, to assure them the Bull Elephant of the Matabele wished to live in peace in the territory between the Magaliesberg and the Limpopo.

In the kraal of enKungwini, Mzilikazi mused over the visit of Schoon and McLuckie. His satisfaction was not wholly complete. He was disturbed by the thought that he, Mzilikazi, Bull Elephant of the Matabele, was as ignorant as ever about the workings of fire-arms.

CHAPTER 12

MOFFAT OF KURUMAN

James Archbell visits Mzilikazi
Matabele dignitaries arrive at Kuruman
Robert Moffat the famous missionary — Moffat brought
to enKungwini

HAVING crossed the Rustenburg and Marico districts and re-entered the arid regions south of the Molopo river, during the latter half of October, Schoon and McLuckie moved on to Platberg, the new mission station of the Rev. James Archbell. They were cordially received by the missionary and, for the first time in four months, enjoyed the luxury of comfortable beds as well as tasty meals prepared by feminine hands.

In the course of their brief sojourn at Platberg, the traders entertained their hosts with anecdotes of their adventures in Matabele territory. Archbell, who had heard only the most bloodcurdling reports of Mzilikazi's tyranny, was amazed to learn the King had actually arranged for Schoon and McLuckie to be conducted to enKungwini and had treated them with respect and kindness.

Archbell was particularly interested to learn that Mzilikazi wanted white men to visit Matabele country. This convinced the missionary he could establish a field for Wesleyan missionary labour in Mzilikazi's domain, and he decided, then and there, to prepare to travel to the Magaliesberg.

Schoon and McLuckie departed for Kuruman, and hardly were their wagons out of sight than Archbell, brimming over with enthusiasm, advised his wife Elizabeth to pack the family luggage. He hastened to the settlement of old Barend Barends to induce the Griqua captain to provide a commando of horsemen as escort for the missionary wagons on the journey to Mzilikazi's tribe. He told

Barends stories about Schoon and McLuckie's pleasant and lucrative visit to the hospitable King of the Matabele, and persuaded the old captain to undertake the journey to the North. The missionary was also fortunate in acquiring the services of an experienced traveller named David Hume, a trader who, like Schoon, enjoyed visiting far-off regions provided the inhabitants were not hostile and the prospects of collecting elephant tusks were good.

Archbell and his family, accompanied by David Hume, Barend Barends and a commando of Griqua musketeers, set out from Platberg and headed for Makwassie. They followed the course of the Vaal and reached that section of the river where the beautiful holiday resort of Parys is situated today. They proceeded due north towards the Witwatersrand and descended into the undulating and wooded country approaching the Magaliesberg.

Archbell was confident he would be well received by the great Bull Elephant. He was to be sorely disillusioned when he entered the land of the Matabele.

Meanwhile Schoon and McLuckie reached Kuruman and brought Mzilikazi's envoys to the mission station of Robert Moffat, the evangelist.

During the years following 1829 Kuruman was to become the most widely publicized mission station in Southern Africa. Situated in the Northern Cape, the territory once included in the Crown Colony of British Bechuanaland, its first buildings were erected by Robert Hamilton, a missionary artisan. The site chosen for the mission station lay to the immediate north of the Eye of Kuruman, an oasis formed by a subterranean river which welled up in a labyrinth of dolomite caves and poured out, daily, about four million gallons of crystal-clear water.

Kuruman was a beautiful settlement. A canal cut from the Eye by Moffat conveyed a strong stream of water to the mission lands, and in the spring of each year cornfields, vegetable gardens, orchards and groves of syringa trees burst into a riot of verdure in the heart of the drab, thirsty surroundings.[1]

1. This lovely old mission station lies about three miles outside the present dust-clad town of Kuruman. The original home of Robert and

In 1829, when Schoon and McLuckie drew up at the mission station to tell Robert Moffat about their journey into Mzilikazi's country and also to introduce him to the Matabele dignitaries who sat perched on the wagons, a new episode in the lives of the missionary and Mzilikazi was about to begin. For, during the next forty years, no white man in Southern Africa would learn to know the Matabele despot as intimately as Moffat. The most extraordinary friendship ever to be recorded in South African history was to develop between these two men.

Moffat of Kuruman was a talented and capable man, ideally suited for the rough-and-tumble accompanying mission work during the last century. Born in Ormiston, in the central county of East Lothian, Scotland, he was the son of poor, simple-living yet pious parents. In 1806, at the age of eleven, Moffat moved with his father and mother to Carronshore, and so intrigued was he by the ships which glided to and fro along the Firth of Forth that he deserted his home and ran off to sea. His career as a sailor was exciting but unsuccessful; before his twelfth birthday he was back at Carronshore attending school at Falkirk.

But as a scholar young Moffat showed little promise, and his schooling lasted only six months. It was only in later years that he acquired the learning that would mould him into one of South Africa's most famous missionaries, an engaging author of ethnographical, historical and geographical records and a translator, into the vernacular, of both the Old and New Testaments.

At fourteen Robert Moffat was apprenticed to a gardener in Polmont, a stern-faced taskmaster who insisted on his workmen rising at four in the morning and toiling almost without a break until sundown. During Scotland's severest winter months there were occasions when the young lad from Carronshore all but succumbed to the duties he was expected to perform: his hands froze, and it was only by hammering his knuckles against his

---

Mary Moffat, with the workshops, outhouses and wagon house built by Hamilton, still stands, and the heavy boughs of the syringa trees, planted by the early missionaries, overhang the great stone church in which David Livingstone and Moffat's daughter were married in 1854.

spade-handle that he managed to keep his fingers alive. Invariably he was hungry and fatigued, yet he forced himself to continue working. After a day's work, when his fellow-labourers lay stretched out on their beds or sat gossiping over a pint of ale in the local public-house, Moffat strove to satisfy his thirst for knowledge by attending Latin and arithmetic classes and learning smithery and other trades.

It was his determination, his positive approach to hardship, and his ceaseless hankering after knowledge that paved the way for Moffat's brilliant career as a missionary. When eventually he qualified as a gardener, and then surrendered his life to Christ, it was only his enthusiasm and almost naive resolve to devote what talents he possessed to serving his Master that induced the Directors of the London Missionary Society to select him, from among scores of applicants, to fill and vacant missionary post abroad.

When, in 1816, a delighted young Moffat boarded the *Alacrity* and sailed for South Africa, he had little to offer his Society other than an iron constitution, a robust frame, a broad knowledge in manual skills and an indomitable desire to carry the light of Christianity to the darkness of pagan South Africa.

In January 1817 the *Alacrity* docked in Table Bay, and Moffat was met at the quayside by the Rev. George Thom, a dominie of the Dutch Reformed Church. It was then that Moffat learned that it had been the decision of his Society to send him to Namaqualand, but that the then Governor of the Cape, Lord Charles Somerset, had refused to allow missionary enterprise in those parts. Over the years Namaqualand had become a refuge for slaves, and criminals who fled the Colony to join the ranks of a notorious half-caste named Christiaan Afrikaner. The Cape Government feared that if white men crossed the western borders into Namaqualand they would be murdered by Afrikaner's desperadoes.

Moffat was taken to Stellenbosch and received lodgings on the farm of a Dutch colonial named Hamman. During the next eight months he and Hamman became close friends, and Moffat devoted his time to mastering the Dutch language.

Meanwhile he set his heart on the calling he believed awaited him in Namaqualand, and with the cooperation of Thom, persuaded the Governor to reconsider allowing white men into Afrikaner's territory. Towards the end of the year Moffat was granted permission to enter Namaqualand. A few weeks later he set out for Afrikaner's haunts.

The hardships he endured through the semi-desert regions to the west might well have discouraged Moffat had he not been a man of such remarkable mettle. In the remoteness of the broiling Namaqualand thirstlands he reached Afrikaner's impoverished, hemispherical huts and met the primitive Hottentot half-breeds who, for two decades, had pursued a career of predatory warfare, taking the lives of all tribesmen who dared cross their path. Afrikaner's followers were disease-ridden nomads, a hostile horde whose sole possessions amounted to the emaciated stock they had plundered, a few scraggy horses, the squalid skins which hung about their bodies and the verminous shelters in which they slept.

For an entire year Moffat lived among these people without a fellow white man to share his aspirations or even to converse with him in his mother tongue. But, imbued as he was with confidence, enthusiasm, faith and the sincerest humanitarian attitudes towards aboriginal peoples, he soon won the affection of Afrikaner and arranged with him to build a classroom and church.

Drought drove the Hottentot nomads from Moffat's first mission station. Undaunted, the evangelist accompanied Afrikaner northwards, hoping to find a more suitable site for a permanent settlement.

Meanwhile, in the Colony a reward of a hundred pounds sterling was being offered for the capture of Afrikaner. When this news reached Moffat he persuaded the bandit to follow him to the Kuruman mission station, and then to hasten to the Cape to surrender himself to the Governor. Arriving with Afrikaner at Kuruman, Moffat was surprised to learn that his reputation as a fearless missionary had spread throughout the territory of the Fish People. He dispatched Afrikaner to the Cape while he himself settled at Kuruman.

In due course Afrikaner came cantering back to the mission station. He reported to Moffat that he had been well received by the Governor, and had been pardoned for crimes committed in the past. The Governor had been greatly impressed by the bandit's voluntary surrender. As a token of goodwill he presented Afrikaner with the £100 reward that for so long had hung over the bandit's head. Now the friendship between Moffat and the Hottentot was sealed, but soon Afrikaner returned to Namaqualand, where he died.

Eventful years lay ahead for Robert Moffat. In 1819 he journeyed to the Cape to meet Mary Smith, daughter of the head gardener for whom he had worked in Scotland. Robert and Mary were married in Cape Town, and early in the following year they set out for the mission station where they were to spend the next fifty years together.

Back at Kuruman, Moffat devoted his energies to diverting the waters of the Eye of Kuruman to the mission fields, laying out gardens, erecting buildings and preaching among the Batlhaping. In 1823 he was responsible for summoning the Griqua of Nicholas Waterboer to repulse the Wild Cat People of Mantatisi at Lithako, and at the beginning of November 1829 he welcomed the traders Robert Schoon and William McLuckie to his home, and also the Matabele dignitaries they had brought from Mzilikazi's royal kraal.

From the moment Moffat was introduced to the Matabele *indunas* he treated them with courtesy and respect, and strove to afford them all the attention they deserved as noblemen of their tribe. One of these *indunas* was uMncumbata who, after Mzilikazi, was the most influential man among the Matabele. The son of Mzingeli – the Hunter – of Zululand, uMncumbata was the Bull Elephant's chief *induna* or Prime Minister of the tribe. Moffat was immediately impressed by uMncumbata, by his colleagues, and also by the *aides-de-camp* who formed the retinue. The missionary confessed that their nudity disturbed him, but, on the other hand, during his sojourn among the tribes of South Africa he had never encountered black men as dignified and polite as these Matabele noblemen.

During the days following the departure of Schoon and McLuckie from Kuruman, Robert Moffat entertained his royal guests by explaining to them the significance of the canal he had built for conveying water from the Eye of Kuruman to the mission gardens, by teaching them the rudiments of enlightened farming methods and by instructing them in the art of masonry.

The *indunas* were reserved and stately, and always profoundly grateful for the hospitality they were receiving from the young white man who claimed to be a priest in the service of the God of heaven. They were fascinated when, for the first time, they saw their own images in one of Moffat's mirrors. The smithy's forge, bellows and the large variety of tools and garden implements also amazed them. They confessed to Moffat that the Matabele were like children when compared with the white man, and they declared emphatically that arrangements must be made for the great Bull Elephant to learn the secrets of the wonders they had seen at Kuruman.

Before a week had passed uMncumbata announced that he and his companions must return to their King. Robert Schoon had arranged with Moffat for a Hottentot servant to conduct the *indunas* back to the Magaliesberg. But uMncumbata disapproved of this arrangement. He requested a private interview with Moffat, and in the mission house he explained that news had reached him of a plot among the Bechuana tribes to waylay the Matabele party on their journey home and to annihilate them. He insisted that Schoon's Hottentot could not provide the *indunas* with adequate protection.

Moffat did not doubt the possibility of such a plot, knowing how bitterly the Bechuana peoples hated the Matabele. Intrigues of this nature occurred frequently throughout the country. He reflected that if Mzilikazi's envoys came to harm, the tyrant's wrath would be unbounded, and not only the tribes in the North but also the Fish People in the vicinity of Kuruman might be subjected to a tragedy similar to that suffered by the Crocodile People four years earlier. After conferring with his colleague Hamilton, and with Mrs Moffat, Robert Moffat decided to accompany the *indunas* as far as Mosega, the new capital village of the Bahurutsi. He brought out his wagon in preparation for the trip and and hired another specially for his guests.

On 9 November scores of black converts gathered at the mission station to wish Moffat, their preacher, Godspeed, and also to present parting gifts to the *indunas* who had spent a few happy days in their midst. On the same day, with a party of volunteers to keep him company, Moffat escorted the wagons on the first stage of their journey to the North.

As the two wagons were almost empty, they travelled with unusual speed over the dry Barolong plains. Ten days after leaving Kuruman they drew into Mosega. Moffat proceeded to the royal kraal of Mokgatla, who since the murder of the Chief of the Bahurutsi by Mantatisi's hordes had been acting as the regent of the tribe. And now having brought uMncumbata's party to Mosega, as promised, and handed them over to the care of Mokgatla, Moffat mentioned that he intended returning immediately to Kuruman.

uMncumbata objected and entreated Moffat not to desert the Matabele *indunas*. Solemnly he recalled the many kindnesses he and his party had received at the Kuruman mission station, the hospitality they had enjoyed and the instruction they had been given in the wonders of the white man's skills. uMncumbata asked Moffat to remember, above all, the friendship between Mzilikazi's *indunas* and the people of Kuruman. The *indunas'* brief stay at the mission station had convinced them not only of Moffat's love for the Matabele, but also his respect for Mzilikazi, the great Bull Elephant.

uMncumbata added demurely that if he, the chief *induna* of the Matabele, returned to enKungwini and reported that he had allowed the white missionary to turn back from Mosega, he would be severely punished by the Bull Elephant, and in all probability he and his fellow *indunas* would be executed.

Moffat was in a quandary. He explained there were many commitments demanding his personal attention at Kuruman and it was imperative that he return as soon as possible. Furthermore, he had brought the *indunas* to Mosega, as arranged, and it was Chief Mokgatla's duty to conduct them safely through Bahurutsi country to the Matabele border.

Trembling at the thought of the responsibility Moffat was

thrusting upon him, Mokgatla entered into the discussion. Visions of the Matabele reprisals which would follow, were any harm to befall the illustrious uMncumbata and his retinue, hovered in his mind. He begged Moffat not to turn back, but to escort the envoys to Matabele territory. If the white teacher refused, he, Mokgatla, would call the Bahurutsi together and flee.

Robert Moffat meditated on the problem confronting him. He could not bear to think his unselfishness might result either in the death of uMncumbata and the Matabele *indunas* or in the flight of the Bahurutsi from their homeland. He consented to accompany the envoys farther to the North, but insisted on taking leave of them as soon as the first Matabele outposts were reached. His decision brought instant relief to Mokgatla and joy to uMncumbata and his companions.

When Moffat had inspanned his wagons in preparation for the second stage of his journey to Mzilikazi's dominions, he was surprised to discover Mokgatla was joining the party. The regent explained that he feared Mzilikazi was contemplating the destruction of the Bahurutsi, and he regarded it as his duty to visit the King in the hopes of soliciting his friendship. Not for a moment did Moffat detect anything but sincerity in Mokgatla's explanation.

The wagons rolled northwards along the trail Schoon had blazed to the Marico river. They turned to the east, approaching the Magaliesberg and the vast country which once had been studded with prosperous Bakwena villages and rambling fields of millet and vegetables.

Moffat reached some isolated settlements of the Crocodile People, dilapidated grass shelters, constructed on poles out of reach of the beasts of prey. He also found the tree-dwellers visited by Schoon and McLuckie a few months earlier. Moffat climbed a tall mimosa, entered one of the primitive huts and shared a bowl of locusts with the timid inhabitants. It grieved the missionary to see the misery Mzilikazi's tyranny was causing these innocent people. He was to be overcome with anguish in the course of the next few days, when he reached the Magaliesberg and inspected the charred ruins of the Bakwena villages with the debris of huts strewn with heaps of human bones and grinning skulls.

A cold loneliness fell over Moffat as, with heavy steps and heavy heart, he plodded beside the wagons on the journey eastwards. Steeped in morbid reverie, his attention was arrested by the approach of a group of Matabele warriors who, on seeing uMncumbata and the other *indunas*, halted and stood motionless in obeisance. Then for the first time Moffat beheld a Matabele kraal. He was happy, for it meant that at last he would be able to leave his charges. Turning to uMncumbata, Moffat expressed his wish to return home. He dared not go on, he said, for there were several important duties awaiting his attention in Kuruman, and besides he had travelled farther than he had ever intended. He also mentioned that Mrs Moffat would by now have become concerned about his safety.

uMncumbata glared at Moffat unbelievingly, and after a brief silence laid his hand on the missionary's shoulder.

'Father,' he said, 'you have been our guardian, and we are yours. You love us; but will you leave us now?'[1]

Moffat's eyes followed a finger uMncumbata pointed to a tint of blue tracing the shape of a mountain range over the distant horizon.

'Yonder dwells the great Mzilikazi,' said uMncumbata impressively, 'and how shall we approach his presence if you are not with us? If you love us still, my father, save us, for when we shall have told him our news he will ask why our conduct gave you pain to cause your return; and, before the sun descends on the day we see his face, we shall be ordered out for execution because you are not with us.'[2]

Moffat searched for words, but before he could reply the chief *induna* continued:

'Look at me and my companions, tell us that you will not go, for then we would choose to die here, rather than in the sight of our people.'

Moffat reasoned, but his words made no impression on uMncumbata.

'Are you afraid?' he was asked by the chief *induna*.

'No,' replied Moffat.

1. Robert Moffat, op. cit., p. 522.   2. ibid.

'Annoyed?' queried another.

'No.'

'Then it remains with you to save our lives,' cried the chief *induna*, skilfully measuring his words; 'you alone can prevent the sorrow our executions will cause our wives and children.'[1]

Moffat had heard enough. Without further ado he agreed to accompany the envoys to enKungwini, where Mzilikazi awaited them.

Robert Moffat and his party continued the journey along the Magaliesberg range, but their progress was impeded by an electric storm followed by a scudding rain that swept across the countryside and engulfed the wagons. And when at last the clouds parted and the sun oozed through, so firmly did the black, gluey soil of the plains cling both to the wagon wheels and the hooves of the oxen that periodic halts had to be called so that the mud could be removed. Meanwhile a member of the group took leave of the wagons and trotted off to enKungwini to report to Mzilikazi that Moffat, the white missionary with whom the Matabele envoys had stayed in Kuruman, was approaching.

Two days of wearisome travelling brought the travellers to the sedgy banks of the Crocodile river. Crossing its menacing flow and descending into a glen, Moffat came suddenly upon a Griqua hunting-party led by old Barend Barends, the man whom the Rev. James Archbell had persuaded to escort the mission wagons from Platberg to the domains of Mzilikazi.

Moffat was delighted to meet his old Griqua friend, and was surprised to learn from him that Archbell, his wife Elizabeth, and David Hume the trader had set out three days earlier for enKungwini. Barends told Moffat it was Archbell's ambition to establish a mission station in Matabele territory, but the prospects of his making friends with Mzilikazi seemed remote. News had been received that the King was furious about the presence, within his borders, of uninvited Griqua horsemen. The Bull Elephant had refused to see Archbell until the *indunas* arrived with the white missionary from Kuruman.

1. ibid.

At this stage of the journey a messenger arrived from enKung-wini bearing greetings for Moffat from Mzilikazi. From Barends' camp Moffat guided the wagons eastwards along a circuitous trail and eventually brought them to the area where Archbell's wagons were outspanned. Moffat strode out to meet Archbell. He listened intently to the news his fellow-missionary told of Mzilikazi's aloofness, and the tyrant's blatant refusal to meet the white men from the Platberg mission station. Archbell was riled by the re-buff. He and Hume were contemplating their return to Platberg at the very moment when Moffat's wagon appeared through the bush.

Moffat persuaded Archbell not to turn back but to follow him to Mzilikazi's royal kraal. Their wagons moved on to the east, winding in and out of the hills and tracing deep tracks through the bush fringing the Magaliesberg. Just before noon on the second day uMncumbata approached Moffat and drew his atten-tion to a long range lying immediately ahead, and also to a Mata-bele kraal barely discernible in the undergrowth.

'There,' said the *induna*, pointing to the settlement, 'there dwells the great King of the Heavens, the Bull Elephant of the Matabele, the Great Lion's Paw.'[1]

Moffat had at last reached enKungwini.

1. ibid., p. 530.

CHAPTER 13

START OF A STRANGE FRIENDSHIP

Mzilikazi is overjoyed to meet Moffat
He leads the Matabele regiments in dancing — He snubs
Archbell — His tyranny shocks Moffat — He sleeps in
Moffat's bed

THE Aapies river lay between the wagons and Mzilikazi's capital. As there was no crossing in the vicinity the wagons proceeded to ford higher up, and Moffat, Archbell and two attendants completed the journey on horseback. They waded through the river and galloped over the veld. The missionaries reached the kraal gates and were conducted to Mzilikazi's cattle-fold, a great palisade enclosure capable of holding at least ten thousand head.

Moffat and Archbell found themselves surrounded by eight hundred of Mzilikazi's warriors, thickset men dressed in kilts made of monkey-skin tails. They were grouped according to the colour and designs of their heavy ox-hide shields. The visitors marvelled at the appearance of Mzilikazi's fighting-men, their superbly proportioned bodies, the profusion of feathers adorning their heads and the tufts of ox-tail hair hanging about their arms and legs.

Moffat noticed that on either side of the gates two groups of warriors were concealed behind a tall fence. On being instructed to dismount, the missionaries and their attendants beheld these warriors bursting through the gates and charging towards them with shields and weapons aloft. For a brief moment the visitors feared for their safety, for the Matabele braves yelled a hideous war-whoop as they advanced, and their entire attitude appeared menacing. However, no sooner had they reached the centre of the kraal, where Moffat and his friend stood holding the reins of their frightened horses, than the warriors swung to the left and the right and joined the ranks of the eight hundred who lined the palisades.

Now for ten long minutes silence pervaded the royal kraal. Not a word was spoken as the regiments stood rigid behind their shields. Suddenly, as if he intended the entire Magaliesberg and the bushveld to hear, a regimental captain raised his face to the skies and bellowed a command. Immediately the floor of the cattle-fold thundered beneath the stamping of warrior feet, and the sur-roundings vibrated with the voices of a thousand men, some sing-ing in harmony, others hissing and others imitating the groaning of dying enemies. This frenzied display of dancing was followed by a brief period of silence. Cheers rose in the farthest section of the kraal and spread throughout the ranks of the warriors as Mzilikazi came swaggering into the dusty arena.

'Bayete!' bawled the regiments, almost hysterical with excite-ment. 'Bayete, nkosi enkulu! – Great King !'

By the descriptions he had received from his *indunas* Mzilikazi recognized Moffat at once. He greeted the missionary with a hearty handshake, and then, assisted by an interpreter standing beside him, he assured the somewhat bewildered group that he honoured its presence in his enKungwini kraal. Mzilikazi turned to a train of menials who had followed him bearing clay pots and baskets on their heads and instructed them to offer beer and food to the white visitors.

Robert Moffat studied the appearance of the tyrant who, during the past decade, had instigated the destruction of tens of thousands of Sotho-speaking peoples throughout the Transvaal. He could not but admire Mzilikazi's friendly disposition, his vigorous person-ality and his scarred yet handsome features. Moffat had pictured Mzilikazi as a surly and arrogant savage, but now that he stood face to face with him he was surprised to find that this notorious conqueror was a soft-spoken person, whose bearing was far more dignified than any other chief or potentate he had met.

While Mzilikazi was chatting with his visitors over a pot of beer, his eyes fell on the white men's 'moving houses' that were being drawn by oxen towards the kraal gates. The King walked with Moffat to the tented wagons, and, although he was fascinated by their great bulk, it was their wheels and the bands of iron surrounding the felloes which captured his imagination. After a thorough inspection of these extraordinary phenomena Mzilikazi was heard to mutter that wonders of this kind were possible only with the aid of the most potent of decoctions. By this time Mzilikazi had linked arms with the missionary Moffat, and the dour Scot felt somewhat embarrassed by the King's sudden display of affection, but he dared not object. He asked Mzilikazi to point out a site where the wagons might be outspanned.

'The land is yours,' grinned the King. 'You have come to visit Mzilikazi, your son, therefore you must sleep where you please.'[1]

Arm in arm the two men strolled back to the kraal. Their appearance at the great circles of beehive huts, and especially at the cattle-fold, brought thousands of cheering subjects to their feet. Dancing and singing commenced. Throughout the late afternoon and almost the entire night, Moffat was obliged to listen to the monotonous rhythm of the drums and the whistling, chanting and animated conversation of the Matabele.

Next day Mzilikazi sent messengers to the neighbouring villages summoning the Matabele to assemble at enKungwini. Meanwhile the *aides-de-camp* of the *indunas* who had visited Kuruman were posted at the wagons to attend to the needs and comforts of the strangers, and also to prevent their being disturbed by inquisitive commoners. An abundance of meat, grain, milk and sorghum beer was delivered to the camp, and messengers arrived at regular intervals from Mzilikazi, who seemed determined his guests should be afforded the best of Matabele hospitality.

A day later, many thousands of people having gathered in a large clearing beside the kraal, and scores of beasts having been slaughtered in order to feed them, Mzilikazi arrived amidst a surge of doting dignitaries and attendants. His stocky body, well smeared with fat, was draped in heavy columns of beads reaching to the ankles. An otter-skin, stuffed to form a solid roll, and pressed firmly on to his head, was punctuated with bundles of the beautiful plumes of the blue jay, Mzilikazi's favourite bird. On this

1. ibid., p. 532.

occasion, instead of the clusters of tails that usually covered his loins, he wore a kilt of multi-coloured beads. Dressed in all this finery, a lion-skin shield on his left arm and a butcher's knife Moffat had given him clutched in his right hand, the King of the Matabele cut an impressive figure, as with his retinue he advanced into the dancing arena.

The missionaries received a royal invitation to the great celebration – the war-dance of the regiments which Moffat facetiously referred to in his memoirs as 'the public ball'.[1] The guests of honour were seated in a section of the arena where they could witness with ease each aspect of the proceedings and especially the important role Mzilikazi would play.

Not for an instant was Moffat impressed by what he saw. Indeed, it depressed him to think that the thousands of people about him worshipped, not God, but a mere mortal, a brutal heathen despot. He watched with reserve the almost incredible command Mzilikazi exercised over every man and woman in the arena. His body drenched in perspiration, Mzilikazi led not only the dancing but also the singing, and he directed changes in tempo and rhythm by the slightest sign from his hand and his head.

And while the dance continued, and the warriors flung themselves with increasing ardour into its tempestuous rhythm, thirty of Mzilikazi's harem women shuffled into the arena and paced backwards and forwards. In contrast with the wild display of the regiments, the stamping of feet, the vaulting, stabbing, parrying, advancing, recoiling and the contorting of bodies, the movements of Mzilikazi's damsels were slow and cumbersome. These women were the overfed, paunchy, heavy-buttocked queens of enKungwini, the mothers of Mzilikazi's increasing progeny.

For hours on end Moffat gazed disapprovingly at the dancers. As he reflected on the energy they were expending on so futile and un-Christian an amusement, his heart overflowed with compassion for them.

Mzilikazi disengaged himself from the dance and seated himself beside Moffat on a lion-skin.

1. ibid., p. 535.

'Is it not fine?' Mzilikazi asked, turning his sweaty face towards the missionary.

Moffat grinned. He was pleased Mzilikazi did not insist on his replying.

The entertainment continued throughout the day. Mzilikazi retired, his breast swelling with pride and his devoted subjects lifted their voices in tumultuous applause: '*Bayete! Bayete! nkosi enkulu!* – Great King! King of Heaven! Bull Elephant of the Matabele!'[1]

A great feast was called. The flesh of the hundreds of oxen slaughtered for the occasion was distributed among the people, and beer flowed from earthenware pots into thousands of dusty gullets. Moffat and his companions were not neglected. To the astonishment of the men who brought them gifts of food, the missionaries declined to partake of a delicacy usually intended only for the privileged warriors – blood.

Among the strangers visiting enKungwini there were two men who enjoyed little of Mzilikazi's company or attention. Mokgatla, the Bahurutsi regent, found himself snubbed, and Archbell, who had been so presumptuous as to bring a command of Griqua horsemen into Matabele territory, was cold-shouldered. During the next day or two Archbell despaired of establishing a mission among the Matabele. He saw no hope of converting a people who looked upon their potentate as a god and allowed their thoughts and actions to be controlled by him. Nothing delighted the Matabele unless they knew it delighted their King. They possessed nothing, not even the crops they harvested, the cattle they herded, the huts they built, the domestic utensils they carved and moulded or the sleeping-mats and baskets they weaved. Nothing. They worshipped their King, extolling his virtues, both actual and imaginary, from sunrise to dark, acclaiming his remarks, humbling themselves in his presence, promptly obeying his commands and accepting any punishment, however unjust, with gratitude.

There was nothing in the Matabele despot Archbell admired save Mzilikazi's excellent physique and his authoritative and com-

1. ibid.

manding manner. The missionary was riled by Mzilikazi's arrogance and by the way the despot hankered incessantly after admiration and praise. As a disciple of Christ, it disturbed Archbell to find at enKungwini a great seraglio in which sixty women, the wives of Mzilikazi, were living in a state of abject servility. He decided to return immediately to Platberg.

Taking leave of enKungwini, he could not resist asking Mzilikazi whether he would welcome a missionary settlement in Matabele country. The King replied with the charm he seemed to reserve exclusively for white visitors: he was anxious for the residence of white men in his dominions, not only because of the messages they would bring from God, but also because of the horses their visitors would bring for the Matabele. Archbell was not amused. He left enKungwini never to see Mzilikazi again, never to bother about pursuing the cause of missionary enterprise among the Matabele.

Robert Moffat was also anxious to return to Kuruman, mainly because he feared that Mary, who had expected him to travel only to Mosega, might be worrying about his prolonged delay. But whereas Archbell had experienced no difficulty in taking leave of Mzilikazi, Moffat was to find that his royal host had no intention of allowing him to return so soon. Mzilikazi had developed an almost childlike devotion to Moffat, a sincere and deep-rooted respect and, above all, he was genuinely grateful for the courtesy and the hospitality the missionary had afforded the Matabele envoys both in Kuruman and also on their journey back to enKungwini. He would not hear of Moffat leaving him after so short a sojourn in Matabele territory, and in his own way Mzilikazi was determined to repay this young white man for the kindnesses shown to his men.

Visiting the wagons, Mzilikazi confessed his love for Moffat. Now he referred to the missionary as Mashobane, his father, for, as he explained in beautiful Zulu idiom, both these men had proved their love for him by feeding him when he was hungry, clothing him when he was naked and covering him with their shields when he needed protection. Mzilikazi pointed to the envoys who sat beside him on the grass.

'These are great men,' he said, 'and uMncumbata is my right hand. When I sent them from my presence to see the land of the white men, I sent my ears, my eyes, my mouth. What they heard, I heard; what they saw, I saw, and what they said, it was Mzilikazi who said it. You fed them and clothed them, and when they were to be slain, you were their shield. You did it for me. You did it for Mzilikazi, the son of Mashobane.'[1]

Moffat was deeply moved. He had not expected these words of appreciation from a despot whose power and authority were such that even his frown was regarded by his subjects as a sign of impending death and destruction. For a moment he forgot his reserve and seized the opportunity to inform the King he had important news to tell him, news of God, the God of the universe who loved all peoples. Moffat might have continued by explaining that, as a preacher in the service of God, he wanted no gratitude for having treated the envoys with respect and kindness, but he noticed Mzilikazi's eyes were focused on a large herd of cattle approaching the kraal, and that his thoughts were being engaged by their beauty. Moffat realized no further purpose could be served by pursuing his discourse on the advantages of seeking God's love, for Mzilikazi bowed politely, swung round and strode off among a throng of gesticulating and applauding courtiers and then disappeared through the gates of enKungwini.

Although his first attempt to speak to Mzilikazi of the wonders of God had proved a failure, Moffat was not disheartened. Soon after, his faith was rewarded by the reappearance of Mzilikazi at his wagons.

'I am come to sit at your feet,' said Mzilikazi. 'I am King, it is true, but you must now talk to me as if I were a child.'[2]

Moffat smiled. He could not but secretly admire this great African conqueror, this haughty despot whose authority held sway throughout the regions between the Limpopo and the Magaliesberg, the entire Transvaal and the highveld plains that stretched out to the Orange river. Moffat could only wonder at Mzilikazi's

1. ibid., p. 538

2. J. P. R. Wallis (ed.), *Matabele Journals of Robert Moffat*, vol. I, p. 15.

effortless ability to switch from the role he played as a tyrant to that of a modest soft-spoken host. The missionary took immediate advantage of the father–son relationship that had grown between himself and Mzilikazi, and he spared no words in reprimanding the King for the many crimes committed by him and his blood-thirsty regiments. He rebuked Mzilikazi for the wars he had waged among innocent peoples, drawing attention to the tumbled-down habitations of the Crocodile People, to the cattle-folds and kraal yards that lay concealed beneath entanglements of skeletons and to the fields, once luxuriant with crops, now untilled and cluttered with weeds.

'Your country mourns,' said Moffat sternly, 'and the bones of your victims call to heaven for vengeance.'[1]

The despot hung on each of the missionary's scrupulously chosen words, neither his eyes nor his face betraying his inner-most thoughts, but when Moffat explained that God, the Supreme Being whom the Matabele obviously did not honour, would demand an eye for an eye and a tooth for a tooth from those who chose to exterminate peace-loving peoples, he interrupted, claim-ing that he was not responsible for the annihilation of the Croco-dile People. It was Mantatisi, the witch-like Queen of the Wild Cat People, who was guilty of these heinous invasions. By con-trast, continued Mzilikazi, somewhat lamely, his was a humane government, and he, as King of the Matabele, strove to avoid wars with neighbouring tribes. He admitted he had captured many of the remnants both of the Wild Cat People and of other tribes, but he had done this simply to prevent the havoc they were wreaking among peace-loving peoples, and also to put an end to the can-nibalism some of them practised.

When next they met, Moffat explained to Mzilikazi some of the first principles of the Christian religion, referring in particular to the immortality of the soul and to the resurrection of the dead.

'Shall all rise from the dead?' asked the King, visibly perturbed.

'Yes,' replied Moffat, 'and all the dust of human bodies scattered by the winds, and all the scattered bones that bespangle your dominions will rise to life and be judged by the Son of God.'[2]

1. ibid.   2. ibid., p. 16.

No more ghastly a thought could have been implanted in Mzilikazi's mind, especially as during the past ten years the numbers of tribes and clans he had butchered had multiplied, and he could imagine the wrath with which they would unite against him if ever they were to find him in the hereafter that Moffat had described.

On the first Saturday after his arrival at enKungwini, Moffat informed Mzilikazi that, as the next day was the Sabbath, he would prefer to be left entirely to himself. The King consented. During the course of the Sunday morning Moffat noticed that the regiments had gathered to dance, sing and feast; his attention was also drawn to the gathering-place of men, the tribal court in which Mzilikazi and his councillors were hearing the case of an *induna* who had been caught in the act of committing adultery with one of the harem women. The penalty for so serious an offence was death, but it pleased Moffat to hear Mzilikazi announce that, as the white preacher from Kuruman was averse to killings, he, the King of the Matabele, had decided to spare the *induna's* life. Instead, said Mzilikazi, the accused would be divested of headring, shield and weapons; his rank would be reduced to that of the lowest in the land, and he would be banished. The *induna* protested bitterly, pleading that, as a nobleman of the royal kraal, he deserved to be spared the humiliation of living among commoners. He had served his King loyally in the regiments, he asserted, but now he chose to die for the betrayal like a warrior.

Mzilikazi granted the *induna* his choice. Executioners bound the adulterer's hands above his head. They led him out of the gates of enKungwini, past Moffat's wagons, over the veld, and to a bank that overhung a deep pool in the Aapies river. Here he was flung headlong into the jaws of waiting crocodiles. Later in the day Mzilikazi's unfaithful wife was fetched from the seraglio and escorted out of the kraal. On a hill near by the executioners dispatched her with knob-headed clubs.

As Moffat mused over the deaths that had blemished his first Sabbath in Matabele country, his mind grew heavy, his spirit despondent. It grieved him further to learn from his *aides-de-camp*

that the Bull Elephant had been magnanimous in his dealings with
the adulterers; Mzilikazi's usual practice was to condemn such
transgressors to the slow and hideous torment of skewering. Although on this occasion Moffat had been spared the horror of witnessing executions of this kind, the day would arrive when he
would encounter individuals reeling in agony with long skewering
sticks, an inch in diameter, beaten upwards through the anus, or,
in the case of women, through the genital organs, into the intestines and chest. Moffat was soon to discover that, when sentencing
his enemies to death, Mzilikazi had several forms of execution
from which to choose. Apart from the culprits he sent to be fed to
the crocodiles, to be skewered or clubbed, there were others whom
he condemned to decapitation, to neck-twisting, genital amputa-
tion, impalement, stabbing and drowning.

Moffat prepared to leave enKungwini, but again he was to be
detained several days longer by Mzilikazi. He noticed that for
some unaccountable reason the King became ever more attached to
him, calling him 'father' and 'Mashobane', welcoming his admoni-
tions and craving his advice on spiritual and other matters. Mzilikazi never tired of prying into the missionary's background. Many
of the questions he asked were puerile, but many led to intelligent
and amusing debate. He could not believe that King George IV
was as great a monarch as he, but when Moffat boasted about the
greatness of the British nation, referring especially to its population, the size of its cities and the vast numbers of cattle that were
slaughtered daily for its subsistence, Mzilikazi was astounded.

'Your nation must be terrible in battle,' he exclaimed. 'Tell your
King I wish to live in peace.'[1]

Now Moffat explained why Mzilikazi could never hope to enjoy
a happy and peaceful reign if he persisted in waging wars and
subjecting his followers to an existence of terror. Shaka's assassination was recalled, and Moffat suggested that had the King of the
Zulu ruled his people justly and sympathetically his brother Dingane would never have plotted his overthrow. This was the fate
awaiting all tyrants, even the great Bull Elephant of the Matabele,
Moffat insisted, and he concluded with the famous words from

1. ibid., p. 27.

Genesis IX, 6, 'Whoso sheddeth man's blood, by man shall his blood be shed.'[1] Mzilikazi listened intently, but seemed unmoved. Perhaps it had already been predicted by his witch-doctors that, although frightful dangers still awaited him, he would survive them all and live to a ripe old age.

The mention of Shaka's death led Mzilikazi to speak of fire-arms. He told Moffat that he expected Dingane's armies to invade Matabele territory, and he wanted not only to arm his own regiments with muskets, but also to fortify the approaches to en-Kungwini with a cannon. Mzilikazi implored the missionary to give him a musket for his personal use. On a previous occasion, when the question of trading arms and ammunition had been broached by Mzilikazi, Moffat had said emphatically that as a man of God, he condemned the use of all weapons of war; now he added he would be violating the laws of the Cape Colony if he supplied fire-arms to any of the tribes of the interior. The King appeared satisfied with this explanation and, although he repeated his intense fear of Dingane, he never mentioned the subject again.

On the morning of the eighth day after his arrival at enKungwini Moffat inspanned his wagons and bade Mzilikazi farewell. He was surprised to learn that the King had decided to accompany him on the first part of the journey through Matabele country. Mzilikazi climbed on the wagon and seated himself beside his missionary friend. This was to be his first trip in a 'house on wheels'. A strong body of armed warriors, together with women bearing food and other essentials, followed the small convoy across the Crocodile river and into the vales that wander with the Magaliesberg ranges into the western bushveld. It was a sultry day and by mid-morning Mzilikazi grew drowsy. He slid from his seat, entered the wagon-tent, flung himself on Moffat's bed and fell asleep. Later, on awaking, he yawningly complimented Moffat on the comfort of his bed, and invited him to lie down beside him. Moffat declined somewhat frigidly, saying that he preferred to study the beautiful scenery, the many species of game and the Matabele cattle-posts that lay to the left and right of the trail. Twilight was beginning to fall when the wagons reached one of

1. Robert Moffat, op. cit., p. 551.

Mzilikazi's royal kraals. Thousands of warriors, women and children came careering through the bush, shouting praises to their King, hailing him with '*Bayete!*' and welcoming him to the settlement.

It was at this royal kraal that Moffat and Mzilikazi parted. After having separated for the night, they met early next morning, precisely at the time when a stream of no less than six thousand cattle, chiefly oxen, were being driven out of the cattle enclosure, past the circles of beehive huts and through the main gates of the settlement. And while the two men conversed, every available space on the wagons was filled with gifts and a variety of foodstuffs. The wagons drew slowly away from the kraal. Beside them strode Moffat, with Mzilikazi, his crestfallen and doting friend, at his side. When only the top-knots of the huts peeped over the foliage of the bush, the King turned to the missionary and took his hand.

'Mashobane, my father,' he said, 'your visit appears as a dream; my heart will follow you. *Hamba kahle* – go well to Kuruman and return soon with your wife, Ma-Mary. Tell your white King I wish to live in friendship, and let the road to Kuruman remain always open. Take with you uMncumbata, my right hand, and let him guide you safely out of my country, and on to the road that leads to your home.'[1]

Moffat listened to Mzilikazi's gentle high-pitched, almost feminine voice. He reflected that had he not known of the tyrant's annihilation of the Bakwena and other tribes, had he not witnessed the brutal execution of transgressors, and had he not tested the King's integrity, thereby exposing him as a hypocrite of the first order, he might well have been tempted to count Mzilikazi among the sincerest of his African friends.

'I shall never forget you,' Moffat replied, 'and I shall pray for you and your people. Perhaps one day God will send teachers to instruct you in wise and happy ways.'[2]

1. J. P. R. Wallis (ed.), *Matabele Journals of Robert Moffat*, vol. I, p. 31.
2. ibid.

At that moment Moffat might not have admitted, even to himself, that he cherished any particular regard for the King of the Matabele, but when his wagons moved away, and he sat listening to the strains of a mournful tribal dirge that Mzilikazi and a group of his men were singing in the white man's honour, Moffat believed there was much to be loved in this wicked, yet genial potentate.

CHAPTER 14

THABA BOSIU—THE MOUNTAIN AT NIGHT

Dingane, new King of the Zulu
The Zulu army attacks the Matabele
Land of broken tribes — Moshesh outwits Mzilikazi's forces

WITHIN a year of Shaka's assassination Dingane, the new King of the Zulu, built emGungundlovu, his capital kraal, in the valley of the ancestral chiefs. Dingane was neither a great warrior nor an outstanding ruler, but, typical of conspirators, he was a bearer of grudges who refused to rest until he had punished those who he believed had wronged him. Throughout his years of service in the Zulu regiments he had hated Shaka and, although careful not to betray his feelings, he had never ceased scheming for the despot's downfall. He had always found Shaka's tyranny intolerable. But, above all else, it had grieved him to think that had it not been for this usurper of the Zulu chieftaincy he, Dingane, would have enjoyed paramountcy over the Nguni peoples to the east of the Drakensberg.

Two of Dingane's closest friends, his brother Mhlangana and an influential *induna* named Mbopha, were his accomplices in Shaka's murder. Together, the three men rounded up and executed Shaka's important supporters, even the chiefs, headmen and military leaders who confessed that they had hated the Zulu tyrant, but had served him loyally only because they had feared him. Dingane's irascible temper and his uncontrollable dislike for all whom Shaka had favoured became a topic of conversation among the courtiers, and especially among the commoners, throughout the territory.

Dingane trusted no one. In his frenzy to rid his dominions of any men who might be tempted to challenge his authority, he butchered some of his lifelong friends. He even strangled his brother Gowujana. With heads toppling freely in the Valley of the Zulu, the King turned upon Mhlangana and Mbopha his faithful henchmen, and ordered their execution.

There seemed no end to Dingane's chain of killings, no reasonable explanation for his dispatching of great men like Matiwane, the chief who had once denounced Shaka and fled from his tyranny, but who had returned from the battlefields of *lifaqane* to pledge his allegiance to the new Zulu potentate.

Early in 1830, at the time when Moffat was back in Kuruman, and when Mzilikazi was preparing to send his regiments on a marauding expedition against the Mashona tribes of Rhodesia, Dingane was telling his people that they could look forward to an era of peace and prosperity. It became known throughout Zululand that Dingane was the liberator of the nation, and that the internecine warfare and the persecutions instigated by Shaka were about to cease. And Dingane was sincere in his intentions, for, having inherited his brother's realm with its huge herds of cattle, its armies and royal harems, he could muster little enthusiasm for an existence other than one of comfort and luxury in his great emGungundlovu kraal.

Now, at the age of thirty, Dingane was corpulent and lethargic. Nothing pleased him more than to pass hours sipping sorghum beer in the company of his favourite courtiers and a bevy of his most beautiful harem girls.

But while Dingane had decided to pursue a sedentary life in his royal kraal, his armies, the invincible regiments of the Shakan régime, grew restless and demanded to be sent into action. The King conferred with his councillors. He announced that if an expedition were to be undertaken into the territories of hitherto unconquered peoples he could think of no tribe whose extermination he would welcome more than the Matabele of Mzilikazi. Dingane looked upon Mzilikazi as Zululand's greatest enemy. He recalled how, as a young fugitive, this grandson of the notorious Zwide had sought sanctuary at Bulawayo, and how, with his charm, he had managed to win Shaka's confidence and friendship.

Dingane could not blame Mzilikazi for treachery to the royal Zulu house, for he himself was tarred with the same brush, but he reflected that had it not been for Shaka's unaccountable affection for the renegade Khumalo there would have been no Matabele tribe, and the royal cattle-fold would have been richer by several thousand beasts. The question of the cattle that Mzilikazi had refused to present to Shaka after the defeat of Ranisi preyed on Dingane's mind. This crime must be avenged, he told his warlords, and Mzilikazi must be taught that he was dealing, not with Shaka, his friend, but with Dingane, his enemy.

In April, at the beginning of the harvesting time, Dingane's army, under the supreme command of a famous *induna* named Ndlela, set out on an expedition against the Matabele.

Meanwhile, since Moffat's departure, Mzilikazi had settled farther north at his emHlahlandlela kraal. It had become his policy never to remain in one place for any length of time. By continually moving about his dominions he was able to inspect all his regiments, his cattle-posts, his crops and granaries, and also keep abreast of developments as well as visit the harems housing his growing collection of wives. This was to prove sound policy, especially as enemies who planned to invade his country could never be entirely sure of his whereabouts.

During the month of May Mzilikazi received a report of the approach of the Zulu army. For the first time in years he found himself in a predicament. A short while before, he had launched an invasion across the Limpopo into the territory of Mgibe, chief of the Mashona cattle-breeders, and with five of his most experienced regiments absent he could hardly hope to defend his country with the forces that remained at his disposal. His home guard consisted mainly of veteran fighters, most of whom had earned the right to don the headring and settle in semi-retirement with their wives and children.

With no allies to call upon for assistance, and with hosts of enemies to gloat over his dilemma, Mzilikazi's position looked ominous. It struck him that the only person who might condescend to join forces with him against Dingane was Sikunyana, the son of Zwide, who since his defeat at the hands of Shaka's

Zulu had retreated to the Eastern Transvaal with the remnants of the Ndwandwe tribe. Until that moment Mzilikazi had never regarded the Ndwandwe as kinsmen or friends, but, with the position as it was, he seemed to believe that because Sikunyana was his maternal uncle and also a victim of the cruel Zulu régime the two armies should unite in battle against their common foe. Matabele envoys hastened to the royal Ndwandwe kraal. In due course Mzilikazi received word from his uncle that under no circumstances would the Ndwandwe take part in the impending struggle. Sikunyana regretted that he should be so unsympathetic towards the grandson of the great Zwide, but he also reminded Mzilikazi that only ten summers ago he, the present King of the Matabele, had fled to Shaka's Bulawayo kraal and had chosen to fight in the Zulu armies against the Ndwandwe. The children of Zwide hated the Zulu, he concluded, but they would never accept the Matabele as their friends.

May merged into June, and now with anxiety mounting in the Matabele kraals a new and unexpected problem confronted Mzilikazi. It was reported to him that certain of his subjects of Zulu extraction had fled across the Magaliesberg and were heading southwards to meet Ndlela's Zulu army and enlist in its ranks. Mzilikazi feared that these deserters would guide the enemy to enKungwini, enDinaneni and emHlahlandlela, and that eventually the entire Matabele tribe would be scattered. He called up every available man, every veteran, every cattle guard, and every servant, and prepared them for action. He led them to the south, and in a clearing between the Mpebane and Bekane streams he detected a large section of the Zulu host resting while awaiting the arrival of the commander-in-chief and his personal contingent. It seems incredible that Ndlela should not have been present to lead the vanguard of Dingane's forces into Matabele territory. Indeed, his carelessness was to save Mzilikazi and his heterogeneous force from a struggle that might easily have ended in their destruction.

The Zulu regiments were taken unawares. Nzobo, the second in command, called his men to order. The two armies faced each other, the *izimbongi*, or praise-singers, on both sides started chanting, and the champion warriors rushed out to engage their opponents in single combat. Gradually, as step by step the Matabele and Zulu advanced, the intervening space between the rival lines of fighters narrowed. The battle began. Stabbing-spear challenged stabbing-spear. Foot to foot the men struggled, parrying assegai thrusts with their huge oval shields, plunging their blades into bodies that for a moment were exposed, and striding over the wounded and dead as they sprawled on the grass.

But the tempo of the battle could not endure. Outnumbered and outclassed, the Matabele were obliged to turn and flee, to lure the Zulu from the open veld into the bush and hills. In this brief but violent encounter many of the Matabele had fallen, but Dingane's forces too had been depleted. During the hours that remained before the sun set over Mzilikazi's country, the Zulu hunted their quarry, but when night approached they abandoned operations and waited for the light of dawn for Ndlela, their commander-in-chief, to arrive.

Meanwhile the Matabele were trekking northwards into the remote bushveld, to the wooded and craggy heights of the Mlula mountain. Next day Ndlela arrived on the scene of battle. He knew at once that his delay had deprived his army of any hope of a decisive victory, and there would be no object in attempting to seek the foe in the sea of bush and hills that extended over the farthest horizons. For miles around the Zulu found no trace of Matabele men, women or children, but within the stockades of some of the deserted kraals there were herds of cattle. Ndlela commanded his men to collect as many herds as they could find, to set fire to the settlements and then to return in haste so that the army might set out to the Valley of the Zulu.

Thus did the Zulu nation retrieve its quota of cattle once stolen by Mzilikazi from Shaka. Thus did the Matabele survive an invasion which might well have resulted in their permanent subjugation.

With the withdrawal of the Zulu regiments from Mzilikazi's country the routine of tribal life returned gradually to the Matabele. For the next year they lived in peace, planting their crops in October, tending them through the rainy season and harvesting during the winter of 1831. Raids into the territories of neighbouring tribes were resumed, and herds were confiscated to be driven to Mzilikazi's cattle-posts. One of these outings is worthy of mention. It took selected Matabele regiments to the land of broken tribes, the Caledon valley, where a few years before the wars of *lifaqane* were raging.

On reaching the Caledon valley the Matabele regiments found that most of the groups of people who populated the outer regions of the country were utterly destitute. When the wars of *lifaqane* had ceased these tribesmen strove to rehabilitate themselves, but three years of drought increased their poverty and they were living on a diet of roots, grass seeds and the little milk received from their hollow-bellied cows. The Matabele did not molest them, for there was nothing among their meagre possessions worth taking. Moving farther to the south the regiments arrived at Umparani, the settlement of Sikonyela, son of Mantatisi, who with a section of the remnants of the Wild Cat People was living on the summit of a mountain. They also found Mantatisi, the old conqueror, now war-beaten and infirm, at Merabing – the Place of the Puff-adder. After becoming involved in a brief skirmish with the Wild Cat People the Matabele withdrew fifty miles farther southwards, to the headquarters of a more prosperous chief named Moshesh.

It will be remembered that in the early years of *lifaqane* Mantatisi, then at the height of her power, had attempted to oust this same Moshesh from his mountain stronghold at Butha-Buthe – the Place of Lying Down. At that stage of his career Moshesh was petty-chief of an insignificant clan of Sotho-speaking cattle-breeders. Having survived the attacks of the Wild Cat People, Moshesh became restless, realizing that sooner or later Matiwane and Mpangazita, the conquerors from Zululand, would besiege him, and that his chances of preventing penetration of his defences would be remote. He sent envoys to the east in search of an impregnable mountain stronghold, and when after a few months they returned to report they had found an ideal refuge for the clan, the young chief collected his subjects and departed.

At length, after a hazardous march through a country swarming with wild beasts, marauders and cannibals, Moshesh and his

clan reached a flat mountain which overlooked the Little Caledon
river. It was a superb stronghold, the heights being crowned with
an unbroken chain of precipices and the base adorned with vast
expanses of fertile soil. Moshesh led his people up one of the
passes approaching the summit. The sun had gone down, and they
settled on the mountain beneath the stars. They named their new
home Thaba Bosiu – the Mountain at Night. This is one of the
most historic mountains in South Africa, for it was on its table-
topped crest in the gloom of night that the Basuto nation, as it is
known today, was born.

Newly arrived on Thaba Bosiu, Moshesh set about building a
village and fortifying his defences by piling mounds of basaltic
boulders along the edges of the cliffs that lined the passes. Life on
the mountain was austere but free, remote from the pandemonium
into which the wars of *lifaqáne* had thrust the people who lived in
the surrounding lowlands. As food supplies dwindled and granaries remained unreplenished, it often became necessary for groups
of his men to rob passers-by, even the rearguard of the armies of
Mantatisi, Matiwane and Mpangazita, and then to retreat swiftly
up the secret passes and back to Moshesh's village. Moshesh
gained stature as a military strategist. When eventually the turmoil ceased and peace returned to the Caledon valley he was
hailed by the survivors of *lifaqane* as the person who could offer
them protection, lands for cultivation and pastures for new
herds. From every direction war-torn wanderers flocked to him
and acknowledged him as their paramount chief. Moshesh even
solicited the confidence of the Bafokeng cannibals, firstly by lur-
ing them from their caves with gifts of cattle and then by offering
them sorghum seed and fields in which to plant it. He gathered
about him a hotch-potch of humanity, the down-and-outs of the
Caledon valley. Then he moulded them into South Africa's
youngest tribe, the Basuto of the present-day British Protectorate
of Basutoland.

But in March 1831 Moshesh was confronted with a grave problem. From the summit of his Mountain at Night he could see the
powerful regiments of Mzilikazi approaching. He feared the Mata-

bele. With his newly founded nation still nursing its wounds he would have preferred to avoid battle, any battle, but especially one against an enemy of Zulu origin. Moshesh watched the regiments as they bivouacked on the banks of the Little Caledon, as they bathed in the shallow waters, as they whetted their assegais and as they lined up towards sunset to take part in a prolonged series of war dances.

And while the Matabele rested beside the river Moshesh and his followers added boulders to the mounds of basalt that already lined the passes on Thaba Bosiu. They were busily engaged when their enemy surged up through the gorge, climbed the hill near the present site of the Paris Evangelical Mission and skirted the base of the mountain in the direction of the steep and treacherous Raputho Pass. The Matabele massed beneath the gigantic precipices escarping the 250 acres of the mountain-top and moved slowly up the tortuous pass. They were allowed to progress far into the rugged slopes of Thaba Bosiu, into that section of the mountain where the pass enters a series of fissures. Now, for the first time, Moshesh's warriors appeared, as, from the vertical heights, they sent a cascade of javelins plunging into the Matabele lines. The boulders came next, a clanging mass of rolling basalt that crushed the van of the invaders and sent the survivors tumbling panic-stricken down the pass. The great majority of the Matabele warriors managed to extricate themselves and then scamper down the lower slopes into the near-by valley.

The Matabele regimental commanders were frantic with rage. They cursed and gesticulated, snatched the war plumes from the heads of their men and trod them into the dust. Cowardice would not be tolerated, they shouted, and nothing must prevent their taking the mountain and destroying the stone-rollers. They regrouped their regiments and prepared for another advance along the Raputho Pass.

This second attempt to reach the summit of Thaba Bosiu was insanely daring, but doomed to failure. The moment the boulders started roaring down the pass the Matabele commanders called a retreat and led their regiments away from the mountain and back to the banks of the Little Caledon. At last they too were convinced that Moshesh's fortress was impregnable and that it would be foolhardy to send the cream of the army to its death.

Next day, as they were about to commence their journey homewards, the Matabele were visited by an envoy from Moshesh. He brought greetings from his chief, and also a gift of a few head of cattle. The great Moshesh wished the Matabele to become the friends of the Basuto, the envoy asserted, and as a token of goodwill he had sent the cattle so that the regiments might not be hungry during their march back to the Magaliesberg.

The Matabele never attacked the Basuto again. Chroniclers and missionary writers have claimed that Mzilikazi was so impressed by Moshesh's diplomacy that he decided to exclude Thaba Bosiu from his itinerary of marauding expeditions. In actual fact the King of the Matabele was too shrewd a tactician to risk his army in further ventures against the defenders of the mountain. In years to come this decision was to prove wise, especially when it is considered that even the armed forces of the Koranna, the British and the Boers could fare no better against the stone-rollers than the Matabele had done in March 1831.

CHAPTER 15

MURDER HILL

*Barend Barends musters an army – Invasion of Matabele
territory – Mzilikazi slaughters the Griqua and Koranna
at Moordkop*

THE reverses suffered by the Matabele in March 1831 at the hands
of the Zulu and the Basuto did not unduly disturb Mzilikazi. His
concern would have been far greater had he realized that during
the past nine months some of the peoples who inhabited the
regions to the south and the west of his dominions had been
planning his destruction. The Bechuana tribes were living in constant dread of a Matabele invasion, believing rumours that floated
through the interior to the effect that Mzilikazi was about to
embark on expanding his dominions, and that the peoples he invaded would be subjected to the same treatment as the hapless
Bakwena. A murmur of discontent arose in every village. The
chiefs complained bitterly among themselves of the incessant
trespassing of Matabele regiments within their borders, of the furtive visits by Matabele spies and of Mzilikazi's interference in their
domestic affairs. The captains of the Griqua and Koranna clans,
and also those of the bands of Bergenaar desperadoes, were especially aggrieved. Before Mzilikazi's rise to power they had been free
to hunt and pillage wherever they chose; now their favourite
haunts were being patrolled by hostile Matabele regiments. In no
part of the plateau forming the central territory of South Africa,
including the country immediately north of the Limpopo, could
there have been a race or tribe without the belief that peace was
impossible so long as Mzilikazi was allowed to live.

Boetsap, the grimy settlement of Barend Barends's Griqua followers, became a centre of intrigue. Ever since his visit the pre-

vious year to the Magaliesberg, when he escorted the Rev. James Archbell to the land of the Matabele, old Barends had been sick at heart for, having been brought face to face with Mzilikazi's ruthlessness, he could not wipe from his mind the memories both of the Bakwena ruins and of the masses of skeletons he had encountered. It riled him to remember Mzilikazi had challenged his appearance at the Magaliesberg. For years the Griqua had hunted elephants in those parts.

Barends recalled that *en route* to Mzilikazi's country he had met his old friend Pilane, Chief of the Bakgatla – the People of the Baboon. Pilane had refused to discuss hunting or even barter, for he declared that Mzilikazi would not hesitate to send a force to wipe out his villages if ever he learned that a friendship existed between the Griqua and the People of the Baboon. Nevertheless, in due course of this brief meeting, Pilane had found sufficient courage to suggest that Barends should raise an expeditionary force, drawn from the peoples of the interior, to be led by the Griqua for the extermination of Mzilikazi and his tribe. This suggestion, allied to his genuine hatred for the Matabele, inveigled old Barends into believing that he, the captain of a powerful section of the Griqua, could be the person to organize the destruction of Mzilikazi's power and so become the liberator of the peoples of central South Africa. Barends reflected that he and other Griqua chiefs had saved the Fish People and the white missionaries from annihilation when, in 1823, they had united to decimate Mantatisi's Batlokoa. Now, if he could stir the leaders of the great tribes of central South Africa into accepting him as their emancipator, Barends would muster a huge army of cavalrymen and warriors to purge the country of its most dreaded enemies, the Matabele.

Barends's scheme proved extremely popular, and in June 1831 Boetsap was thronged with a multitude of fighting men, a miscellany drawn from the Lion People, the numerous Griqua and Koranna clans, the Barolong and almost every other Bechuana tribe. The old Griqua convened a council of war, and impressed upon his military leaders the magnitude of their joint undertaking. Shortly after, this great army swaggered out of the dust-drenched

. A Matabele warrior sketched by Captain William Cornwallis Harris
uring his visit to Mzilikazi in October 1836.

2. A Matabele cattle post on the north side of the Magaliesberg range.

3. While hunting elephant in Mashonaland, Henry Hartley discovered gold in abandoned mines. (From a painting by Thomas Baines.)

4. Mzilikazi (seated in chair) receives Dr Andrew Smith (with top hat), Moffat (with long black beard) and members of the scientific expedition in the Marico district.

5. Mzilikazi (fourth from right) leading his warriors in a war dance (1835).

6. Women and children of the Bakwena, or Crocodile People, take refuge from Mzilikazi's regiments on the banks of the Marico river.

7. Matabele warriors escorting a train of Bakwena captives with supplies for Mzilikazi.

8. Matabele warriors on the attack.

9. Matabele war dance.

10. Boer men and women defending the laager at Vegkop against the Matabele army. (15 October 1836.)

11. Execution of a prisoner. His legs and arms bound, and a stone tied round his neck, he is about to be thrown into a pool in the river.

12. A prisoner, found guilty of witchcraft, being taken to his execution.

13. The prisoner is unconscious and will now be skewered. Note the skewering stick in the executioner's left hand.

14. Mzilikazi (seated in the wagon) listens to an *induna* as he praises two herdsmen for saving the King's cattle from being attacked by a lioness. The head, tail and paws of the lioness have been presented to Mzilikazi.

15. Matabele men dosing an ailing ox.

16. Robert Moffat in his declining years.

17. Jan Viljoen, famous Boer hunter and close friend of Mzilikazi.

18. Thomas Morgan Thomas, missionary of Inyati, who attended Mzilikazi during his last illness.

19. Inyati, the mission founded by Robert Moffat in Matabeleland (*circa* 1862).

20. Kuruman, Robert Moffat's mission station founded in 1820.

21. Robert Moffat's original home at the Kuruman mission station as it is today.

22. The church built by Moffat at Kuruman. In 1835 Mzilikazi helped the missionary to select rafters for the roof.

23. Nyamazana, the Antelope, in 1922. Originally a Swazi queen, she became one of Mzilikazi's wives.

24. The grave of uLoziba, Mzilikazi's favourite wife. Photograph taken by the author in 1960.

25. The main pass leading to the summit of Moshesh's mountain stronghold, Thaba Bosiu.

26. The author's guide at enTumbane, Mzilikazi's sepulchre in the Motopos, Rhodesia. Note how the mouth of the sacred cave has been sealed with stones.

settlement, headed by a commando of a thousand horsemen and followed by a long procession of wagons bearing rifles, ammunition and provisions.

Meandering eastwards along the course of the Vaal, the expeditionary force reached Makwassie. And there it bivouacked while Barends sent out spies. Within a few days the spies returned with the heartening news that Mzilikazi's crack regiments were away on a raiding excursion into Bamangwato territory, and that veterans and untrained youths alone remained to defend the kraals, the cattle-posts and the herds that swarmed the vales and the hill slopes. The army prepared to advance.

Barends held a second council of war, at which he announced that his old age and precarious health would not permit him to travel farther north with the forces. He had decided, he said, to remain at Makwassie, where he would await tidings of the extermination of the Matabele. The old man exhorted his men not to fear Mzilikazi, but to crush him and drive the remnants of his tribe across the Limpopo. He added that nearly all the Matabele cattle once belonged to the Crocodile People and other Bechuana tribes. He promised to return the cattle to the rightful owners once the campaign was over. With these last words the meeting closed, and the allied army set out towards the Magaliesberg.

Travelling mainly at night and taking shelter in the bush during the day, the army reached the southern confines of Mzilikazi's country within five days. Spies crept through the Magaliesberg, observed the exact positions of the outposts and hastened back to report to the main force that the Matabele were unaware of the impending invasion. The allies advanced swiftly. Their horsemen swooped down on the kraals, killing herdsmen, capturing women, firing huts and rounding up cattle for the footmen to drive to the south. For hour after hour thousands of Mzilikazi's cattle were stampeded through the ranges and it struck the leaders of the commando as strange that not a single Matabele warrior appeared to challenge them. They did not guess that Mzilikazi had no intention of exposing his men to their musket-fire, and that he had already organized the withdrawal of his people to the depths of the bushveld. For the Griqua and Koranna, whose avarice for cattle was unrivalled in South Africa, this visit to Mzilikazi's kingdom was a delightful adventure. They soon forgot the original purpose of launching the expedition to the north, and they decided to postpone their extermination of the Matabele. They also agreed unanimously that the idea of handing over the Matabele cattle to the Bechuana tribes was ridiculous, merely a product of Barend Barends's addled old mind.

During the following days the cattle-thieves hustled their herds towards the Vaal. Their scouts hung back to watch for the approach of Mzilikazi's regiments, but when at the end of the third day there was no sign of the enemy the captains believed that their commandos were beyond reach of an attack. Therefore, when by twilight they reached a conical-shaped hill that dominated the immediate surroundings, they halted at its base and pitched camp. Fires were kindled and beasts slaughtered in preparation for a feast.

The women prisoners, who by this time had confessed to their captors that they were happy to be free of Mzilikazi's tyranny, were alarmed at the carefree attitude pervading the camp. They approached Gert Hooyman, one of the captains, and advised him to picket the encampment lest the Matabele arrive during the course of the night. The young regiments or day-fighters were in Bamangwato country, they said, and the veterans who operated only after dark had remained behind to defend the kingdom. The women suggested that if Mzilikazi had decided to retaliate his veteran regiments would travel by night. For a while Gert Hooyman was moved by the logic of the women's warnings, but he was scoffed at when he conferred with his colleagues. A Griqua named Jan Pienaar was particularly amused at the absurdity of Hooyman's fears. By midnight the revelry ceased and sleep descended upon the thousand men.

In the meantime, beyond the Magaliesberg, Mzilikazi fumed over the losses his herds had suffered at the hands of his enemies, the yellow-skinned horsemen. When he learned that the stockthieves had left his country, heading southwards with the cattle, he called his warriors to arms and dispatched them in hot pursuit under cover of darkness.

For three days the Matabele stalked the marauders, remaining well out of sight. At nights they were always within striking distance of the Griqua and the Koranna, and Matabele spies skulked about the fringes of their bivouac. Then on the third night, when it was found that the encampment was unguarded, the veterans formed a great circle about the sleeping horde and sat on their haunches in silence.

Just before daybreak, as the waning moon was sinking behind the crest of the hill, the Matabele rose and padded forward. When they were within two hundred yards of the first row of sleepers a Griqua detected them and sounded the alarm. The Matabele charged, whooping, beating their shields with their stabbing-spears, and hissing sibilant war chants. Gert Hooyman, the Griqua, a Korranna named Haip and a third man managed to jump on to their horses and break through the converging circle of warriors, but before the rest of the camp had time to fling aside their karosses they were being butchered by assegai blades. Many reached for their guns only to have them wrenched from their hands before a shot could be fired; many grasped their muskets but were so overcome with fright that they fired indiscriminately, and killed not only Matabele warriors but also their own people. By sunrise the entire commando lay slain at the foot of the lonely conical hill. Only three men had escaped to gallop away to Makwassie, there to break the tragic news to old Barend Barends.

During the day some of the Matabele rummaged for booty through the carnage, while others collected cattle. Then the warriors returned to the Magaliesberg to take part in the greatest victory celebrations ever to have been held by the tribe.

Mzilikazi himself visited the scene of the slaughter. It is said that as he strode through the agglomeration of decomposing bodies, many of which had already been reduced by the vultures, jackals and hyenas to white polished skeletons, he was jubilant. For years afterwards traders, travellers and hunters passed this battlefield and inspected the bones of the men and horses, the tattered saddles, the rotting karosses and the rusting guns.

To this day this historic spot is known in South Africa as Moordkop, or Murder Hill.

CHAPTER 16

THE INVASION OF BECHUANALAND

Mzilikazi conquers the tribes of Bechuanaland
French missionaries settle at Mosega
Jean Pierre Pellissier held by Mzilikazi
Warclouds in Bahurutsi territory – Matabele exodus

IN the years following Mzilikazi's destruction of Barend Barend's army Matabele warriors travelled hither and thither like hornets whose nest had been disturbed, never ceasing to attack neighbouring tribesmen, never settling in one particular place for any length of time.

During the five years after Mzilikazi's arrival in the Rustenburg district, the Bechuana tribes had feared the Matabele tyrant would unleash his armies in a full-scale invasion of the regions to the south and west of the Magaliesberg. Their fears became a reality when the Matabele advanced westwards and swooped down on the great villages of the Bangwaketsi.

The Bangwaketsi, ruled by Chief Sebego, were a prosperous tribe. Many thousands of their rondavel huts, identical in style to those of the Crocodile People of Bechuanaland and the Magaliesberg area, were grouped in large settlements throughout Sebego's country. The Bangwaketsi were also considered a powerful tribe, especially as in 1823 they had repulsed Mantatisi's Wild Cat hordes, and in 1826, with the support of Andrew Geddes Bain, they had defeated the Makololo of Chief Sebitoane. It is interesting that Mzilikazi should have decided to invade the far-off territories of the Bangwaketsi first when there were relatively defenceless tribes living immediately beyond the Matabele borders. One may assume the King believed that if once he subjugated the Bangwaketsi, the other tribes would yield quickly to Matabele supremacy.

It is unnecessary to describe fully Mzilikazi's conquest of the Bangwaketsi, for it follows almost to a detail the pattern of the Matabele campaign against the Crocodile People. The veteran Matabele regiments attacked at night, firing villages, cutting off the flight of residents as they came tumbling terror-stricken out of their huts, butchering aged men and women, dispatching infants and capturing the young men and women they considered suitable as warriors and mothers of their tribe.

During the day the veterans rested and the cream of Mzilikazi's army rose to continue the onslaught. Then there was no question of surprise attack, and whenever the Bangwaketsi stood their ground and faced their foe a mass slaughter took place. The cumbersome javelins of the Bangwaketsi, their battle-axes and their clubs, proved futile against the sturdy ox-hide shields and the long-bladed stabbing-assegais of the Matabele. Within a few days the Bangwaketsi were fleeing in every direction, their country overrun by the Matabele conquerors, and vultures were skidding down from the skies to feast on corpses.

Streams of Bangwaketsi refugees poured westwards into the adjoining desert, past present-day Maokani and Dikgomo Dikayi towards Ghansi. They struggled through the plains of the Kalahari, carrying their impedimenta on their shoulders, and driving their cattle before them. But soon the thirstland took toll not only of the Bangwaketsi and their beasts, but also of a Matabele regiment sent to destroy them. Matabele spears, thirst and the heat of the desert broke the power of the Bangwaketsi in Bechuanaland. In some remote part of the desert Chief Sebego died. His grave was dug with javelin blades in the blistering sands.

With the dispersal of the Bangwaketsi, Mzilikazi's armies turned on the Bakgatla – the Baboon People, a comparatively defenceless Bechuana tribe inhabiting the regions about the Notwani and Marico rivers. This campaign was brief: the Baboon People offered no resistance. Smoke clouds rose above the bushveld, conveying a mute message to tribesmen watching from afar that the Bakgatla villages were being laid waste, the inhabitants massacred and the cattle-folds pillaged.

When the Baboon People were crushed, their young men and women taken prisoner and their herds driven across the Magaliesberg to Mzilikazi's cattle-posts, the Matabele advanced to the north-west and fell upon that section of the Crocodile People inhabiting Northern Bechuanaland. Once again Mzilikazi's regiments encountered a minimum of opposition and swept through the country, leaving desolation and misery in their wake.

Their mission of destruction accomplished in the land of the Crocodile People, the Matabele headed homewards. For years to come the Bakwena were homeless and broken of spirit. Famine ravaged this decimated tribe. Prodigious fortitude alone saved them from extinction.

By the end of 1831 Mzilikazi had included a great section of Bechuanaland within his domain, but the richest prize of all, the fertile, well-watered country of the Bahurutsi, was yet to be taken. Mzilikazi decreed that the Bahurutsi must be wiped out before the next autumn, but his plans were temporarily thwarted by the unexpected arrival at Mosega, headquarters of Chief Mokgatla, of white men from across the seas.

During March 1832 three Frenchmen, Prosper Lemue, Samuel Rolland and Jean Pierre Pellissier, arrived at Mosega to establish a mission station on behalf of the Paris Evangelical Mission Society. On two previous occasions Lemue and Rolland had visited Chief Mokgatla, hoping to find a site for the church, the school and the house they intended building. But so great was the chaos among the Bahurutsi, as a result of the havoc Mzilikazi's armies had wrought among the Bechuana tribes to the immediate north, that the Frenchmen decided to join Robert Moffat at Kuruman, and to wait until peace was restored in the interior.

Letters arrived from the directors in Paris who, growing impatient, were urging the three evangelists to find, without delay, a suitable field for mission work among one or other of the Bechuana tribes. Eventually, when Lemue, Rolland and Pellissier learned from Chief Mokgatla that in recent months there had been no further signs of a Matabele invasion, they set out again from Kuruman to open their mission station in the Bahurutsi capital. But they arrived at Mosega at a most inopportune time.

In his kraal Mzilikazi was discussing with his warlords the campaign he intended launching against the Bahurutsi. He knew about the movements of the French missionaries, and had he not been aware of their association with his friend Moffat he would not have hesitated to drive them from Mosega. Mzilikazi was suspicious of these white men, and even accused them of taking part in the launching of Barend Barend's allied army. Perhaps what annoyed the King most was the fact that the Frenchmen had chosen to settle in Bahurutsi country, in the capital of an inferior chief like Mokgatla, when they might have followed the example of the other white teachers who had sought to work among the Matabele. Mzilikazi felt slighted. When news reached him in March that the missionaries were actually building a house at Mosega he postponed his attack on the Bahurutsi and decided to summon the Frenchmen to his royal kraal.

Therefore, only three weeks after their arrival at the new mission station, Lemue, Rolland and Pellissier were visited by eight Matabele envoys, who instructed them to proceed immediately to Mzilikazi's kraal. Pellissier, an enthusiastic young novice, had already contemplated investigating the potentialities for mission work among the war-like Matabele, and he volunteered to accompany the envoys to the north while his colleagues continued their building programme at Mosega.

He set out by ox-wagon on what was to prove a hazardous journey. Arriving at length at the Matabele capital, Pellissier found Mzilikazi sitting in the company of his ring-headed councillors, his courtiers, jesters and warriors in the shade of a tree. The young missionary was conducted to Mzilikazi, and was pleasantly surprised when the tyrant cordially welcomed him.

Pellissier was impressed by Mzilikazi's charm, his good looks, his ready smile, his well-proportioned body and dignified bearing, but as a shrewd judge of character the missionary regarded these attributes as the veneer beneath which the tyrant concealed the traits that had earned him the reputation of a ruthless destroyer.

In a letter to his directors Pellissier described Mzilikazi as a ruler whose authority and power were so great that the populace hardly dared breathe without his permission. Mzilikazi's subordinates, irrespective of status, were his slaves, and in his presence they trembled. His whims and moods so dominated the tribal court of justice that it was not uncommon for an accused man to be found guilty of some trivial misdemeanour and to be executed without the right of uttering a word in his own defence. Could one not compare the authority Mzilikazi exercised over the tribes with that which Napoleon enjoyed over the kingdoms of Europe? asked Pellissier. He hastened to add that he regarded the French Emperor's brand of despotism as lenient when compared with that of the King of the Matabele. Mzilikazi was the sole owner of everything in his domain, every cow and every ox; he even determined when men might marry. When, on rare occasions, he did condescend to allow distinguished veteran warriors to marry, he first selected the flower of the eligible young women for his own harems.

Tyrants like Mzilikazi were never at ease, wrote Pellissier, referring especially to the King's policy of moving from one kraal to another lest his enemies might learn of his whereabouts. Mzilikazi trusted no one, and, in turn, not a soul trusted him. He was also a hypocrite. Usually he flattered and fêted those whom he hated most, only to murder them when they least expected it. And often, when he intended invading foreign territories, he first sent envoys to the chiefs, bearing messages of goodwill, and then his regiments followed, bearing weapons of destruction.

Pellissier was delighted to learn that Mzilikazi was eager to have missionaries among the Matabele. The King assured him that he himself was anxious to learn about God. As time wore on, the young missionary became apprehensive, for it suddenly struck him that Mzilikazi was far more interested in the lessons the Matabele would receive in the handling of fire-arms than in the teachings of Christ. Nevertheless, Pellissier and Mzilikazi selected a site for a mission station, a spot where water and wood were plentiful and where the soil was best suited for the cultivation of gardens. Mzilikazi assured his white guest that as soon as he and his fellow-teachers left the Bahurutsi and settled among the Matabele they would have as many servants as they needed. Mzilikazi promised he would attend personally to the missionaries' requirements and comforts. Pellissier dreamed of the flourishing mission station rising in Matabele country. But then he received a rude awakening.

He informed Mzilikazi that the time had arrived for his departure to Mosega. The King became aloof and uncooperative, and insisted that he alone would decide when Pellissier might leave. He advised the missionary to send a message to the white men at Mosega, letting them know that he had not been killed by the Matabele. He instructed Pellissier to collect the servants who had accompanied the missionary wagon into Matabele territory, and to clean a stack of fire-arms which the Matabele regiments had taken from the Griqua and Koranna. Pellissier could not refuse, and during the next week, while engaged in the task assigned to him and his party, he was virtually a prisoner. Time and again he wondered whether he would live to see Lemue and Rolland.

Pellissier reflected on Mzilikazi's sudden change of attitude, and was convinced that ominous developments were afoot in Matabele country. He also believed there would be little scope for mission work in those parts in the immediate future. Eventually, when Mzilikazi allowed him to leave, Pellissier hastened to Mosega as fast as his wagons could carry him.

Back in Mosega, Pellissier fell into the routine of building the home in which he and his colleagues would live. Among the Bahurutsi rumours were still rife that Mzilikazi was planning to invade the country, and one day, when six Matabele warriors were found prowling about the outskirts of Mosega, the settlement seethed with suspicion. The warriors were captured and dragged before Mokgatla, the Chief, who convened his court of justice and charged the unwelcome strangers with espionage.

The trial was brief and decisive: the men were found guilty and sentenced to death. Lemue, Rolland and Pellissier feared the consequences of Mokgatla's hasty and somewhat hysterical action, but before they could express their opinions the spies were executed and their blood-drenched corpses carried to a spot where the birds and beasts of prey could devour them. No man knew better than Pellissier what Mzilikazi's reaction would be to the news of the death of his spies. He realized that the tyrant regarded Mokgatla with contempt, and would never allow so blatant an insult to remain unavenged.

Throughout May the Bahurutsi lived on tenterhooks. False alarms occurred frequently, and on one occasion even the familiar cheering of a group of locust-collectors was interpreted as the war-whoop of the advancing Matabele regiments. In June there was consternation in Mosega when a Matabele deputation arrived at the mission station and instructed Lemue, Rolland and Pellissier to present themselves at once before Mzilikazi. Now rumours spread that Mzilikazi was planning to murder the white men, and that his attack on the tribe would follow their death. The people pleaded with the missionaries to flee while there was yet time. The Frenchmen gathered their belongings, packed their wagons and departed for Kuruman. They decided to abandon all hope of establishing a mission in the land of the Bahurutsi.

At Kuruman, Lemue, Rolland and Pellissier were received by the sympathetic yet incredulous evangelists of the London Missionary Society. Robert Moffat in particular urged them to return to Mosega and he even offered to take them to Mzilikazi. The Frenchmen refused to undertake so foolhardy a venture.

After lengthy discussion it was decided to send a deputation to the Matabele King to ask him if he wanted missionaries to settle in his country. The messengers set out, but when four months passed and not a word was received from them Moffat and his friends feared they had come to grief.

Had Moffat been able to visualize what was happening beyond the Magaliesberg he would not have bothered to send his messengers to Mzilikazi's royal kraal. The King had not the slightest intention of allowing missionaries in his country, and as he was on the verge of attacking the Bahurutsi and annexing their country he would not have allowed the Frenchmen to remain at Mosega. His reasons for sending envoys to summon the three missionaries to his kraal will remain a mystery, but had Mzilikazi not done this, had he decided instead to pour his regiments into the country of the Bahurutsi, he might have suffered the most disastrous defeat of his career. At that very time, whilst Mzilikazi was waiting patiently for his men to return from Mosega, Dingane's Zulu army was advancing towards the Magaliesberg.

It was almost spring when the Zulu reached the first Matabele settlements. Bearing in mind the relative ease with which they had put the Matabele to flight in 1829, and then absconded with several of their herds, the invaders pressed on, sacking outposts and slaying the terrified inhabitants.

News of the arrival of the Zulu reached Mzilikazi and before long the Matabele regiments were streaming from their barracks and trotting behind their commanders to a meeting-place their King had named. The full weight of the Matabele army bore down on the Zulu, checking their advance, and even compelling them to fall back a short distance. The Zulu forces then stood firm and faced the Matabele. The two most powerful armies in Southern Africa moved forward, collided and became entangled in a bloody struggle.

The Zulu were the first to call off the battle, not because they were being defeated, but because they were in foreign territory and their enemies showed no sign of succumbing to their onslaught. They managed to break through and disperse a section of the Matabele army made up mainly of veteran warriors, but then three of their own regiments were wiped out almost to a man, and there was no knowing whether the cunning Mzilikazi was holding back reserves to be sent into the field at a moment's notice.

After this battle both the Zulu and the Matabele claimed a victory, but in actual fact this struggle ended in a stalemate and both sides were relieved when it was over. Dingane's forces returned to Zululand and the Matabele to their barracks.

This episode did not unduly disrupt the tribal life between the Magaliesberg and the Limpopo. If anything, it served to confirm Mzilikazi's belief that the Matabele army was invincible. Mzilikazi reprimanded his veteran regiments for having allowed the

Zulu to break through their lines. He accused them of cowardice, and for reasons best known to himself he decided to postpone punishing them.

During the next few weeks Mzilikazi's thoughts were engaged by an ambitious project. The King planned not only to destroy the Bahurutsi, but also to move the entire Matabele tribe into the fertile Marico district and the well-watered regions embracing it.

The summer rains came, and in Bahurutsi country the planting season commenced. Mzilikazi waited. He dared not be impatient, for if he attacked the Bahurutsi prematurely, thereby preventing them from sowing their sorghum, there would be no crops in the Marico district for the Matabele to reap in the coming winter.

When eventually Mzilikazi's army did advance over the border it found the outlying Bahurutsi villages deserted. The farther the Matabele proceeded to the south the more apparent it became that news of their approach had leaked out and that the Bahurutsi were already in flight.

The Matabele found the settlements surrounding Tshwenyane, the historic Little Baboon village, intact, as well as the rambling villages flanking the sorghum fields at Mosega. Far sooner than they had expected, the Matabele added the territory of the Bahurutsi to Mzilikazi's expanding dominions.

Towards the close of the year Mzilikazi announced, throughout his domain, that he had decided to move the Matabele tribe into Bahurutsi territory.

Thus, on an appointed day, a great exodus began. The Matabele dignitaries, the harem women, the royal children, married men and their families, the retainers, slaves and herdsmen, collected their belongings and followed their illustrious Bull Elephant out of the old country of the Crocodile People to a land they believed promised even greater prosperity. The women carried the sleeping-mats, baskets of grain, bundles of household articles, utensils and hoes. The men drove the herds, a multitude of almost a hundred thousand beasts, and scanned the surroundings for enemies who might arrive to challenge the tribe's safe passage to the west.

And as the Matabele surged into the beautiful, wooded regions and the luscious plains of the Marico district, and took possession of the deserted Bahurutsi villages and fields, another important period in their history drew to a close.

With most of the tribes of Bechuanaland and the Transvaal, as well as small sections of Southern Rhodesia quaking beneath his tyranny, Mzilikazi must have looked on the past with satisfaction and to the future with confidence. But within the next few years disaster would befall his great Matabele tribe.

CHAPTER 17

THE MATABELE OCCUPY THE MARICO DISTRICT

Mzilikazi fortifies the Marico district
Truey and Willem Davids taken prisoner
Andrew Geddes Bain's narrow escape
Mzilikazi and Moffat travel together

AS a result of Mzilikazi's efficient planning the Matabele were able to spread out and settle in the vastness of the Marico district with the minimum of confusion. The King and his councillors had apparently decided beforehand that the most vulnerable parts of the country should be guarded by a chain of powerful military stations, and the most inaccessible sites were set aside for kraals and cattle-posts. Mosega, the Bahurutsi capital, became Mzilikazi's most southerly settlement, the official headquarters of the Matabele tribe and the site of Mkwahla, the regimental barracks. Mkalipi, one of Mzilikazi's astutest generals, commanded this station, and built his personal kraal, Mastenyaneng – My Mother Goes in There – in the heart of the valley.

Fifteen other Matabele kraals rose in the fertile cornfields and pastures of Mosega. This great settlement, flanked south and west by a series of wooded and boulder-crested ranges, by Tsebe Khama – the Hartebeest Ear mountain – and by marshes and lakes became Mzilikazi's pride, a stronghold that would guard his newly acquired domains from enemies who might advance across the Vaal and Molopo rivers. Mkalipi and his regiments reconnoitred the southern confines of Mzilikazi's country, but they were also responsible for protecting Matabele kraals as far afield as present-day Vergenoegt and Mamanato in the north.

At Tshwenyane – the Little Baboon village – Mzilikazi established another military station, and chose as its commander Marapi. Marapi was a Bechuana captive, who over the years had proved so loyal and redoubtable a warrior in Mzilikazi's army that the King had allowed him to rise to the rank of a Matabele general. The stronghold at the Little Baboon village was considered almost as important as Mosega, for not only did it guard a great section of the eastern flank of the country, but it also protected the people Mzilikazi had settled in the districts known today as Rooisloot, Enselsberg, Leeufontein and Kleinfontein.

Some thirty miles to the immediate north of Tshwenyane, on the slopes of an isolated dome-shaped hill, a division of Matabele warriors was garrisoned under the command of a general named Kampu. This section of Mzilikazi's army traversed the central areas of the country, but it was also assigned to patrolling the banks of the Marico river. On occasions it joined forces with the regiments of a second station commanded by Kampu at Koppieskraal.

Not fifteen miles from Kampu's headquarters the Great Marico river flows leisurely westwards. In close proximity to its sedgy course three conical hills rise abruptly from the veld and gaze down on the site where Mzilikazi built eGabeni, most northern of his royal kraals.

eGabeni was a colossal settlement with circles of beehive huts enclosed by a broad, thorn-tree hedge. Within the kraal a tall, irregular palisade isolated both Mzilikazi's royal lodge and harem from the cattle-fold and the living-quarters of the courtiers, retainers and warriors. Sibekhu was in command of the regiments of eGabeni and, with Kempu, he operated in the northern and eastern limits of Mzilikazi's new domain.

In the western regions, where the danger of invasion from the broken Bechuana tribes was remote, and where the extreme heat and dryness of the country served as natural defences, Mzilikazi posted smaller concentrations of warriors under the supervision of Kabalonta, one of his closest friends. Mzilikazi's armies guarded the frontiers of the entire country. In the circle formed by the military posts the bulk of the population lived under appointed *indunas* and headmen.

There were also special kraals where only women resided. Several of these housed widows and young girls eligible for marriage. There were a few kraals that had been set aside by Mzilikazi for the wives of the veteran warriors who in 1832 had failed against the Zulu army. After that memorable battle against Dingane's forces Mzilikazi had chosen to postpone punishing the veterans, but then in his new kingdom he decided that as these warriors had obviously allowed themselves to be tempered by the luxuries of married life they must return for an indefinite period to the bachelors' barracks.

In specially guarded cattle-folds in the securest parts of the country Mzilikazi grouped his most cherished herds according to colour, sex and shape of horns, but along the outer fringe and in regions vulnerable to attacks by marauding armies he placed the Bechuana and other alien members of his tribe. By the beginning of 1834 the Matabele were firmly established in the Marico district, and Mzilikazi was continuously engaged in visiting the military kraals, cattle-posts and royal harems of which he was the supreme master.

Early in 1834, after the Great Nxwala or First-Fruits ceremony had been celebrated by the Matabele, Mzilikazi dispatched his regiments on raiding expeditions. Mkalipi's first project was to wipe out a section of the Barolong tribe settled to the north of the Molopo river. He razed their villages, butchered their fighting-men, captured their young women and cattle and drove the survivors westwards into the Kalahari.

But Mkalipi's foremost duty, as commander-in-chief of the military settlement at Mosega, was to guard the southern approaches to the Matabele kingdom. The King decreed that no strangers could cross the Vaal without permission, and he instructed Mkalipi to patrol the river area regularly and annihilate all trespassers. In 1834 Mkalipi sent a patrol to the Vaal, and in the course of their march along the river bank the warriors came upon some Griqua hunters and their families. The Matabele attacked. They slew the women and children and also the men who chanced to be in camp, but they spared the lives of a young Griqua girl named Truey and a boy named Willem.

Truey and Willem, the daughter and nephew of Peter Davids, leader of the Griqua party, were taken post-haste to Mosega. In years to come they were to find themselves intimately associated with Mzilikazi – Truey as a concubine in one of the despot's harems and Willem as a headman of the tribe.

With news of the presence of the yellow-skinned hunters on the Vaal, Mzilikazi became more insistent than ever that his regiments should be constantly on the alert for intruders. He believed that, if he was to succeed in maintaining his paramountcy over all the tribes he had subjugated, he dared not allow strangers, other than those recommended by Robert Moffat of Kuruman, to cross the Vaal or Molopo.

Therefore it was an unfortunate coincidence that at this time Andrew Geddes Bain, the Graaff-Reinet trader, accompanied by a small group of Griqua and Koranna servants, should have undertaken a trip towards the Molopo. Bain had set out on a commission from American clients to collect trophies and skins of lion, giraffe, rhinoceros and other animals. He was foolhardy in allowing a party of Griqua hunters to join his wagons as they trekked to the north, otherwise his trip could well have proved the most lucrative of his career.

In the vicinity of the Meritsane river Bain and his motley group discovered a sandy trail newly trodden by a herd of cattle stolen by a band of Bahurutsi from a Matabele outpost. To Bain the cattle spoors signified danger. He hastened towards the Molopo realizing that the Matabele were expert trackers and it would not be long before a search-party would arrive. He decided to visit Mzilikazi at Mosega and ask permission to hunt in Matabele country. But before he could set out he found to his horror that some of his Griqua had deserted and turned from hunting to raiding the Matabele cattle-posts.

He knew that his wagons would soon be discovered, and the Matabele would punish him for the crimes committed by the Bahurutsi and the Griqua servants. Three days later he reached a sultry valley on the Molopo. On the morning of the fourth day he was sitting in his wagon when his attention was attracted by a Griqua horseman galloping across the veld.

'Get your guns and horses ready,' the man shouted. 'Mzilikazi is close upon us.'[1]

Across the valley Bain saw a Matabele regiment descending at full speed upon his outspan. His thoughts turned immediately to the valuable collection of zoological specimens aboard his wagons and the chest in which he had hidden his money and papers. A second glance at the advancing regiment, and especially at its right wing already spread out to encircle the encampment, convinced him that if he intended escaping there was not a moment to spare. He snatched his double-barrel, sprang on to his horse, and galloped after his servants, who by this time had fled into an adjoining thicket.

The Matabele pursued the fugitives across the Molopo, but when Bain and a Griqua named Hendrik Klaas opened fire on them they wheeled about, covered their backs with their shields and trotted towards the wagons. Eventually they set out for Mosega to deliver to Mzilikazi the cattle, sheep and the heavily laden wagons of the strangers who had ventured into Matabele territory.

Bewildered and dejected, Bain retreated down the left bank of the Molopo and turned homewards. He reflected that had it not been for the avariciousness of his Griqua companions he would have returned to Graaff-Reinet the richer by a thousand pounds.

Early in 1835, not three months after Bain's mishap on the Molopo, messengers arrived from Kuruman to ask Mzilikazi whether he would allow Robert Moffat and a party of Colonials and their coloured servants to enter Matabele territory. Without the slightest hesitation Mzilikazi consented. In fact, the thought of a visit from his missionary friend delighted him.

Meanwhile, in Kuruman, thirteen white men and a retinue of twenty-three Hottentots awaited Mzilikazi's reply, and were enjoying the hospitality of the missionaries. They were the mem-

1. M. H. Lister (ed.), *Journals of Andrew Geddes Bain*, p. 143.

bers of a scientific expedition organized by the Association for the Exploration of Central Africa, to amass knowledge about the tribes, the geographical features, the natural resources and the flora and fauna of central South Africa. The commander was Dr Andrew Smith – later Sir Andrew Smith, K.C.B., Director-General of the Medical Department of the British Army, and the men accompanying him included Captain Edie of the 98th Regiment; John Burrow, surveyor and astronomer; George Ford, draughtsman; Charles Bell, artist and handyman; B. Kift, an experienced traveller and friend of Andrew Geddes Bain; C. Hartwell and the trader hunters Robert Schoon and David Hume, both of whom had already met Mzilikazi in the Magaliesberg.

Moffat agreed to accompany Smith as far as Mzilikazi's country, primarily because the missionary knew his friendly relationship with the despot would prove invaluable to the success of the expedition. But there were other important reasons : he was eager to select timber in the Marico district for the church he was building at Kuruman, to induce Mzilikazi to release Truey and Willem the Griqua children, and also to retrieve Bain's wagons, money and zoological specimens. When word was received from Mzilikazi the expedition set out to the North.

At the Molopo river Smith and his party were met by Mkalipi and four other Matabele dignitaries sent by the King. The white men learned that a mysterious epidemic was raging in Mosega, and, for fear of being infected by it, Mzilikazi had decided to withdraw to an outpost beyond the military kraal of eGabeni. During the next ten days the dozen tented wagons trundled through the Marico district, skirting Mkwahla, the military settlement at Mosega, and scraping through the bushveld thirty miles to the east of Tshwenyane. On 8 June the wagons struggled across the shallow waters of the Marico river and during mid-morning on the following day they reached the Tolane stream, where Mzilikazi's temporary headquarters were situated.

Mzilikazi, who had just returned from taking his bath in a pool below the huts, strode out to welcome Moffat with outstretched hands.

'Moshete, Moshete !' he exclaimed, his voice tense with excitement. 'Now my eyes see you again, and my heart is white as milk.'[1]

During the next hour or two Mzilikazi was so affable, so blatantly humble and almost puerile in his desire to please his dour missionary friend, that he astounded Moffat's Hottentot servants, who hitherto had only known of the Matabele King as a butchering tyrant. One of these men confessed later he had found Mzilikazi's *naïveté* pathetic to watch.

During the first few days of their sojourn on the Tolane members of the expedition watched in amazement as Mzilikazi followed Moffat among the wagons, holding the missionary's hand like a doting child and even playing with his beard. Any doubts about Mzilikazi's strength of character or his qualities of leadership vanished when, at a special meeting held in the kraal, Dr Smith ventured to hint at the atrocities the King and his people had committed over the years.

Presenting Mzilikazi with a medal and chain, tokens of goodwill from the Cape Government, Dr Smith announced that the British authorities were determined to punish all chiefs who invaded and pillaged the territories of peace-loving peoples. He referred in particular to the marauding excursions the Matabele were undertaking to the South, and recommended that Mzilikazi surrender Truey and Willem Davids immediately, as well as the wagons taken from Bain. Though annoyed by this unexpected interference in the domestic affairs of his tribe, Mzilikazi did not lose his composure; nevertheless, he assured Dr Smith that the Griqua children and the wagons had been taken according to the rules of war and would only be released after the payment of cattle. As Mzilikazi seemed reluctant to pursue the subject any further, Smith brought the meeting to a premature close.

Dr Smith and his party took leave of Mzilikazi and departed for the regions about the Tropic of Capricorn. Moffat remained at Tolane, and for two long months Mzilikazi fêted him, bestowed gifts upon him and even performed rituals in his honour in the cattlefold. But even Mzilikazi's intense devotion and respect for

1. J. P. R. Wallis (ed.), *Matabele Journals of Robert Moffat*, vol. I, p. 73.

Moffat did not deter the despot from attending assiduously to the affairs of his kingdom, from receiving messengers from and dispatching them to his military stations, and from presiding over urgent cases in the tribal court.

Although he knew that Moffat abhorred all forms of violence and killing, Mzilikazi decided on 2 July to skewer eight alleged traitors. On the same day he had two female defaulters lashed to a tree and their eyes torn out; then they were strangled and their bodies taken to the veld for the beasts of prey to devour.

Invariably Mzilikazi was inundated with a host of problems demanding his personal attention, but he found time to visit Moffat's wagons daily. The King spared no efforts to please his white guests, and even decided to accompany Moffat in a search for timber for the Kuruman church.

But the King would not tolerate interference, not even from Moffat, in Matabele affairs. When one day the missionary pleaded that he be allowed to take Truey and Willem back to Peter Davids, Mzilikazi retorted that he himself would decide both the time and the terms for the release of the Griqua children. Nevertheless, the King promised his white friend he would take good care of the children while they remained his hostages.

At a kraal in the neighbourhood of eGabeni Moffat was allowed the privilege of inspecting Bain's wagons and also a few others the despot had apparently taken from his Griqua enemies. The vehicles were in a sorry state of dilapidation, and their contents, although untouched by the Matabele, were being destroyed by rust, moths and mice. In vain Moffat tried to persuade Mzilikazi to let him repair Bain's wagons and return them to their rightful owners in the South. Mzilikazi replied brusquely that he had decided to send envoys to the Cape Government to find out why nothing was being done to prevent the Griqua, the Koranna and white travellers from attacking the Matabele. The King assured Moffat that if the envoys received a favourable explanation from the white Governor he, the Bull Elephant, would consider surrendering the booty his regiments had taken legitimately in battle.

Moffat and Mzilikazi travelled slowly by ox-wagon through the Marico district, past Mosega and southwards towards the

Molopo river. Together they selected trees to be felled for the rafters of the Kuruman church.

On reaching the banks of the river, where they were to part company, Mzilikazi presented Moffat with an ox, three cows and several bags of corn. Then the two friends said farewell. As Moffat struck out homewards he was contented, for at last he had found the timber he needed to complete his church. But one anxious thought lingered in the missionary's mind: he knew that if strangers from the South continued to cross the Vaal river without Mzilikazi's permission there would always be bloodshed in the interior of South Africa.

CHAPTER 18

ARRIVAL OF THE BOERS

Mzilikazi enters into an agreement with Sir Benjamin
D'Urban – Americans settle at Mzilikazi's capital
The Boers are attacked by Matabele regiments
Cornwallis Harris arrives from India – Massacre at Vegkop

WHEN Dr Andrew Smith returned from exploring regions far
beyond the Marico river, he brought his party to Mzilikazi's kraal.
Before departing for the Colony, Smith was asked by Mzilikazi to
allow a Matabele delegation headed by uMncumbata, chief
induna of the tribe, to accompany the expedition's wagons to the
South. The white man consented. A few months later when Dr
Smith reached the Cape he conducted Mzilikazi's envoys to the
Governor, Sir Benjamin D'Urban.

In March 1836 uMncumbata drew a cross on a treaty the Cape
Government placed before him. In so doing, the *induna* pledged on
behalf of Mzilikazi that the Matabele would become allies of the
Colony. The terms of the treaty demanded that, unless invaded,
the Matabele were to abstain from waging war, and in addition
Mzilikazi must protect all white visitors, missionaries and other
persons who with the King's consent were resident in Matabele
territory.

Travellers engaged in activities beneficial to mankind were to be
assisted and defended in times of danger, and all hostile movements among peoples of the interior were to be reported to the
Colonial Government. At all costs the Matabele were to cultivate
and encourage peace.

In turn, according to the terms of the treaty, the Governor
would agree to accept Mzilikazi and the Matabele tribe as friends
of the Colony, would supply the King with gifts and consider his

request to send a white official, perhaps a missionary, to reside in Matabele territory.

Two months later, as a result of a recommendation from Robert Moffat, Mzilikazi allowed three white men and their wives, members of the American Boards Mission, to resuscitate the ill-fated French mission station at Mosega. These people were Dr Alexander and Jane Wilson of North Carolina, Daniel and Lucy Lindley of Ohio, and Henry and Martha Venable of Kentucky. The Americans set about preparing their homes and making acquaintance with the Matabele living in and about Mkalipi's great military barracks. They were intensely happy; but they were unaware of the grave dangers then looming over the southern Matabele frontiers and the tragedy that was to overwhelm the Mosega settlement.

In the eastern districts of the Cape Colony the Great Trek was already in progress. Convoys of tented wagons bearing Dutch Colonials, their wives, children and household goods, were travelling northwards towards the Vaal river. As the Boer emigrants trekked from their farms and away from the British, under whose rule they had never been happy, they looked to the future with pleasant expectation. Devout Christians, the Trekkers prayed that in the interior of South Africa they might find a peaceful hinterland where life could be started afresh.

In the early months of 1836 Louis Trichardt's Trekkers, accompanied by those of Jan Van Rensburg, slipped across the Vaal into Matabele territory. They escaped the notice of Mzilikazi's patrols and pressed on to the Zoutpansberg and Delagoa Bay. In due course, somewhere along the route, they were wiped out almost to a man by fever and by unknown hostile tribes.

At about the time when Mzilikazi's envoys were visiting the Cape Governor a Trekker party, under the leadership of a distinguished Boer named Hendrik Potgieter, had already reached the banks of the Vaal. In the country between the Vaal and the Vet rivers, the domain of an impoverished section of the Bataung tribe, Potgieter's party split into family groups, each herding its own sheep and cattle beside separate wagon encampments. Taking eleven chosen horsemen, Hendrik Potgieter set out across the Vaal and moved northwards in search of a country where his followers might settle permanently. This small group of riders was trespassing in the territory claimed by the Bull Elephant of the Matabele.

Meanwhile, at Aliwal North, a Boer named Stephanus Erasmus decided to take advantage of the presence of the Trekkers along the Vaal by organizing a hunting-trip into Mzilikazi's territory. With his three sons, Piet Bekker and his son, Jan Claassers, Karel Kruger, some coloured servants, eighty slaughter-oxen and fifty horses, Erasmus stole across the river.

One morning, leaving five wagons in the care of the servants, Erasmus and his fellow-hunters set out in different directions in search of game. Towards sunset he and one of his sons returned to camp and found the wagons surrounded by six hundred Matabele warriors. From the commotion the Boer hunter knew the coloured servants were being butchered, but he did not realize that his own two sons and also Karel Kruger had already been captured and murdered in the veld by the Matabele.

Piet Bekker and his son came galloping along to join Erasmus. They reported that they had narrowly escaped the encircling swoop of the horns of a Matabele regiment, and that Claassens, a member of the hunting-party was missing. Indeed, Jan Claassens was never seen again.

Stephanus Erasmus's thoughts flashed to the scattered groups of Trekkers encamped along the banks of the Vaal. Digging his heels into his horse's flanks and calling his son to follow, the Boer galloped away from the scene of destruction and headed for that part of the river where Parys stands today. Before daybreak he reached the camps of the Botha and Steyn families, blurted out the news of the tragedy, and announced the advance of the Matabele.

In a bend in the river the Bothas and Steyns drew their wagons into laager formation. Meanwhile young Dolf Bronkhorst had raced off to alert the Liebenberg families, also outspanned close to the Vaal. At about ten in the morning the Matabele arrived and fell upon the laagers of the Botha and Steyn families, but although the regiments flung their full weight into the attack they could not penetrate through the volleys of bullets. By mid-afternoon, when a third of their number lay dead about the wagons, the Matabele withdrew, taking with them droves of Boer cattle. The thirty white men in the laager suffered no casualties, but a young herdboy who had been cut off from the wagons was killed. The Matabele had also captured and murdered Bronkhorst.

The Liebenbergs were taken unawares by a large section of Mzilikazi's marauding regiments. Old Barend Liebenberg, patriarch of the family group, was murdered, and also three of his married sons, a daughter, a daughter-in-law and Jan du Toit, a son-in-law. The Matabele also killed McDonald, the party's schoolmaster, as well as four children and twelve coloured servants, but they spared three of the Liebenberg children – two girls and a boy – and carried them off as presents for the Bull Elephant. Although in later years news was frequently received about the presence in Matabele country of white children, the Boers never set eyes on these three members of the Liebenberg family.

Before this disastrous week was out Hendrik Potgieter, leader of the Trekkers, returned from his excursion to the North. Essentially a man of action, he gave himself wholeheartedly to the plight of his followers and set about devising a scheme to ensure their safety. He ordered the van of the emigrant farmers to withdraw from the Vaal and sent messengers to advise all the Boer families to remuster and form up in laagers. One half of Potgieter's people converged on a selected spot on the banks of the Vet river; the other, under the Boer leader's personal supervision, formed a laager between the Renoster and Wilge rivers, at a knoll which was soon to be named Vegkop – Battle Hill.

Believing Mzilikazi would not be satisfied until all the Trekker parties had been exterminated, Potgieter prepared his own wagon fortress with deliberation. He had eight tented wagons drawn into a ring, and around these another circle of fifty. All the vehicles were securely bound together with chains, and every gap, save one narrow entrance, was tightly packed with thorn-bush branches. Then Potgieter looked to his arms and ammunition. Every available utensil was filled with slugs or gunpowder, and every able-bodied man was given two or three muzzle-loaders. The womenfolk and the reliable girls and boys were instructed in the art of loading rapidly, for if the Matabele attacked it would be the task of these members of the laager to provide the men with guns ready for firing. The inner circle of wagons was set aside as a shelter for the old people, expectant mothers and infants.

During all these preparations, Potgieter and his followers paused regularly to bow their heads in prayer and listen to the words of encouragement from the Bible read by their preacher, Sarel Cilliers.

At Mosega the American missionaries watched the movements of Mkalipi's regiments with bewilderment. For some time they had heard rumours concerning the massacre of white colonials in the South, but they did not realize the magnitude of the danger until they saw looted cattle arriving at Mosega and Stephanus Erasmus's wagons being drawn into the settlement. The Americans' position became desperate when all the missionaries and their wives, except Dr Alexander Wilson, contracted fever. In mid-October Jane Wilson died, and was laid to rest in a cornfield adjoining the mission station. Jane, originally a citizen of Virginia, became the first white woman to be buried in the Transvaal.

A few days after her funeral the wagons of William Cornwallis Harris, a captain in the Indian Army, lumbered into the Mosega valley and wound their way among the kraals and cornfields to the home of Dr Wilson. Recently granted two years' leave from his regiment, Cornwallis Harris was spending a holiday hunting and sketching in South Africa. His hunting-party included William Richardson of the Bombay Civil Service, an Indian named Nasserwanjee and a group of coloured servants recruited in the Cape with Robert Moffat's cooperation. Harris had received Mzilikazi's permission to enter Matabele country and although aware of the unrest among the Matabele, he was determined to allow nothing to thwart his plans for a successful trip.

The American missionaries welcomed Harris and his party to the mission, but advised them to seek hunting-grounds in some other part of South Africa far removed from Matabele territory.

Dr Wilson told Harris that Mzilikazi was living at his eGabeni kraal and that Mkalipi, the commander-in-chief of Mosega, had left some days before, with six thousand warriors, to attack the emigrant Boers on the banks of the Vaal.

Harris was not to be dissuaded. With one of Mzilikazi's *indunas*, a resident of Mosega, to guide his party, the hunter returned to the valley, passed the enclosure housing Stephanus Erasmus's wagons and then departed northwards for the royal kraal of eGabeni.

Meanwhile, at Vegkop, Hendrik Potgieter and his men were keeping vigil over their wagon fortress. For hours on end they stood scanning the surrounding plains, puffing their pipes and wondering when the Matabele would launch an attack.

On the afternoon of 15 October a group of Bataung tribesmen running towards the laager shouted hysterically that, not five hours' march from the wagons, a great Matabele army was approaching. A brief service was conducted by Sarel Cilliers. Then a party of Boers galloped out of the camp to meet the foe.

It was late afternoon when the Boers located Mkalipi's throng – six thousand warriors grouped in regiments according to the colours and designs of their ox-hide shields. At sunset the Boer patrol returned to the laager. Grave yet undaunted, Potgieter's Trekkers awaited the night and the perils about to befall them.

For some unaccountable reason Mkalipi did not employ the conventional Matabele tactics of attacking under cover of darkness. In fact, when eventually the Matabele army converged on the laager the sun had already climbed high. At the head of twenty horsemen Hendrik Potgieter rode out cautiously. The Matabele halted, sank on to their haunches and covered their bodies with their shields. In silence the warriors glared at Potgieter, who from his saddle was calling the commanders, advising them to avoid bloodshed and to lead their regiments back to their kraals.

Suddenly Mkalipi signalled his army to rise. The Matabele surged forward. Potgieter and his men raised their guns, discharged a volley, withdrew swiftly to a safe distance, reloaded and again opened fire. The Boers fired and retreated repeatedly until they reached their laager.

At this stage the horns of the Matabele spread out and formed a circle round the Boer wagons. Then the regimental commanders gathered to discuss tactics and the warriors sat down and nonchalantly whetted their blades with stones. This lull ended when suddenly the Matabele rose with a muffled roar, drumming their shields and clattering their spear-shafts.

The warriors charged, brandishing their weapons above their plumed heads, and were within thirty paces of the laager before the Boers opened fire, sending the first two score of Mkalipi's men plunging into the dust. The Matabele reached the wagons, tugged at their wheels in an endeavour to separate them, climbed up the sides and struggled to drag the thorn-bush branches from the gaps.

A vicious fusillade tore incessantly into the ranks of the Matabele host. As one after another of Mkalipi's men was bowled over, they started flinching, then hesitated, and finally withdrew rapidly out of range.

Soon after this setback the Matabele army launched its second attack. Throwing caution to the winds, one section of the army sent a deluge of stabbing-spears into the laager while another clung to the wagons, ripped the sails from the frames and strained to break through the thorn-bush defences. But so accurate was the aim of the Boers and so consistent their fire that, although barely an hour had passed since Mkalipi's first onslaught, several hundred Matabele corpses lay heaped about the laager.

The Matabele called off the battle and retreated. They rounded up a hundred horses, five hundred head of cattle, fifty thousand sheep and then moved away through the highveld plains to Mosega.

Hendrik Potgieter and his people looked upon their triumph at Vegkop as the first step towards the overthrow of Mzilikazi's tyrannical rule. The Boers joined their leader in rejoicing and in praising God for delivering them. Among the Trekkers who took part in the service of thanksgiving was a little boy who in the course of time was to win fame as a President of the South African Republic. His name was Paul Kruger.

CHAPTER 19

THE BOER–MATABELE WAR

Cornwallis Harris reaches eGabeni
Mzilikazi's army returns from Vegkop
Potgieter and Maritz destroy Mosega
Last battle between the Zulu and Matabele
The Boers invade Matabele country
Mzilikazi driven from the Transvaal

EIGHT days after the battle at Vegkop Captain Cornwallis Harris, Richardson and Nasserwanjee arrived at the gates of eGabeni. uMncumbata, chief *induna* of the tribe, came out to greet them and assure them that Mzilikazi approved of their presence in Matabele country, and would be arriving soon to welcome them. After a long delay the King's approach was heralded by a yelling and chanting chorus. Mzilikazi appeared at the wagons amidst a procession of gesticulating warriors, fully armed and attired in their regimental regalia. On identifying Mzilikazi in the throng, Harris reflected that the King was far more corpulent than he had anticipated – undoubtedly the result of Mzilikazi's decision to withdraw from active service in the Matabele army and also of his fondness for food and sorghum beer. Nevertheless, Harris conceded that in his kilt of leopard-tails, his headdress of green parakeet feathers and his blue bead necklace the King cut a most distinguished figure.

At the time of their meeting neither Mzilikazi nor Harris knew the outcome of Mkalipi's expedition against the Boers, but on 25 October messengers arrived at eGabeni to report that the regiments were returning with a large haul of cattle, sheep and horses. eGabeni seethed with excitement. From information Harris gleaned from the men of the tribe there was no doubt in his mind that the Boers had been routed. Although he would have welcomed more news about this recent clash between the Matabele and the Boers, Harris was far too discreet to broach the subject, or even to allow Mzilikazi to know that he had seen Erasmus's wagons at Mosega. Harris did not mention he had heard of the massacres that had taken place some months earlier along the Vaal. For this reason, and also because of the many gifts he lavished upon Mzilikazi, Harris' brief sojourn at eGabeni was a pleasant one.

It amused the hunters to watch the bulky despot swaggering about in a duffel coat, lined and trimmed with scarlet shalloon, that Harris had brought him from the Cape. When Mzilikazi was not shuffling in and out of the coat, he was discarding his leopard-tails and putting on a tartan suit Mrs Moffat had sent him. Dressed in these different costumes he admired himself in Harris' mirror. Harris, Richardson and Nasserwanjee found the King an entertaining host, except when he absconded with Nasserwanjee's silk braces and pocket-knife, and Harris' shoes, silk waistcoat, woollen night-cap and many other articles that chanced to catch his eye.

Far less amusing was the hunters' visit to the interior of the royal kraal. They trudged through an agglomeration of skulls, paws and the tails of lions to the seraglio, where thirty swarthy wives, grossly plump and with enormous pendent breasts, watched over their royal master while he took an afternoon nap in one of Andrew Geddes Bain's captured wagons. It was here, while taking a meal of stewed beef, that Harris and his friends were served by Truey the Griqua. As one of Mzilikazi's concubines, Truey was extremely unhappy. She wept as she begged Harris to convey her greetings to Peter Davids, her father. Willem, Truey's cousin, was also at eGabeni, but on the day the hunters arrived Mzilikazi sent him to a distant kraal to deliver two Boer children taken prisoner by the Matabele. This information puzzled Harris, for at that stage he had not heard of the capture of the Liebenberg children.

Three days after arriving at eGabeni Harris took leave of Mzilikazi, crossed the Marico river and pressed on to the Tolane. Near this stream his wagons were intercepted by an 'aristocratic and intelligent'[1] boy who introduced himself as Mzilikazi's son. From Harris's description of the lad it may be assumed that he was Kulumane, the heir-apparent to the Matabele throne.[2] Moving on, the hunters found the 'traders' road', a rugged trail along which the faintest vestige of the pioneers' wagon-tracks were still to be seen. It was the 1st of November, and they were travelling almost due south to avoid a barrier of mountains looming up ahead of them. To their consternation they came upon a section of Mkalipi's army returning from the battle at Vegkop.

'Nothing could be more savage, wild and martial,'[3] wrote Harris, referring to the hostile attitude of the Matabele on discovering his tented wagons. Some of the warriors carried wounded comrades; others were laden with odds and ends of accoutrements. Harris knew immediately that the warriors belonged to Mkalipi's regiments, for many carried shields holed by musket-balls, and many were engaged in driving a great herd of looted cattle before them.

Although at one stage Harris feared the Matabele would exterminate his party, the tension was eased when the white men explained that they had only recently been Mzilikazi's guests at eGabeni. The warriors moved on to the west, and the three gentlemen from India proceeded on a trip that was to prove one of the most fruitful in the annals of South African hunting.

In the meantime the Trekkers were stranded in the plains around Vegkop. Hendrik Potgieter sent his brother, Hermanus, to the South to solicit the assistance of James Archbell, now resident at Thaba Nchu. Hermanus's arrival at Thaba Nchu coincided with that of a third party of emigrant farmers under the leadership of Gerrit Maritz, a former wagon-maker from Graaff-Reinet. With the minimum of delay Maritz had oxen driven to Vegkop, and the herd included teams provided by Archbell and also by Moro-

1. Captain W. C. Harris, *Wild Sports of Southern Africa*, p. 162.
2. After Moffat's visit in 1829 Mzilikazi decided to nickname his heir Kulumane, after the Kuruman Mission.
3. ibid., p. 178.

ko, Chief of the Barolong tribe. Potgieter's people were brought back to Thaba Nchu, where they merged with their countrymen recently arrived from the Colony.

But the Trekkers had no intention of settling in those parts. Having returned a month ago from an excursion as far as the Zoutpansberg ranges, Potgieter was able to tell the Boers about the vast expanses of fertile and unpopulated hinterland awaiting their occupation. He insisted that the Trek must continue, but if it was to succeed Mzilikazi's despotism must first be crushed and his tribe dispersed. Both Potgieter's followers and those of Maritz agreed that not a single wagon must venture across the Vaal until the Matabele threat had been removed.

During November and December Potgieter and Maritz devoted their energies to organizing an expeditionary force. They conferred with Peter Davids, the Griqua captain, who in the hope of rescuing his daughter and nephew agreed to send the Boers forty armed horsemen. Matlabe, a petty Barolong chief who knew the old Bahurutsi country thoroughly, was persuaded to act as guide and to provide the expedition with a group of herdsmen and spies. Finally, Potgieter and Maritz received the support of six Koranna, members of the fearsome marauding bands of former years, and also of Sikonyela, son of Mantatisi. On 2 January 1837 this heterogenous army, headed by 107 mounted Boers, set out for Mzilikazi's kingdom.

Two weeks later, having travelled through hundreds of miles of desolate country, Potgieter and Maritz crossed the Malmani stream and sank cautiously into Bobbejaansgat – Baboon Hole – a great hollow bounded by four hills and situated immediately south-west of Mosega. That night, in the bivouac, a council of war was held and final plans drawn up for the assault.

Early the following morning the Boers accompanied their leaders to the summit of a hill known as Anntjieskop. Descending swiftly into the cliffs through an entanglement of bush, they halted as the first light of dawn filtered into the valley. With the assistance of Matlabe, their guide, they identified Mkalipi's stronghold of Mkwahla and several Matabele kraals, barely discernible in the sorghum fields. They approached the Tsebe Khama hill and split into two columns, Maritz leading his men along a circuitous route to the right and Potgieter advancing directly to Mkalipi's barracks.

When Potgieter reached the first row of Mkalipi's beehive shelters he was surprised to find the warriors were not yet astir, but as he and his men sat watching the kraal from their saddles they saw a man crawl from a hut and rise to urinate beside its entrance. Potgieter raised his elephant gun and fired, and before the echoes had faded in the hills the regiments came pouring out of their huts with their shields and spears. They were driven back by a hail of slugs and by the flashes and the thunder of the elephant guns. Time and again the Matabele rallied and attacked, but so fierce was the fire of the Boer guns that they retreated panic-stricken through the settlement and fled helter-skelter into the valley. Then the fugitives careered into Maritz's commando and scattered before a series of fusillades. Women and children came screaming from the huts, but the Boers galloped past them, concentrating only on picking off the warriors in the fields of sorghum.

By mid-morning the entire population of Mosega was in flight to the north, and twenty-one riders under a Boer named Steyn were hunting out tribesmen thought to be hiding in the surrounding bush. In the vicinity of present-day Zeerust the Matabele mustered and attempted a last desperate stand. It was a feeble effort, for they could never come to grips with the Boers, who fired upon them with unflagging persistence. The Matabele turned and followed a disorderly stream of fugitives through Jacobsdal. They struggled into the wooded slopes in the north, and streamed eventually into Marapu's military kraals at Tshwenyane – the Little Baboon village.

Realizing that their horses were too fatigued to carry them into the rugged heights ahead, the Boers trotted back to Mosega. At the American mission station they met Dr Wilson and his colleagues, who asked the Boers to allow them to return with the commandos to Thaba Nchu. In the seven months the American missionaries had laboured among the Matabele they had experienced a succession of hardships, hazards and heartaches. For, apart from the bouts of fever that ravaged them and the sudden death of Jane Wilson, they had been shunned by Mzilikazi from the start, and had often found cause to fear for their safety. Now that the Matabele had been dispersed there was no point in keeping the mission open at Mosega. Furthermore, the Americans believed the despot would accuse them of having instigated the Boer invasion. In the course of conversation with the Boers the missionaries reported that Mkalipi, commander of Mosega, was not among the fugitives who were heading northwards. Some days earlier he had been summoned by Mzilikazi to the royal kraal of eGabeni.

Potgieter and Maritz decided that, in view of the poor condition of their horses, they would not attempt to invade the interior of Mzilikazi's kingdom. Instead they led the Boers into the Mosega valley, ransacked and fired the kraals, collected seven thousand head of cattle and seized Erasmus's wagons. In the course of looting the Boers searched for the Liebenberg children, but found no evidence that they were still alive.

As clouds of smoke drifted across Mosega, the Boer commandos departed, leaving a deserted mission station, a solitary missionary grave and four hundred corpses of the Matabele warriors who had sought to exterminate the defenders of the Vegkop laager.

The defeat of the Matabele was celebrated among all Mzilikazi's subjugated tribes. In Zululand Dingane reacted to the news by mobilizing his army and preparing it for an expedition into Matabele country.

At the grave of Senzangakhona, Shaka's father, Dingane offered up sacrifices to the ancestral spirits, calling on them to strengthen the Zulu army and to protect it from harm. Dingane also had his regiments ceremoniously cleansed by instructing the witch-doctors to sprinkle the warriors with magical decoctions. With a host of boys to carry the sleeping-mats, karosses, earthen cooking-pots and provisions, the Zulu crossed the Pongolo river in May 1837 and turned westwards into the Transvaal highveld.

A month later Dingane's forces approached the outskirts of Mzilikazi's kingdom and were detected by Matabele spies, who hastened to the military kraals and sounded the alarm. A Matabele division crossed the Marico river to meet the foe, and before long, for the third time in eight years, the two most powerful tribal armies in Southern Africa were engaged in hand-to-hand battle.

At first the Matabele were no match for the Zulu. Mzilikazi's famous iziMpangele or Guinea Fowl regiment was slaughtered almost to a man, and vast herds of Matabele cattle were captured. But then the Matabele rallied, drove the enemy back, inflicting heavy losses and recapturing most of Mzilikazi's beasts.

Towards the end of the year when the Zulu army arrived back at emGungundlovu, Dingane's royal kraal, it claimed to have defeated the Matabele. But as Mzilikazi's regiments also took part in victory celebrations, it may be concluded that neither of these great tribes had won a decisive victory and that there was little to choose between the might of Mzilikazi's and Dingane's armies. This was the last battle ever to be waged between the Zulu and the Matabele.

Soon after dispersing the Matabele at Mosega, the Trekkers moved in convoy from Thaba Nchu to the Vet river, and they founded the village of Winburg. Then petty jealousies crept up between Potgieter and Maritz, and the two leaders became involved in a prolonged series of altercations. The disagreement spread, and the Trekkers formed themselves into rival political parties.

Potgieter grew impatient. He decided he would endure the bickering among the emigrant farmers no longer, and that he would prepare the way for settling his own followers in the country over which Mzilikazi claimed sovereignty. He convened a meeting of his menfolk and announced that he intended leading a second expedition against the Matabele.

And while these discussions were in progress, Pieter Uys, another of the Trekker leaders, arrived with his party and joined forces with Potgieter.

In October 1837 Potgieter and Uys led a commando of 360 men and a convoy of horse-drawn wagons over the Vaal. On the north bank of the river some of the wagons were left in the charge of thirty men while the rest of the commando moved on along the route followed by the Boers at the beginning of the year. On reaching Mosega on 2 November, the commando found the valley desolated, the kraals in ruins and the fields infested with weeds.

Potgieter ordered his men to bivouac at Kameeldoring on the outskirts of Zeerust, and at sundown on the following day he led them as far as Rooisloot, a seasonal stream tracing a sandy course through dense bushveld, rugged hills and sultry vales. The Boers approached Tshwenyane, the site of Marapu's military station, and there divided into two columns, one advancing to the left along the base of a chain of hills, the other to the right through subtropical bush. The sun had not yet risen when the Boers converged on Marapu's settlement. The commandos took up positions around the circles of beehive huts and waited for Potgieter to fire the first shot.

When the Matabele were awakened by the blast of the muzzle-loaders, they snatched up their weapons, poured out of their huts and launched a haphazard attack. The Boers drove them back in confusion, reloaded and waited for the Matabele to charge again. Row upon row of warriors fell before the remorseless onslaught of the horsemen. Marapu, commander-in-chief of the military settlement, was away at eGabeni answering a summons from Mzilikazi, and the efforts of the regimental commanders to maintain discipline among their men proved futile.

The slaughter ended momentarily when the Matabele fled to some adjacent kraals where many of the survivors of the battle of Mosega were housed. The Boers sacked Marapu's military settlement and advanced along the hills, destroying every kraal they came upon and firing upon every warrior they saw. By sunset the entire population of Tshwenyane was in flight to the north. Hundreds lay dead, and every hut and granary was smouldering in a heap of ashes.

The next day was Sunday. Although normally it would have been unheard of for the Boers to devote the Sabbath to any activity other than meditation with God, on this occasion they were sent by Potgieter and Uys to scour the bush and hilltops for fugitives. On the Monday morning the commandos trekked in a south-westerly direction past Koppieskraal to Pagskraal and pitched camp. Then the Boers prepared to advance on an isolated hill where Kampu commanded a powerful Matabele garrison.

By this time, unknown to the Boers, Mzilikazi had commanded all his regiments to assemble at this hill. The King, Marapu and Kampu mustered the army in the traditional crescent formation: the middle section, known as *isifuba* (or chest) guarding the kraals and the *izimpondo* (or horns) spreading out across the veld in readiness for the encircling swoop that would cut off the Boers from escape.

Tuesday the 7th brought the Boer commandos into the treeless flats surrounding Kampu's military kraal, the black-soiled turf of which stretched out to the north of eGabeni as far as the Marico river. Anticipating that the Matabele would attack in crescent formation, the Boers decided to spread out in a long line, and to have two groups of horsemen guarding their flanks. Slowly they advanced towards the Matabele awaiting them in silence.

The Matabele attacked with a sudden rush. The horns of the army spread out and then converged swiftly on the Boers. The body of riders on either flank of Potgieter's line galloped out to meet the tips of the horns, and blasted them asunder before they could meet in their encircling movement. Then the entire commando opened fire, concentrating on the chest of the crescent, while the men on the flanks continued to shatter the menacing horns.

The battle was brief but bloody. The Matabele lines buckled, and some of the regiments started breaking away from the main body to form up in platoons. The Boers surged forward, driving their opponents backwards to the base of the hills and cutting down those warriors who were scrambling up the rocky slopes. Forsaking all hope of surrounding the Boers or of checking their advance, Mzilikazi and his generals led the regiments to the west, in headlong flight, and struck out for the marshes about Alwyn-spoortjies.

When, after a while, the Matabele realized that the Boers were not pursuing them, they halted, reformed their crescent and waited. They saw sheets of flame engulfing Kampu's stronghold. Heavy smoke-clouds drifted across the plains. Then, out of the screen of smoke, the Boers came galloping towards them. Again as the horsemen drew near the Matabele army advanced, its horns spread out to encompass the foe. Again it failed. The Matabele disintegrated, the regiments turned tail into the marshes.

Throughout the day the Boers stalked the Matabele through the reeds on foot. This was a risky undertaking, for they often almost trod on their quarry before detecting them. Potgieter, who controlled the operation from his saddle, narrowly escaped death when a stabbing-spear flung by an unseen warrior whizzed past him. The hunt continued until sunset, when the Boers withdrew, mounted their horses and cantered back to the wagons. During the night the Matabele streamed into eGabeni, where they found their King in discussion with his council of war.

Potgieter's assault on eGabeni, Mzilikazi's last stronghold, commenced on the morning of 9 November. Realizing that at least twelve thousand warriors under the command of Mzilikazi, Mkalipi, Marapu, Kampu and Sibekhu would be awaiting the Boer advance, Potgieter led his commando to the north with the utmost caution.

When the Boers reached the outskirts of eGabeni, they were puzzled to find not Mzilikazi's great crescent-shaped army blocking the approaches to the royal kraal, but a huge herd of cattle. It never occurred to Potgieter that Mzilikazi had forsaken the tactics he had employed during past days and had decided to precede the Matabele attack by a stampede of oxen.

The cattle broke loose. The Boers retreated, turned, galloped towards the bewildered beasts and fired. They withdrew to reload and then fired another volley. They repeated this procedure until they succeeded in driving the animals back towards the Matabele. As the herd dispersed, the Matabele ranks were exposed and the Boers inflicted heavy losses on the regiments, who had already started bolting for the sedges flanking the Marico river. Mzilikazi's army was in flight, and the women, children and greybeards whom the King had long since sent into the depths of the bushveld were instructed by messengers to move with their animals and household goods through the Dwarsberg in the North.

During the remainder of the day the Boers continued to hunt down the warriors in the bush. They returned at dusk to set fire to eGabeni, and to rest for the night.

The Dwarsberg runs in three parallel ranges across the most densely vegetated and rugged regions of the Marico district. Most of its summits are inaccessible, but the Marico river cuts through the ranges, leaving three precipitous passes through which footmen may travel with comparative ease. On 10 November the Matabele struggled northwards with the Boers in hot pursuit. They negotiated the first pass next day, and the second on Sunday the 12th. The Boers watched the Matabele streaming through the gorge severing the last range of the Dwarsberg. So fatigued were the Boers' horses and so treacherous the terrain that lay ahead, that Potgieter decided to turn back. The Boers retraced their steps along the tortuous course of the Marico river, destroyed a kraal they recognized as Mzilikazi's former refuge and winter lodge, and returned to eGabeni.

Collecting whatever was left of Mzilikazi's herds, the Boers moved southwards to the isolated hill where Kampu's great military station lay in ruins. On reaching the battlefield at the foot of the hill they were amazed to find that the vultures, hyenas, jackals and maggots had already reduced most of the Matabele corpses to skeletons. The Boers named this place Maaierskop, or Maggot Hill. Indeed, to this day the Maggot Hill bears mute testimony to one of the most bloody battles ever fought between the white and black races of South Africa.

The defeat and dispersal of the Matabele and the ending of Mzilikazi's tyrannical reign brought immediate changes to the way of life of the tribes inhabiting the central plateau and the western reaches of South Africa. The downtrodden Bechuana tribes emerged from the Kalahari, where for several long years they had eked out a precarious existence in the wastelands; the scattered Sotho-speaking clans filtered back into the desolate Transvaal plains, and the slaves Mzilikazi had taken from among the Bakwena, Bangwaketsi, Bahurutsi, Barolong, Bapedi and other tribes were set free and returned to start life afresh. Gradually these peoples, broken in spirit and haunted by the memory of the misery inflicted upon them by Mantatisi and other *lifaqane* conquerors, and especially by Mzilikazi, regained their courage and threw themselves with ardour into restoring their huts, their cattle-folds and fields.

Fresh from their victory the Boers laid claim to the Northern Free State, to the regions between the Limpopo and the Vaal, to Bechuanaland as far as the Kalahari in the west and the Batlhaping border in the south – in fact, to almost the entire empire Mzilikazi had amassed since his flight from Zululand.

Eventually the Boers were to trek northwards and fan out over the entire Transvaal, and in the course of the years they and other white colonists would cross the Limpopo and claim the beautiful country that is Southern Rhodesia today.

But one important factor thwarted their ambitions: Mzilikazi was still alive.

PART THREE

CHAPTER 20

MATABELE CONQUESTS NORTH OF THE LIMPOPO

The Matabele are divided
Mzilikazi becomes a wanderer in the desert
He reunites his tribe and executes his indunas *and sons*
He conquers the tribes of Southern Rhodesia and establishes
Matabeleland
Defeat of the Matabele expedition to the Zambezi

IN the flight of the Matabele from the commandos of Potgieter and Uys the non-combatants of the tribe were conducted northwards by a body of warriors of the Amnyama-Makanda, or Black Heads division, under the command of an *induna* named Gudwane Ndeweni. They reached the third pass in the Dwarsberg, far in advance of the army, and continued to the north believing that eventually Mzilikazi would overtake them and assume command. Somewhere beyond the Dwarsberg, in the labyrinth of bush and kopjes, Gudwane lost contact with Mzilikazi; nevertheless he pressed on lest the women, children, the old people and the stock he had in his charge should fall into the hands of the Boers.

When Mzilikazi crossed the third pass he veered to the left and hastened with his army into Bechuanaland. The Matabele were then divided into two sections, and as the days merged into weeks the gap between the army and the followers of Gudwane became so great that the people despaired of living again as a united tribe under the sovereignty of Mzilikazi.

Months of wandering through the bushveld took Gudwane's party into the Rustenburg district, the old country of the Crocodile People, through the Waterberg district and over the lofty

Zoutpansberg ranges to the Limpopo. In these northern reaches of the Transvaal, where Bapedi, Bavenda and Lobedu settlements were plentiful, the warriors stripped the fields of crops, raided the cattle-folds, ransacked the huts and emptied the granaries. Without challenge from the tribes they pillaged, the emigrant Matabele crossed the river and streamed into the wooded regions of what is now Southern Rhodesia. Before long they passed through Gwanda, skirted the Sizeza mountain, and on reaching Entabenede in the Bushtick area selected a spot where they built a temporary settlement and planted their crops. This Matabele kraal in Southern Rhodesia was named Gibixhegu – Take Out the Old Man – after the famous Zulu military settlement where Mzilikazi once had been stationed as a young commander of one of Shaka's regiments.

Meanwhile, the Matabele army was trudging over the austere flats of Northern Bechuanaland, through a country scourged by heat. In the region of Shoshong, they were attacked by the Bamangwato, whose Chief, Seghoma, believed the power of the Matabele had been broken by the Boers. But the Matabele put the Bamangwato to flight, pillaged their kraals and captured substantial herds of cattle. Then they moved on, foraging here, raiding there and sleeping each night beneath the stars.

Several months after his flight from the Marico district Mzilikazi was leading his men through wastelands inhabited by Bushmen, hardy desert nomads who neither planted crops nor herded stock, but who managed to subsist by hunting and snaring game, by collecting insects, edible berries, roots and bulbs and by storing, in ostrich eggshells, what little water they were able to suck up from the isolated pans. This was undoubtedly the most arduous march Mzilikazi had ever undertaken, but the King's determination to find a new country for his people somewhere in the well-watered regions about Lake Ngami, the Okavango swamps or even the lush approaches to the Zambezi compelled him to keep moving northwards.

Somewhere beyond the Okavango Mzilikazi encountered the Makololo tribe, a branch of Mantatisi's Wild Cat People. It will be remembered that in 1826 the Makololo, led by Chief Sebitoane, deserted Mantatisi, routed the Bangwaketsi and invested Lithubaruba, capital village of the Crocodile People of Bechuanaland. This was the same Makololo tribe Andrew Geddes Bain had blasted out of Lithubaruba, and Mzilikazi had attempted to destroy as they fled northwards. Mzilikazi had never forgotten how Sebitoane managed to elude the Matabele regiments, and now, thirteen years later, he rejoiced at the thought of being able to crush him.

Little is known about the battle waged on the Zambezi between the Matabele and the Makololo, except that it ended as an undecided affair, and that Mzilikazi withdrew swiftly to the south when he learned that his army was in the land of the tsetse-fly where cattle died of *nagana* disease and men of sleeping-sickness.

Two seasons passed, and the two sections of the Matabele tribe remained separated. At Gibixhegu the people were growing restless and demanded that Gudwane confer with his fellow-*indunas* and choose a successor to Mzilikazi. For some time now they had been plagued by rumours that Mzilikazi had decided to abandon them, and recently scouts had learnt from wandering Bushmen that the King and his army had been annihilated.

Some of the *indunas* asserted that it was not customary for a tribe to remain so long without a ruler, and that as Kulumane, heir-apparent to the Matabele throne, was resident at Gibixhegu he should be declared the new King, and a regent should be appointed to watch over the affairs of state until Kulumane had attained his majority.

Other *indunas* insisted that Mzilikazi was still alive, and scoffed at the suggestion that he would forsake his wives, children and subjects. These *indunas* demanded that before steps were taken to proclaim Kulumane the new King of the Matabele a search-party should be dispatched to scour the country to the west and to return with concrete evidence either of Mzilikazi's death or of his reluctance to assume sovereignty over the tribe. Although this suggestion did not meet with unanimous approval, at least Gudwane was prudent enough to order the postponement of further deliberations until word had been received of the Bull Elephant. He appointed a delegation and sent it to the west to find Mzilikazi.

During the early months of 1840 Mzilikazi and his weary, crestfallen army were located on the fringe of the desolate part of Northern Bechuanaland known as the Makarikari Salt Pans. Until this momentous meeting with Gudwane's men the King had heard nothing of the women and children of his tribe, and he was delighted to learn they were safe and settled in a luxuriant country lying only ten days' march towards the rising sun. The thought of relinquishing his throne had never entered his mind; in fact, when he was told that some of the *indunas* were planning to install Kulumane in his stead, he was thunderstruck, and demanded to be conducted by the shortest route to his people.

Not twelve miles from the present Southern Rhodesian city of Bulawayo, to the left of the main road leading to Salisbury, two hills stand side by side, dominating the wooded surroundings. One hill is elongated and table-topped, the other narrow and conical-shaped. It was at this spot, after leading his army through the Plumtree and Figtree districts to the east, that Mzilikazi decided to establish a settlement. Then he summoned Gudwane from Gibixhegu and accused him of conspiring with his fellow-*indunas* to overthrow the old régime and also of seeking to promote Kulumane to the chieftaincy of the tribe. Learning from Gudwane that the protagonists in the plot were the *indunas* Kanye, Mafu, Dlodlo, Mkwanazi and Dambisamahubo, he commanded that they be arrested and brought to the settlement to stand trial for treason in the tribal court.

The trial was brief. Together with Gudwane, the accused were found guilty and were executed in the vicinity of the flat-topped hill which to this day bears the name of Ntabazinduna – the Hill of the Indunas.

Then Mzilikazi ordered two of his executioners to capture Kulumane and kill him. Bearing in mind that on occasions such as this it was not customary to spill royal blood, Mzilikazi decreed that the young prince be strangled, or his neck twisted. Kulumane was fetched from Gibixhegu, bound to a tree and put to death. Still plagued with suspicion, Mzilikazi bade the executioners rid the tribe of two more of his sons, who stood in the direct line of succession to the Matabele throne. The first, Ubuhlelo, suffered a similar fate to Kulumane, but the second, an infant named Lobengula, was smuggled out of the kraal by his mother and was taken into hiding. Years later, when Mzilikazi's wrath had subsided, Lobengula was revealed to his father. The boy became the King's favourite, the heir-apparent, and, as history was to prove, the second and the last of the Matabele despots.

Having purged his tribe of the so-called conspirators, Mzilikazi turned his attention to settling both the civilians and the fighting forces in strategic positions. During his march from the west to the Hill of the Indunas the King had taken care to watch the reaction of the tribes he encountered, and there was no doubt in his mind that the Matabele armies would prove invincible in this new territory.

In 1840 Southern Rhodesia was inhabited by a miscellany of insignificant tribes, each governed by a patriarchal chief, each cultivating its crops and tending its cattle, goats and sheep. Occupying the immense stretch of country between the Maclautsi river in the south-west and the main watershed in the north, the Tuli river in the east and the Matengwe in the north-west, were several of these tribes, who for the sake of convenience ethnologists have termed the Makalanga. About Gibixhegu and in the region of the Matopo ranges small scattered groups of Barozwi lived under their *mambos*, or chiefs, while in the great plateau extending to the north-east were located a hotch-potch of tribes known collectively as the Mashona.

During the past century and a half the Barozwi had ruled supreme over the other tribes of Southern Rhodesia, but only four years before Mzilikazi's arrival in the territory Zwangendaba, a fugitive from Zululand, had invaded and crushed them and then moved northwards to found the aNgoni tribe of Nyasaland. Among Zwangendaba's host was a Swazi queen named Nyamazana – the Antelope – who preferred not to proceed to the Zambezi but to settle in the Matopo region. On meeting her, Mzilikazi married her and housed her in one of his harems. The King incorporated the queen's followers in his tribe and bestowed upon them the honour of joining his *Abezansi*, the inner circle of aristocratic and privileged Matabele.

Ignoring for the time the indigenous inhabitants of the country, Mzilikazi established Mahlokohloko, his first capital, at Ntabazinduna. At this important settlement a section of Mzilikazi's three hundred wives was settled, and also the Mahlokohloko regiment under the command of Mbambelele.

Gibixhegu was abandoned. Selecting temporary boundaries within which he would settle his people, Mzilikazi divided the territory into two main sections. The first, which included the Bulalima-Mangwe and Nyamayendlovu districts in the west, was occupied by the regiments of the Amnyama-Makanda, the Black-headed division, and the other, which extended to the Gwelo district in the north, by the regiments of the Amhlophe or White division.

This country, to which we will refer as Matabeleland, was divided by the King into subdistricts. Over each of these small areas an *induna* was placed to conduct the affairs of the Matabele kraals, to preside over the inferior courts of justice and to report all matters of importance to Milikazi. At all the military barracks there were royal harems, and it was the prerogative of the women to acquaint the King with titbits of gossip concerning the capabilities and the loyalty of the *indunas* of the settlements.

Within the first year of Mzilikazi's arrival in the country embracing the Matopos, tribal life had returned to the Matabele: the fields were cultivated, the cattle tended both at the kraals and in the bush and plains, and daily sittings of the tribal courts were conducted.

But during the next five years there was to be carnage in Southern Rhodesia and the tribes were to buckle beneath the might of the Matabele army. The Barozwi settlements were invaded, the once autocratic *mambos* ousted from their thrones and the huts, cattle-folds and granaries pillaged and destroyed. The Barozwi, once the conquerors of the ancient Monomotapa dynasty, a proud ruler-tribe of farmers, expert hunters, smiths and artisans, were swept out of Matabeleland into the tsetse country fringing the Zambezi. Their ranks decimated, their young women taken prisoner and their men enslaved, the Barozwi tumbled into the jungle country to the north in a bid to elude the Matabele regiments. The relentless onslaught of Mzilikazi's forces eventually compelled the Barozwi to cross the Zambezi and seek a new home among the tribes of Northern Rhodesia.

One section of these people fled from the Matopos to the sources of the Tati river, and the *mambo*, an influential ruler, took to the hills with his servants and wives to seek shelter in a cave. Looking on to the slopes below him, the *mambo* could see the Matabele approaching, and rather than fall into their hands he decapitated his wives and then allowed himself and their corpses to be consumed in the flames of a brushwood pyre.

The Makalanga tribes suffered a fate similar to that of the Barozwi. Until the latter half of the seventeenth century they had been the rulers of Southern Rhodesia under the Monomotapa dynasty, but on being conquered by the Barozwi armies they became so oppressed by the *mambos* that they degenerated into a timid and inoffensive people. The Makalanga were butchered by the Matabele; indeed, the atrocities that took place followed the typical Mzilikazian pattern of the past, except that by this time the Matabele tyrant had decided to leave several of the settlements unscathed so that the inhabitants might be allowed to breed conscripts for the Matabele army and also produce crops and herds for their overlords.

Although the Makalanga were among the least warlike tribes the Matabele had ever encountered in Southern Africa, they had an extraordinarily high reputation for their powers in witchcraft and magic. Their diviners and hereditary priests led the tribes in the worship of Mwari, a deity they believed had created the universe, controlled rain and dwelt in an inaccessible fastness in the Matopos.

Mzilikazi regarded the Mwari priests with the deepest respect, never attempting to injure them, and lavishing gifts regularly upon them. Often the Matabele heard Mwari, the great god, speaking oracularly in the Matopos. They were awestruck, for they did not know that the mysterious voices were in fact those of the priests, who were masters in the traditional art of ventriloquism. Although eventually the Makalanga tribes were subjugated by the Matabele and forced to pay tribute to Mzilikazi, their magicians enjoyed the privilege of being summoned periodically to the capital to give advice on important religious matters.

The Mashona tribes who populated the regions to the north-east of the Matopos succumbed to the Matabele army, but not without offering desperate resistance. These were an industrious people who hunted with bows and arrows, cultivated crops about their rondavel-style clay huts, and herded stocky sheep, long-haired goats and a species of dwarf cattle.

Mashona kraals were laid out haphazardly, and had no protective hedges about them; therefore it was customary for the inhabitants to bring their fowls, dogs, sheep and goats into the huts at night. The Mashona also venerated the Mwari deity, and offered sacrifices and prayers to their ancestral spirits. They conducted rituals similar to the Nxwala, the Matabele ceremony of the First-Fruits, but their lives were pervaded by superstitions and fears of the evil influences of sorcerers and also of the many animals and reptiles they believed possessed supernatural powers. At hunting, fish-trapping, carving, pottery, weaving and smithery the Mashona were unrivalled in Southern Rhodesia. They were also expert musicians who played a variety of percussion instruments and a xylophone, the keyboard of which consisted of strips of iron and the resonators an assortment of calabashes.

When the Mashona were invaded by the Matabele, they withdrew northwards in confusion. But the survivors fled into the hilly country taking refuge in caves, rolling boulders on their pursuers and driving them back with volleys of arrows. Mashona women who had avoided capture fought side by side with their men, some hurling stones at the enemy, others hurling rocks over the edges of the precipices. The Matabele deliberately bypassed some of the Mashona settlements, but arrived eventually to subjugate the inhabitants and compel them to become tributaries of the King.

In the course of time, apart from the rebels who clung to their mountain fortresses, all the Mashona tribes became subservient to the Matabele. But because of his fear of the tsetse-fly Mzilikazi never established cattle-posts farther north than half-way between the Matopos and the Zambezi.

Although over the years the Matabele never ceased raiding their Mashona and Makalanga vassals, they failed to capture the people who had fled into the mountains. This section of the Mashona became as elusive as the rock-rabbits, sharing their cliffs and caves, and there were occasions when they boldly made sorties into Matabeleland.

During one of their outings the Mashona captured some Matabele women at an outpost, hacked off their arms and legs and left them to bleed to death. On learning of this atrocity, Mzilikazi retaliated by having the identical punishment meted out to a group of Mashona women, and also by sending a punitive force to wrest the culprits from their lofty hideouts. But the rebels possessed ladders they could hang over the faces of the cliffs and draw up at a moment's notice. They were always out of reach of the Matabele, whom they bombarded with stones and iron-headed assegais.

The reverses the Matabele suffered at the hands of the Barozwi, the Makalanga and the Mashona were negligible, but during this time Mzilikazi met with one of the most disastrous defeats of his career.

Ever since his meeting on the Zambezi with the Makololo tribe, the King had been plagued by a stubborn urge to destroy Sebitoane and his people. He mustered two thousand warriors and sent them along the courses of the Umbusa and Gwaai rivers in search of the Makololo. All along the route the Matabele captured cattle for slaughtering and fed on the grain they looted from Mzilikazi's tributaries. The army reached the Zambezi in the pink of health, and followed the river's south bank, hoping to come upon the Makololo and annihilate them. But Sebitoane was no longer in Southern Rhodesia. Since his last encounter with Mzilikazi he had left the tsetse-infested Chobe regions, subdued some of the river tribes, crossed the Zambezi in canoes and settled in the lush, undulating plains in the Kafue Highlands.

On learning of the arrival of the Matabele, the Makololo hastened to the Zambezi. The two armies stood on the banks of the great river hurling insults at each other across the water, brandishing their weapons and issuing challenges. They might never have come to grips had the Matabele not seized upon the idea of contracting with some river-dwellers of the Batonka tribe to paddle them in their canoes to an island in midstream. By nightfall half the Matabele army was landed safely, and according to the agreement the remainder were to be fetched the following day. The plan was that when the whole Matabele army was on the island the ferrymen would start paddling batches of warriors across the relatively narrow strip of water to the opposite bank, drop them and then hurry back for more.

During the night, when the Matabele regiments on the island were asleep, the ferrymen disappeared. When the sun rose and the warriors realized that they had been deserted, they searched frantically along the shores and in the undergrowth for canoes, but none were to be found. Their dilemma was frightening, for their rations could not last more than a day, or at the utmost two, and none of them could swim. As the days passed the Matabele consumed what edible vegetation and insects there were. Most of them were dead when the Makololo landed on the island and carried off the emaciated survivors to the Kafue Highlands, there to be resuscitated and then inducted as new members of Sebitoane's tribe.

The other half of the Matabele expeditionary force abandoned all hope of crossing the Zambezi and withdrew to the haunts of the tsetse-fly – the swamp country in the south. This proved a hazardous journey: the Matabele were repeatedly harassed by hostile tribes, they became enfeebled with hunger and most of them contracted malaria fever. Batches of warriors fell out along the route and were left to die. Those who struggled on into the drier regions farther to the south were so weak that they became ready prey for lions. Wasted by fever and starvation, a small remnant forged through the heat of Northern Bechuanaland and turned eastwards towards Matabeleland. Eventually, eight of the original two thousand staggered into Mahlokohloko to relate to Mzilikazi and his councillors their tale of woe.

Not a word of sympathy did the survivors receive from the King. Indeed the three regimental commanders who were among the survivors were accused of shirking their responsibilities – thereby contributing to the fiasco – and were sentenced to death.

Apart from the series of butcherings the Matabele had suffered at the hands of the Boers, this expedition to the Zambezi was undoubtedly the severest setback ever to befall Mzilikazi since his flight from Shaka, but it was to mark the last of the despot's truly great military ventures and also the beginning of an era of comparative tranquillity and security. Within a decade Mzilikazi had established himself as the supreme ruler over all the inoffensive tribes of Southern Rhodesia, a despot who at any time could demand tribute from the peoples he allowed to live in the vast block of Africa situated between the Limpopo and the Zambezi.

The Matabele flourished. About the military kraals, the settlements of the married ringheads and the cattle-posts, sorghum, melons, pumpkins, marrow and sweet reed were cultivated by the women and then harvested in autumn by both the men and the women. The herds and flocks multiplied. Meat was plentiful, for Matabeleland teemed with game, and hunting became a popular pastime.

In the past, during turbulent times the Nxwala had often been allowed to lapse, but now each year when the sorghum grew heavy in ear the people waited for the moon to wax full in December and then prepared themselves for the solemn ritual of the First-Fruits. Dressed in their finery the entire tribe converged on the capital, danced, sang Nxwala hymns and feasted in the company of their monarch. During the three days of the Nxwala the Matabele would extol Mzilikazi's virtues, enshrouding their illustrious Bull Elephant in glory, praising him for providing the country with abundant rains, blessing him for protecting them in times of danger, and revering him for the role he had played in converting them from an insignificant band of Khumalo fugitives into the powerful and prosperous Matabele tribe.

At this stage of their history, had the Matabele been ruled by a King less capable than Mzilikazi they might well have followed the pattern of so many tribes of Southern Africa and sunk into a sedentary and uneventful way of life. Fearing that his people would become indolent, Mzilikazi insisted not only that the regiments keep in training, but also that they undertake regular excursions in all parts of the country and never cease raiding the tribes the Matabele had subdued.

The King conducted periodic tours through his domains, inspecting his military stations, visiting his harems and presiding over trials in the tribal courts. When reports of witchcraft reached him he assembled his people, ordered his witch-doctors to conduct smelling-out ceremonies and condemned the culprits, many of whom were innocent victims of intrigue, to gory deaths.

But while Mzilikazi would not allow indolence or misconduct among his people, he himself became increasingly less active and exercised his royal prerogative by living a life of luxury. With no complicated intrigues or ambitious military projects to occupy his mind, he gradually became a slave to the beer-pot, the food-bowl and the sleeping-mats that bedecked the hut floors of his many harems.

CHAPTER 21

MOFFAT'S THIRD VISIT TO MZILIKAZI

The Boers advance into Matabeleland – Gun-running among the tribes – Potgieter and Mzilikazi make peace Moffat reaches Matabeleland and finds Mzilikazi broken in health – Moffat and Mzilikazi set out with provisions for Livingstone

DURING the ten turbulent years following the flight of the Matabele from the Marico district Mzilikazi lost contact with the half-caste Griqua and Koranna clans, the Bergenaar *banditti*, the Zulu army, the white traders and missionaries and the Boers. But, throughout the time when he was wandering with his army in the Northern Kalahari, the Lake Ngami area, the swamp regions, the Makarikari Salt Pan, and while he was subjugating the tribes of Southern Rhodesia in establishing his kingdom in Matabeleland, a series of events was taking place far to the south which would bring the King face to face with the Boers, his most dreaded enemies.

In 1837, after driving Mzilikazi and his tribe from the Marico district, Potgieter, Uys and their commandos returned to their families. At the small settlement of Winburg they met Pieter Retief, leader of a party of Trekkers, originally from the Winterberg area in the Cape. From Retief the Winburg Boers learned that Dingane, King of the Zulu, had promised to grant the emigrant farmers a tract of land between the Tugela and the Buffalo rivers. Most of the Trekkers were keen to leave Winburg with Retief and settle in Zulu territory, but Potgieter refused to join them, insisting that the recent Matabele war had been waged so that eventually the Trekkers could settle in peace in the country north of the Vaal. Potgieter declared he was not prepared to risk the lives of the families in his charge in a strange land dominated by a tribe as powerful and warlike as the Zulu.

Retief set out with a thousand tented wagons and crossed the Drakensberg into the uplands of Natal. Leaving his people on the banks of the Bluekrans and Bushman rivers, he moved on, accompanied by a commando of sixty-six Boers and thirty-three Hottentots. They headed for emGungundlovu, the royal kraal of Dingane. At the capital the Boers were cordially received, and Dingane requested Owen, the resident missionary, to draw up a treaty ceding Natal to the Boers.

At length, when the time arrived for their departure, Retief and his men entered the kraal to bid Dingane farewell. They were seized, dragged out of the gates and clubbed to death by executioners on a nearby knoll.[1]

Then Dingane unleashed ten thousand warriors and dispatched them to the south, where the wagons of the Trekkers dotted the uplands of Natal. In the carnage that followed, white men, women and children, as well as their coloured servants, were massacred along the river banks, and only those who had time to draw up their wagons into laager formation were saved from annihilation.

Receiving news of the tragedy, Potgieter and Uys, each heading a commando, galloped off to the relief of the distressed Boers. Travelling ahead of Potgieter, Uys and his men cantered into an ambuscade, and before they could retreat to safety the horns of a Zulu division encircled them. The Boers swerved, opened fire, and blasted a path through the Zulu lines. All but ten managed to escape, but among the dead were Pieter Uys and his fifteen-year-old son Dirk. Potgieter's commando withdrew rapidly as the Zulu army turned and surged towards them. The Boers abandoned the idea of proceeding to the relief of Retief's followers, and hastened back to Winburg.

Potgieter was condemned by all his own followers for failing

1. Retief and his followers were murdered on the exact spot where Dingane put Matiwane, the *lifaqane* conqueror, to death. To this day the historic place is known as kwaMatiwane.

to bring help to the Trekkers of Natal. He was also accused of cowardice and blamed for the disaster which had befallen Uys's commando. Disillusioned, Potgieter gathered his people and trekked away from Winburg into the Transvaal highveld. And while Potgieter's wagons were trundling to the north, the Boers in Natal were joined by Andries Pretorius, a dauntless leader from the Colony, who mustered the fighting-men and prepared for war against the Zulu army. Under his command the Boers crushed the Zulu on the banks of Blood river, sacked emGungundlovu and drove Dingane across the Pongolo into Swaziland.

Dingane, the conspirator, the assassin, the usurper of the Zulu throne, was murdered soon after his escape by members of the Nyawo tribe. During his reign he was the only potentate Mzilikazi had feared, but now with Dingane's departure to the realm of ancestral spirits, there was no greater African conqueror in all Southern Africa than Mzilikazi, son of Mashobane.

Sixteen thousand Boers spread over the vast unpopulated interior of South Africa, and on the Mooi river Potgieter founded Potchefstroom, the first permanent European settlement north of the Vaal. In 1840 at about the time Mzilikazi was reuniting his tribe about the Hill of the Indunas, a party of Boer scouts reached the Bapedi tribe in the Northern Transvaal and learned from them that the Matabele had settled to the north of the Limpopo. The Boers also heard that two white children were living among the Matabele. Potgieter thereupon sent a commando to locate the Matabele and also to bring the children, whom he guessed were the Liebenbergs, back to Potchefstroom. This commando penetrated the unexplored regions to the north, and although one of its black guides claimed to know the kraal in which the children were being held captive, the Boers found no trace of the Matabele and turned back to the Mooi river.

Mzilikazi had already embarked on the subjugation of the tribes of Matabeleland when Potgieter moved from Potchefstroom to the Magaliesberg. In 1845 Potgieter trekked towards the Zoutpansberg, his aim being to settle beyond reach of the Cape of Good Hope Punishment Bill, which placed all inhabitants of the subcontinent as far as 25 degrees longitude beneath the jurisdiction of the British Government. Potgieter also aimed to open a trade route to one of the Portuguese ports in the east. He founded the picturesque town of Ohrigstad, and although he believed he had chosen its situation wisely he was to change his mind when the intense heat of summer arrived, accompanied by an epidemic of malaria.

Two years after arriving in Ohrigstad, Potgieter planned an expedition to Inhambane, a small port on the Moçambique coast. During the early winter he set out with more than two hundred riders, many of whom had served under his command in the wars against the Matabele, and also a squad of Bapedi tribesmen. After crossing the Zoutpansberg the Boers turned to the north-west, crossed the Limpopo and entered the part of Mzilikazi's country inhabited by the Makalanga tribes.

It seems strange that the Boers should have taken this circuitous route when Inhambane lay to the east, but apparently they wished to avoid the Limpopo valley, which they knew to be fever-ridden. Leaving their wagons under guard at the Shashi river, the Boers proceeded through the Mangwe Pass towards Matabeleland. They resolved to take Mzilikazi unawares, to re-capture the cattle and sheep still owing to them and to find the Liebenberg children.

Reports of the approach of 'Ndaleka' (Hendrik Potgieter) swept through Matabele country and reached Mzilikazi on the Ingwig-wisi river, where he had recently arrived at the kraal of his Inyati or Buffalo regiment. Meanwhile Mbigo, commander of the newly conscripted Zwangendaba regiment, set out immediately with his warriors to investigate the movements of the Boers. They came upon the Boer commando whilst it was pillaging cattle-posts and sending herds of Matabele beasts back to the wagons on the Shashi. A skirmish took place during which the Matabele were compelled to retreat rapidly into the bush.

Night fell, and with the Boers bivouacked on a hill beside the Khami river the Zwangendaba regiment crept out of its hiding-place to massacre the Bapedi herdsmen, who with hundreds of Matabele cattle in their charge had lain down to sleep in the open. At dawn the Boers found the mangled corpses of their servants, but not a single head of cattle looted on the previous day. Potgieter's command set out to the Matopos, and on finding Mahlo-kohloko – the royal kraal – deserted, contented themselves with looting. Then the Boers retraced their spoors into the Makalanga regions, through the Mangwe pass and back to the Shashi river.

At this stage Potgieter decided the horses were too fatigued to continue the journey through the rugged country inhabited by the Matabele, and for the time being the attempt to reach Inhambane would be postponed. The Boers proceeded to Ohrigstad, and peace returned to Matabeleland.

The discovery of his new kingdom by Potgieter caused Mzilikazi grave concern, but, as events were to prove, this recent incident heralded an era of comparative peace and friendship between the Matabele and the Boers.

This change in the relationships between Mzilikazi and the Boers was indirectly due to the aspirations of David Livingstone, resident missionary among the Bakwena, the Crocodile People of Bechuanaland. A staunch partisan of the cause of the black man of South Africa, Livingstone criticized and opposed the Boers' claim to authority over the peoples Mzilikazi once had subjugated, and because of his interference in their affairs the Boers regarded the missionary's movements with suspicion.

In 1849 a series of discussions with Sechele, Chief of the Bakwena, awakened in Livingstone an urge to find the great lake said to lie in the heart of the Northern Kalahari. In years past, tales about this fabulous lake had intrigued the Rev. John Campbell, Dr Andrew Smith, David Hume, Captain Cornwallis Harris and scores of other pioneer travellers, but no one had ever ventured into the Kalahari in quest of it. So convinced was Livingstone that he would overcome the hazards to be encountered in the desert that he prepared his wagons and departed in the company of W. Cotten Oswell and Mungo Murray, well-known British hunters. Two months later, after facing death on several occasions, Livingstone and his companions discovered Ngami, the lake reached by Mzilikazi and his army a year or two after their defeat by the Boers in the Marico district.

As an immediate reaction to Livingstone's achievement, traders, hunters and adventurers, both white and dark-skinned, prepared to follow the newly plotted trail to the lake and seek their fortunes in the ivory trade. Joseph McCabe, an Irishman who for some years had been known as a trader-hunter both in the Colony and in the territories occupied by the Boers, reached Lake Ngami in 1852, and was followed by Fred Green, Sam Edwards, a party of Boers under Hermanus, brother of Potgieter, and a succession of other hardy travellers. Loads of barter goods were distributed among the indigenous peoples of the interior, in exchange for greater loads of elephant tusks. Many of the tribesmen and especially their chiefs, who until recently had never set eyes on a white man, became wily *entrepreneurs*, refusing to part with their stocks of ivory unless given arms and ammunition in exchange. And although most of the visiting traders refused to take part in this illegal traffic there were undoubtedly others who used it as a means for accumulating wealth in the shortest time possible.

The fact that the tribes of Bechuanaland and the Northern Kalahari were receiving fire-arms perturbed the Boers, who in the meanwhile had gained independence from British rule and had proclaimed the Transvaal a republic. Their first step towards combating this problem was to attempt to close the Missionaries' Road through Bechuanaland and to decree that trading with tribesmen could be conducted only by approved individuals.

The Boers accused Livingstone not only of supplying the Bakwena with arms, but also of stirring them into revolt. Furthermore, when Hermanus Potgieter returned from Lake Ngami he reported to his brother that Joseph McCabe had carried several cases of guns to the north-western tribes, and had delivered four small cannons to Sebitoane, Chief of the Makololo in the Chobe district. Hermanus also claimed that Green and Edwards had been seen with wagons loaded with ivory they had exchanged for fire-arms. He reported that the Griqua hunters were the most assiduous and unscrupulous among the gun-runners he had encountered.

As Hermanus's evidence was based on hearsay, no steps were taken by the Boers to punish the alleged transgressors. Tension mounted when it became apparent that, if ever the gun traffic spread into Matabeleland and Mzilikazi's army was equipped with muzzle-loaders, the safety of the numerically inferior Boer Republic would be placed in jeopardy.

Therefore in 1852 Hendrik Potgieter sent a party of burghers to interview Mzilikazi and tell him the Boers wished to enter into a peace treaty with the Matabele. Few details concerning this meeting with the despot exist, but there is no doubt the Boers' mission was successful, for in December of the same year a group of Matabele dignitaries, headed by Marapu, the military commander, arrived at the Zoutpansberg, where Potgieter had recently founded a settlement.

Mzilikazi's envoys found Potgieter in a pitiable state of health. Fatigued, prematurely decrepit and invalided by persistent bouts of fever, he was a dying man. The Matabele listened intently while the Boers told them about the gun-running among the Bechuana tribes. The envoys agreed that unless they accepted the friendship of the Boer Republic Mzilikazi's country might well be overrun by tribes once subjugated by the Matabele.

On behalf of Mzilikazi, Marapu and his colleagues accepted the treaty proposed by the Boers. In future Mzilikazi would promise to allow no traffic in fire-arms and ammunition within his dominions; he would be expected to take into custody all traders and hunters found smuggling guns to the Matabele, and would deliver the culprit together with their possessions to the nearest Boer magistrate. If the Republic were invaded Mzilikazi would be expected to supply the Boer leaders with auxiliaries. He would also be required to afford protection to Boer hunters and traders seeking to enter Matabeleland. Finally the King would be free to trade with the Boers provided the goods exchanged were not contraband.

The treaty was signed early in January of the new year. Hendrik Potgieter died a month later.

The first Boers to organize a hunting-trip into Matabele territory were Pieter Jacobs, Jan Abraham and three brothers named Piet, Jan and Frans Joubert. Crossing the Limpopo river, they were intercepted by Matabele scouts, who instructed them to report to Mzilikazi. At Mahlokohloko, the royal kraal, the King received the Boers kindly and even presented them with valuable gifts of elephant tusks.

Mzilikazi asked the Boers whether they had news of Robert Moffat, for he wished to see his old missionary friend once again. The King said he had striven to keep the road through Bechuanaland open, so that Moffat could visit him. Indeed, only recently he had sent six warriors and ten Makalanga subjects on a friendly mission to Chief Seghoma of the Bamangwato tribe, asking him to direct Moffat to Matabeleland if ever the white man chanced to arrive in those parts. Seghoma murdered the messengers, Mzilikazi declared, and nothing could be done to avenge this insult for fear Seghoma might prevent Moffat from travelling through Bamangwato country along the road leading to Matabeleland. The Boer hunters confessed they knew nothing about Robert Moffat, but then the Jouberts, who hailed from Natal, said they knew of a missionary working among the Zulu in Port Natal. To the best of their knowledge he was the white man Mzilikazi was looking for. One of the Joubert brothers offered to escort a small party of Matabele warriors to the missionaries at Port Natal. A few months later the Jouberts and Mzilikazi's warriors reached what is today the city of Durban, and met not Robert Moffat but Daniel Lindley, the American missionary who fled from Mosega after the Boer invasion in 1837. Lindley assured them that Moffat was still stationed at Kuruman.

On the return journey to Matabeleland Mzilikazi's men were crossing the Transvaal when they learned, from numerous sources, that Robert Moffat was dead. They reported to Mzilikazi, who refused to believe their story and dispatched them instead to Kuruman while he himself slaughtered oxen, conducted sacrificial ceremonies in honour of the ancestors and called upon the spirit of Mashobane to send Moffat to Matabeleland.

Incredible as it may seem to the European reader, the spirits answered Mzilikazi's prayers, for at that moment, in the company of Sam Edwards and John Chapman, Moffat was travelling northwards to the Matabele kingdom along the sandy track known as the Missionaries' Road.

It had long been Moffat's intention to visit Mzilikazi in Matabeleland, but his work of translating the Old Testament into the vernacular had prevented his leaving Kuruman. It was only recently, when his health grew precarious, that Moffat decided to set his translation aside. He resolved to regain his strength by undertaking a wagon-trip into the new domains of the Matabele tyrant.

Included in the baggage Moffat had in his wagons were parcels of clothes, preserved and dried foods, and books and letters he hoped to deliver, with Mzilikazi's cooperation, to David Livingstone, who was exploring the Zambezi regions. By the beginning of July 1854 Moffat had passed through Shoshong, crossed the Maclautsi and Shashi rivers and entered the Makalanga section of Mzilikazi's dominions.

Following Moffat's trail in the hope that the missionary's friendship with Mzilikazi would help them gain entry into Matabeleland were two parties of hunters: one under Seepamore, a coloured from Kuruman, and another under three Englishmen named Reader, Connolly and Clarke. In Makalanga country Moffat also met Lucas Marthinus Swartz, a Boer hunter who was returning to the Republic after visiting Mzilikazi at Mahlokohloko.[1]

On 17 July Moffat reached Mahlokohloko. This royal kraal had only recently been moved from the Ntabazinduna area, and was being built beside the uMkosa river. Amidst a host of warriors dressed in their finery, and women naked to the waist, Moffat was conducted into the royal kraal, where sixty dignitaries awaited his arrival. Silence fell over Mahlokohloko as eyes were focused on the missionary and also the gateway through which Mzilikazi would make his appearance. Suddenly the people raised their voices in praise of the King, and Moffat was amazed to see a group of courtiers carrying Mzilikazi to a kaross spread out on the ground. The missionary could hardly believe his eyes: on the kaross sat not the straight, robust and eager-eyed conqueror he had

1. Recently Swartz's name has been added to the list of pioneer travellers reputed to have reached the Victoria Falls before Livingstone.

known some twenty years ago, but a paunchy old man, his drooping frame buried in rolls of fat, his face bloated and his feet swollen and lame.

'Moshete, Moshete, Moshete,' the despot cried, his anguished voice barely audible. Mzilikazi took the hand Moffat proffered, but as tears welled up in his eyes he released the hand and drew his mantle across his face. Regaining his composure the King peeped over the mantle, grasped Moffat's fingers, turned to uMncumbata, the chief *induna*, and confessed how happy he was to see his old missionary friend.

'I have come to see you before I die,' said Moffat. 'God has preserved us both to see each other again.'[1]

But Mzilikazi would not speak of death, and refused to admit that Moffat had aged despite the fact that since last they met the missionary's flowing beard had turned from black to white. The King thought of the aches besetting his own weary body, and asked Moffat to give him medicines.

'Your God has sent you to help me,' Mzilikazi insisted. 'Yes, he has sent you to heal me.'[2]

Moffat diagnosed the King's condition as dropsy. When night fell, and the wagons were brought into the royal kraal, the missionary searched his wagon chest for medicines. Then, day after day, he strove to relieve Mzilikazi's discomfort. Moffat dosed him with mixtures, massaged his feet and cheered him by recalling the happy times they had spent together in the past. But he also reprimanded Mzilikazi for over-indulging in food and beer. Within ten days the King was hobbling about, unaided, on his swollen, aching feet.

Mzilikazi's ill-health did not deprive him of the smallest fraction of the authority he had always enjoyed as the ruler of the Matabele. In the tribal court he cut a pathetic figure, but his decisions, however cruel, were applauded by the councillors and subjects, and defaulters accepted their punishments with grati-

1. J .P. R. Wallis (ed.), *Matabele Journals of Robert Moffat*, vol. I, p. 230.
2. ibid.

tude. Tyranny still held sway among the Matabele. Suicides were common occurrences. Some men took their own lives because they had transgressed and feared the wrath of the King; others because they had grown old, or, being stricken with disease, realized they could no longer be of service to the tribe. One of the warriors, detained for some petty offence, set fire to the hut in which he awaited his trial, and perished in the flames rather than face Mzilikazi in the tribal court or endure the death he believed he would suffer.

Early in August Moffat announced his intention to move on towards the tsetse-fly country. He asked Mzilikazi to provide an escort of warriors, and also a party of bearers whom he could send to the Zambezi with provisions for Livingstone. Mzilikazi was taken aback and refused to comply. Was not Moffat his father, he inquired irascibly, and should not a father know better than to desert an ailing son? Taking the King by the arm Moffat explained that Livingstone was his son-in-law, and that if he returned to Kuruman without attempting to see the explorer, or to receive news from him, he would be failing in his duty as a parent. But the more Moffat tried to reason with Mzilikazi the more irritated and unco-operative the despot became. Three weeks of haggling followed.

Mzilikazi resorted to playing on Moffat's kind nature. He said the Mwari witch-doctor who had attended his illness in the past was incompetent and the medicines Moffat was giving him were restoring his health. Mzilikazi also tried to dissuade Moffat from undertaking the journey to the west by telling him about ghastly conditions along the trails, about diseases fatal to man and beast, about crocodiles preying on all who crossed the streams and about hostile tribes who butchered all strangers venturing into the territories. The stalemate ended when Moffat, growing determined to leave Mahlokohloko, decided to get the provisions to Livingstone without Mzilikazi's help.

On the morning Moffat was due to leave, Mzilikazi hobbled towards the wagons, struggled up the steps and settled on the driver's seat. For a moment the missionary thought the King intended accompanying the wagons to a kraal along the route. He was soon to realize his mistake, for during the entire journey to the west Mzilikazi remained his constant companion.

As the wagons drew out of the royal kraal, almost the whole male population followed. Included in the procession were the King's retainers, old uMncumbata, a group of important *indunas* and also thirty yapping dogs. Mzilikazi's retinue multiplied as it was joined by men bearing lion-skins and leopard karosses, women balancing large calabashes of beer on their heads, and herdboys driving slaughter cattle and goats.

Finding the wagon seat uncomfortable, Mzilikazi rose laboriously, shuffled into the wagon-tent, and dropped into Moffat's bed. Supine, he fingered an assortment of beads and baubles received from Sam Edwards. The King issued occasional instructions both to Moffat and the Matabele attendants and often he dozed while the wagon wheels creaked and the bedstraps groaned in his ears.

The wagons headed westwards through Makalanga country. Each evening when a halt was called the warriors cut branches and thatching-grass and erected makeshift huts. Moffat and Mzilikazi occupied separate wagons, but the missionary enjoyed little sleep, for at nights the camp resounded to the singing, dancing and animated conversation of pleasure-seeking warriors, the inarticulate soliloquizing of befuddled dagga-smokers and the yelping and snarling of dogs fighting incessantly over the bones of the slaughtered beasts. But amidst this hullabaloo Mzilikazi slept soundly. Indeed, as the days passed and Moffat showed signs of exhaustion, the King's health seemed to improve.

At the beginning of September the wagons approached the Gwaai river over the series of gulleys conveying an overflow of water into the Khami river. A week later, when crossing the Nata stream, Moffat's wagon sank axle-deep into the sands, and the oxen could not budge it. Mzilikazi commanded his warriors to pull the wagon over the river bed on to the opposite bank. Then as the last of the Matabele cattle-posts came in sight and the scouts reported there would be no trace of water ahead for days, Mzilikazi suggested that Moffat should return with him to Mahlokohloko.

Moffat refused. He said he would continue on foot, for, come what may, the provisions must be taken to Livingstone. Again the two friends started arguing. But Mzilikazi was bent on remaining with Moffat and declared that as he was in no fit state to walk his warriors would carry him wherever the missionary journeyed. Moffat agreed to return to Mahlokohloko provided the King found reliable bearers to proceed with Livingstone's goods. This suggestion delighted Mzilikazi, who called his retinue together, selected twenty men, and briefed them on the important journey they would undertake to the North.

Under the leadership of an *induna* named Mondane, the men set out with seventeen bundles, and although they were to struggle through desert flats and tsetse-infected country, they reached the Makololo tribe on the Chobe river, who, on taking over the provisions, delivered them eventually to Livingstone.

Meanwhile, Moffat had returned with Mzilikazi to Bobampeng, a kraal situated some seven miles outside Mahlokohloko. On the last Sabbath in September he experienced the joy of preaching a sermon from the Book of Genesis to one of the largest tribal congregations he had ever seen in Southern Africa. This was the outcome of his mentioning to Mzilikazi that before his return to Kuruman he would like to convey the wisdom of God's word to the Matabele. Immediately, the King ordered the inhabitants of Bobampeng as well as the regiments of the neighbouring villages to assemble at Moffat's wagons.

On that eventful Sunday morning hundreds of warriors listened confusedly but in silence to the missionary's teachings. Their eyes fixed on Moffat and on Mzilikazi, who sat beside him, the Matabele strained their ears in an effort to catch each word. It was imperative that they should understand the sermon, for Mzilikazi had decreed that if any man was guilty of forgetting Moffat's message he would be put to death.

Spring slid into Matabeleland and the vicious heat of the sun entered the kraals. Fearing that the rains would soon arrive to prolong his stay with the Matabele, Moffat hinted at his return to Kuruman. The King would not hear of Moffat's departure. Mzilikazi assembled his subjects not only on Sundays but also on weekdays, and insisted that the missionary should preach to them. Always a member of the congregation, Mzilikazi derived little pleasure from Moffat's teachings, and on 1 October he was visibly shocked when for the second time in his life he was obliged to listen to a lengthy discourse on the Resurrection and the punishments awaiting sinners after death.

Next day Moffat set out for Mahlokohloko, and along the road his wagons were approached by Truey, the Griqua, daughter of Peter Davids. Like her cousin Willem, whom incidentally Moffat had met on several occasions during the past few weeks, Truey had almost forgotten her mother tongue, and had adopted the mode of life of the Matabele. She pleaded with Moffat to ask Mzilikazi to set her free so that she could return to her people. Promising to speak to Mzilikazi on her behalf, Moffat took leave of Truey and continued on his way to the Matabele capital.

Moffat spent six uneventful days at Mahlokohloko, and on the second Sunday of the month, having preached again to a great gathering of warriors, he asked the King to allow Truey to accompany the wagons to the South. At first Mzilikazi refused, saying, among other things, that his women were as valuable to him as his cattle, and that it was Peter Davids' duty, not Moffat's, to negotiate for Truey's release. Eventually the King agreed to release Truey, for on the eve of Moffat's return to Kuruman there was nothing Mzilikazi would not do to please the white friend whom he loved above all other people.

On the last night at Mahlokohloko, Mzilikazi slept in a wagon drawn up close to those of Moffat and his party. In the early hours of the morning Sam Edwards was awakened by a commotion in the cattle enclosure, and flinging his bedclothes aside he strode into the darkness to investigate. He found, not a lion, among the cattle as he had expected, but Mzilikazi. Edwards chuckled. The old King was hobbling about the enclosure trying to drive out the oxen. Mzilikazi had planned for the beasts to disappear mysteriously during the night so that Moffat would not be able to leave on the morrow.

The sun rose and the wagons pulled out of Mahlokohloko. At

the gates of the royal kraal Moffat paused to say farewell to Mzilikazi, who was unusually silent and dispirited. They shook hands,
exchanged a few final words and parted. Neither believed they
would ever meet again.

CHAPTER 22

THE STRICKEN KING

Mzilikazi bewitched – His health deteriorates
He snubs Robert Moffat

MOFFAT'S departure was followed by one of the most prosperous seasons the Matabele had known. The harvests were abundant, the routine raids into the territories of the Makalanga and Mashona tributaries fruitful and the danger of being invaded by powerful enemies remote. In almost every way 1854 was a happy year. Mzilikazi, commander-in-chief of the armies, chief priest, supreme judge, King of the tribe, was extolled by his idolizing subjects. The soaking rains, the good fortune granted to the tribe by the shades of ancestors, the peace and security enjoyed in every kraal and cattle-post – all these benefits were attributed to the astute leadership of the great Bull Elephant.

This was also a busy year. In the vicinity of the huts of the ring-headed patriarchs, the married women hoed the fields, brewed beer, prepared meals, suckled their babies, made bead ornaments, moulded and baked clay utensils and winnowed, stamped and ground the corn. The menfolk enjoyed long spells of idle gossip and beer-drinking beside the cattle-folds, but also repaired and erected huts, hedges and game-traps, supervised the herding and milking of the cattle, carved wooden ornaments and utensils and built watchtowers beside the ripening crops. They attended sacred ceremonies and feasts at the capital, and also trials in the tribal courts of justice.

But while the Matabele were enjoying this spate of good fortune, the elders of the royal kraal could not fail to notice the change that had come over their ageing King. For some time they had been concerned about the decline in Mzilikazi's health, and discussions led them to believe that the King was bewitched. That Mzilikazi should have grown stoop-shouldered and rotund, that his legs should have become swollen, his feet nodular and his hands trembling and weak was cause enough for his associates to shake their heads in despair, but it was the sudden change in the King's nature, his spasms of moodiness, his despondency, his irrational decisions in the tribal court and his prolonged spells of brooding that mystified the Matabele dignitaries. This change induced in them a fear that their King was the victim of sorcery.

Furtive eyes searched among the courtiers for suspects. The elders noticed that the man most frequently at the King's side was Mzilikazi's uncle. They held him responsible for Mzilikazi's illness and, arresting him, brought him before the tribal court.

Mzilikazi was loath to believe that the greybeard who always had attended him faithfully could be guilty of witchcraft, but to be on the safe side he agreed eventually to exile his uncle to Mashona country. Even old uMncumbata, senior *induna* of the tribe and Mzilikazi's oldest friend, was named by the elders as a likely sorcerer. But Mzilikazi refused to be persuaded that uMncumbata would want to destroy him, so the famous Matabele dignitary was never charged.

During 1855 Mzilikazi exhausted the supply of medicines Robert Moffat had left him, and as the months passed his health deteriorated. He lamented the fact that no longer had he stocks of the remedies to alleviate his aches and discomfort, but at the same time he ignored Moffat's solemn warnings to abstain from drinking beer and to reduce his consumption of fatty meats and starches soaked in rich gravies. Nowhere in the writings of pioneer missionaries and adventurers is mention made of the source of Mzilikazi's dropsical condition, but a close study of the symptoms of the illness suggests that he was suffering from cirrhosis of the liver.

Apart from the devouring unhappiness his ill-health was causing, Mzilikazi was for ever pestered by visions of white men travelling into Matabeleland along the tracks Moffat's wagons had left. He ordered the regiments both in the South and to the West to watch the borders and to stop all strangers venturing into

Matabele territory. In 1855 he was informed that the Boer Lucas Marthinus Swartz was hunting along the opposite bank of the Shashi, and in the following year he was shocked to learn that the same white man had crossed the river and had been captured while travelling through the bushveld regions of the Makalanga tributaries. Mzilikazi reprimanded Swartz, but set him free when the Boer promised to bring the King nine guns and a goodly supply of ammunition to compensate for the elephants poached in the hunting-grounds forbidden to all people other than the Matabele.

Meanwhile, across the seas, events were unfolding which in the course of time would lead to the infiltration of white men into Matabeleland. David Livingstone had returned to Britain after exploring the continent of Africa from Loanda on the west coast to Quelimane in the east. He fascinated the entire civilized world with reports of his adventures and achievements, and especially with his discovery of the Victoria Falls. Britain was ebullient with excitement. Livingstone was acclaimed a hero, presented with the freedom of cities, fêted both by scientific and commercial bodies, and awarded honorary degrees by the Universities of Oxford and Cambridge. He addressed a succession of meetings, enthusing his audiences for more and more knowledge about the hitherto unknown continent of Africa. Livingstone painted so colourful a picture of the tribes he had encountered that he succeeded in resuscitating the urge of enterprising young men to carry the light of Christianity to the darkest depths of pagan countries.

The directors of the London Missionary Society conferred. So impressed were they by Livingstone's account of the potential for missionary labour among the black peoples of Africa that they decided to write to Robert Moffat of Kuruman, instructing him to prepare the way in Matabeleland for evangelists. In this letter the directors also mentioned that Livingstone would be responsible for introducing a group of missionaries to the Makololo tribe living north of the Zambezi.

Reluctantly Moffat prepared his wagons for the trip to Mzilikazi. His erstwhile zest for long-distance travel had forsaken him.

Forty-one years of missionary labour among the Batlhaping – the Fish People – in the dry, sun-scorched country surrounding Kuruman, had drained his energies, and his prolonged and unstinting devotion to the translation and printing of the Bible had robbed him of the health he had enjoyed in former years. Bearing in mind the history of the ill-fated French and American mission stations at Mosega, and the fact that Mzilikazi had always been averse to the permanent settlement of white men among the Matabele, Moffat feared there would be little scope for successful mission work in Matabeleland. Nevertheless, towards the end of July 1857 he took leave of Mary, his wife, and proceeded along the crude Missionaries' Road curling northwards through Bechuanaland.

On reaching the Bakwena tribe, Moffat met Chief Sechele, who asked the missionary to persuade Mzilikazi to release from military servitude a young tribesman named Matsheng. Apparently, years ago, when the Matabele invaded Bakwena country, they found among the captives a boy whom they learned was Matsheng, heir to the Bamangwato throne. It was an unfortunate coincidence, Sechele explained, that the little prince should have fallen into Matabele hands, for at that time Matsheng and his mother were enjoying asylum among the Bakwena. They had fled from their own country when conspirators arrived to kill Matsheng and install a usurper as King of the Bamangwato. Seghoma, the present Chief, was merely the regent, Sechele added, and he was an unpopular and corrupt ruler. Therefore it was essential that Matsheng, the rightful King of the Bamangwato, be returned to the Shoshong and placed on the throne. Moffat promised to discuss the matter with Mzilikazi, and struck on towards Matabeleland.

Crossing the Maclautsi river and then the Shashi, the missionary followed the trail he had taken three years before through the rugged bush-country of the Makalanga tribe. He called at the first Matabele outpost and paid his respects to Makhobi, the vassal chief whose duty was to guard the southern approaches to Matabeleland. Sending runners ahead to report his progress to Mzilikazi, Moffat left Makhobi's kraal, followed a twisting path round the bases of the boulder-crested hills, crossed the Mangwe pass and entered the flats reaching out to the Matopos and the heart of Mzilikazi's kingdom.

Messengers from the Matabele capital arrived to guide the missionary to the capital. Moffat was surprised to find Mahlokohloko in ruins, and he learned that the King was resident in a new Mahlokohloko, built but recently a few miles farther north. Moffat drew up his wagons in a suitable camping site and followed his guides into the royal kraal.

On previous occasions when Moffat had visited Mzilikazi he had been struck by the crowds of dignitaries, courtiers, warriors and commoners who gathered to welcome him. There had been dancing, singing and feasting, and when the missionary had stepped forward to meet Mzilikazi a tumultuous ovation had greeted him. Now Moffat was being conducted, unheralded, past the huts and the cattle-fold, and only a few inquisitive inhabitants turned from their activities to hail him. He found Mzilikazi hunched up in an old armchair, three of his wives fussing about him and a servant or two waiting to attend to his needs.

The King was gravely ill, thought Moffat, as he took the hand his old friend proffered. Moffat was thankful to find Mzilikazi alive, but it grieved him to see the suffering the King was compelled to endure. Mzilikazi and the missionary sat talking for several hours. They were glad of each other's company, and yet their conversation was devoid of the repartee they had enjoyed in years gone by.

Moffat remained at Mahlokohloko for two and a half months and in all this time he did little else than attend to Mzilikazi's fading health. He dosed the King with mixtures, and prepared liniments for easing the pain in his swollen legs and gouty joints. And the more Moffat tried to help him, the more he was angered to watch Mzilikazi guzzling beer, gorging beef, and taking snuff. Indeed, Moffat knew that unless his patient curbed his insatiable appetite for food, and especially for beer, he would never regain even a modicum of his former strength.

Mzilikazi drank all day, every day. Moffat gave him pills to cause a revulsion towards the brew which enslaved him. Yet the King persisted in drinking, and kept his wives busy by calling them incessantly to assist his trembling hands in lifting the beer-pot to his mouth. Time and again Moffat ventured to mention establishing a mission station in Matabeleland, but so besotted was the King, and so confused his reasoning that the discussion was seldom pursued beyond a few sentences.

In an entry in his journal Moffat complained that as Mzilikazi was in his dotage, it was difficult to convey even the simplest message to his befuddled brain. The missionary grew impatient. Whenever he saw the King he rebuked him for his excessive drinking. But all Moffat's nagging proved of no avail, for soon he discovered that Mzilikazi no longer wanted his medicines. Instead, the King was reverting to the concoctions of his witch-doctors.

Although temporarily snubbed by Mzilikazi, Moffat was asked to attend to three corpulent royal women, who for some time had been complaining of pains in the chest, of headaches and of spasms of dizziness. Moffat examined them in the seraglio and then bled them. When the women responded by heaving up large quantites of beer, he concluded that their disorders, like those of Mzilikazi, were the results of habitual intemperance.

During the first week in October a letter reached Mahlokohloko from a trader named Collins, who, on reaching the southern border of Matabeleland, had been detained by a body of Mzili-kazi's warriors. Addressed to Moffat, the letter asked that Collins and a Boer hunter named Jan Viljoen be permitted to enter the Matabele kingdom. Although the missionary had met neither of these men he had often heard favourable reports about them. Collins, Moffat recalled, had once been kind to his son, Robert Moffat Junior in Natal, and Jan Viljoen, field-cornet of the Transvaal Republic, was the owner of the farm Vergenoegt – Far Enough – in the Mosega valley where Mzilikazi's great military settlement had stood until 1837. By reputation Moffat knew the Boer as a man of good character, God-fearing, friendly, sympathetic towards tribesmen and hospitable and cooperative towards travellers of both Boer and British descent. Listening to the contents of the letter, Mzilikazi agreed to let Collins proceed to headquarters, but refused to allow Viljoen to cross the border. Mzilikazi was averse to the presence of white men in his dominions, but this did not deter him from sending an *induna* with nineteen elephant tusks for the purpose of purchasing a wagon, ten trek-oxen and two guns from Jan Viljoen. So greatly did this transaction please the King that within the next few years he was to welcome this same Boer hunter to Matabeleland.

In the course of discussing with Mzilikazi the arrival of Collins and Viljoen on the border, Moffat took the opportunity to ask the King whether he would sanction the permanent settlement of missionaries among the Matabele. He was surprised when, with apparent enthusiasm, Mzilikazi said: 'Let me have teachers. My land is yours. You must do with it what you think.'[1]

But the missionaries would require a piece of land beside a perennial spring, replied Moffat somewhat apprehensively. They would need a suitable site for building homes, cultivating gardens and addressing congregations. Moffat added that it was not his but the King's prerogative to decide where such a place would be found. Mzilikazi grew impatient, and dismissed the subject by declaring that as there were no springs within reach of Mahlokohloko Moffat must journey into the interior and search for one.

The old missionary withdrew from the King's presence. Dejected, he decided to postpone his quest for a mission site until such time as he brought his colleagues to Matabeleland. He remained at Mahlokohloko until 9 December. Before braving the homeward journey through the heat of the subtropical sun and the blast of the summer storms, he succeeded in gaining the release of Matsheng, future King of the Bamangwato tribe.

Moffat was pleased to be returning to Kuruman. Nevertheless, his heart filled with sorrow when he took leave of Mzilikazi and beheld the anguish the old King's many afflictions were causing him. He wondered whether this, his fourth visit to the founder of the Matabele tribe, had been worth while.

1. J. P. R. Wallis (ed.), *Matabele Journals of Robert Moffat*, vol. II, p. 83.

CHAPTER 23

THE INYATI MISSION

*Missionaries arrive in Matabeleland – They are ignored by
Mzilikazi – They establish a mission station at Inyati*

No sooner had Moffat reached Kuruman than he prepared to
travel to the Cape in order to meet the evangelists selected by the
directors of the London Missionary Society for the Matabele and
Makololo missions. He set out with Mary, his wife, and reached
Cape Town in time to see Livingstone, who, bound for the mouth
of the Zambezi, had touched at Table Bay. In mid-July 1858 the
new missionaries arrived on South African soil, and during the
next few months they crossed the Orange River and proceeded to
Moffat's home in Kuruman.

The familes destined for Matabeleland were John Smith Moffat
(Robert's son) and his wife Emily; Mr and Mrs Thomas Morgan
Thomas and their infant son; and William Sykes, whose wife had
recently died. The members of the Makololo mission were Mr and
Mrs Holloway Helmore and their four children, Mr and Mrs
Roger Price and their baby daughter, and Mr and Mrs John
McKenzie. Early in July 1859 the Helmores and the Prices set out
for Makololo country, leaving McKenzie and his wife to follow.[1]
The Matabele missionaries, headed by Robert Moffat, left Kuru-
man three weeks later, and followed the wagon-rutted road
through Bechuanaland into the southern reaches of Mzilikazi's
kingdom.

1. On reaching the Chobe river the Makololo missionaries became
gravely ill, and by the time McKenzie arrived to join them all except
Roger Price, two of the Helmore children and a few servants had died.
Although it has been claimed that the party were poisoned by the
Makololo, it seems more likely that the deaths were caused by fever.

It was early spring when Moffat and his party crossed the Shashi river and outspanned at Makhobi's kraal, the most southerly of the Matabele outposts. Already messengers had been dispatched to Mzilikazi, informing him of the approach of the missionaries Robert Moffat had promised to bring to Matabeleland. A few days later a body of warriors arrived from headquarters with greetings from the King and with instructions for the missionaries to continue immediately into Matabeleland.

To his dismay Moffat discovered that the trek-oxen were infected with lung-sickness, a contagious disease which during the past year or two had been sweeping the Cape Colony, and also the central plateau of South Africa. The missionaries dared not move on for fear of spreading the scourge to the hundreds of thousands of Matabele cattle. Moffat sent runners to report the position to Mzilikazi and to ask him to arrange for the missionaries' wagons to be fetched.

Moffat's party were not stranded for long. A regiment headed by an *induna* and accompanied by a diminutive witch-doctor arrived to pull the wagons over the tortuous track leading through the Matopos to Mzilikazi's royal kraal. But before the warriors were instructed to form up behind the yokes, the witch-doctor announced that it was imperative he perform a purifying ceremony. With a tail of a gnu he sprinkled a black, oily decoction over the missionaries, the oxen, the wagons and every item of luggage thought to be contaminated by the sickness. The white strangers were shocked by the indignity of the ritual, but, when eventually the wagons were being drawn to the north-east by teams of loping and chanting warriors, the women tittered over their extraordinary introduction to Matabele customs.

On reaching the hub of Matabeleland the missionaries were taken, not to Mahlokohloko, as Moffat had expected, but to the outskirts of a modest cattle-post situated on the south bank of the Bembesi river. The sun was setting when the *indunas* arrived at the wagons to escort first Robert Moffat and then his son John to Mzilikazi, who awaited them in the kraal.

Moffat found the King seated in his old armchair, a heavy duffel coat draped about his body and a highland cap perched back to front on his head. Mzilikazi was happy to see his missionary friend, and expressed pleasure at meeting John. But with darkness descending over the kraal the King was in no mood for talking, and dismissed his white guests promising to see the rest of the party on the morrow. Moffat and John returned to the wagons and that night, when the old missionary sat down to enter the events of the day in his journal, his final thoughts turned to Mzilikazi's health: 'To me he looks much aged,' he wrote, 'he looks infirm. . . .'[1]

It was the end of October. A still, humid heat enveloped the missionaries' encampment, and thunder-clouds were gathering. In such conditions the travel-weary missionaries were naturally eager not to delay unduly their departure to the site Mzilikazi would provide for a mission station. They dreamt of the homes they would build and the comforts and amenities they would enjoy. But as the days passed, they realized that the King was in no hurry to allow them to move, or even to know where in Matabeleland they would be given a plot of ground. For three weeks they strove to negotiate with Mzilikazi, but found him elusive, stubborn and uncooperative, quick to demand presents, yet reluctant to discuss their aspirations for mission work among the Matabele. The missionaries grew despondent, especially when it became clear that even Moffat had lost favour in the eyes of the King.

One morning they were awakened by confused noises from the direction of the cattle-post. They saw Mzilikazi's wagons accompanied by a host of armed warriors, servants and women, and also droves of cattle and sheep moving northwards into the bush. Moffat, who had not expected this sudden development, mounted a horse and galloped off to find out where Mzilikazi was bound, and what plans the King had made for the missionaries. But he was not allowed to speak to the King, and he returned crestfallen and as confused as his companions. The missionaries were stranded, for the only oxen they had were those left at Makhobi's kraal a hundred miles away.

For three long days Moffat and his party sat beside the wagons

1. J. P. R. Wallis (ed.), *Matabele Journals of Robert Moffat*, vol. II, p. 204.

pondering the problem confronting them. When the situation appeared most gloomy they were relieved to see a man named Monyebe, one of Mzilikazi's most influential *indunas*, approaching with a companion. Monyebe told them he had been sent by the great Bull Elephant to speak with Moffat. The King was displeased with the white teachers, and feared that they, like the American missionaries who once had settled in Mosega and eventually had chosen to join the Boers, were spies who were preparing the way for aggressors to destroy the Matabele. Why had Moffat not brought Mzilikazi guns and ammunition, asked Monyebe.

Before Moffat could reply Monyebe's companion spoke up: the missionaries' wagons were loaded with goods belonging to Mzilikazi, he rasped, and must be forwarded to the rightful owner without delay. Astonished, yet composed, Moffat refuted these accusations. He assured the messengers that the King would never be given fire-arms by the missionaries. Then Monyebe announced there were other matters of importance he had been instructed to convey to Moffat and his party: Mzilikazi demanded payment for bringing the missionaries' wagons from Makhobi's kraal to Matabeleland; he would allow no fishing, hunting or bartering with tribesmen, and Moffat's people must keep away from the river lest they be tempted to kill a crocodile in order to remove its liver for medicines to bewitch the Bull Elephant.

The missionaries were bewildered. They called a meeting to discuss leaving Matabeleland and establishing a mission station with a ruler more enlightened and cooperative than Mzilikazi. Steadfast in their belief that by returning to Kuruman they would be shirking their duty to the cause of Christianity, they prepared to remain where they were and face whatever hardships confronted them. Two weeks of hunger and privation followed and then one afternoon Monyebe appeared again at the wagons with three slaughter-oxen and a goat from Mzilikazi. The missionaries were surprised yet extremely happy to learn from the *induna* that trek-oxen would be arriving to fetch the wagons to Inyati, headquarters of the Buffalo regiment, where Mzilikazi was living in the royal kraal with uLoziba, senior Queen of the tribe. Wary of Mzilikazi's whims and moods, the missionaries doubted the sincerity of Monyebe's message. But on 15 December the trek-oxen arrived and the wagons were taken from the 'open-air prison' on the Bembesi river to Inyati, the most important of Mzilikazi's military settlements in the north.

Inyati was an enormous kraal. A sturdy hedge encircled row upon row of beehive huts, which in turn embraced a cattle-fold capable of holding three thousand beasts. The seraglio in which Mzilikazi resided with uLoziba and seventeen other royal wives was cut off by a tall stockade from the homes of the warriors, retainers and courtiers.

Barely had the missionaries reached Inyati when they were summoned by the King. They found Mzilikazi reclining in one of his wagons, his wives sitting close by, waiting to fulfil his demands for beer. He beamed with happiness when he saw the white men approaching and, rising laboriously in his bed, he hailed Moffat heartily, offered him his beer-pot and invited him to select a portion of cooked beef from a large wooden trough.

With an air of reserve Moffat seated himself on the wagon shaft and listened to the words of flattery with which Mzilikazi placated him. Too long a time had elapsed since their last meeting, cried Mzilikazi, and now that Moffat had come his fretting heart had grown white with pleasure.

For half an hour Mzilikazi dominated the conversation and, although obviously tipsy, he succeeded in convincing Moffat that he earnestly wanted the missionaries to settle in his country. The King grew uneasy when reminded of his false accusations, his unreasonable demands and unfriendly treatment of his white guests. Mzilikazi was unaccustomed to reprimand; indeed, he forestalled further discussion on the matter by informing Moffat that Monyebe had already been instructed to show the missionaries a site selected for them. There seemed nothing more that either Moffat or his black friend could add to this happy announcement. Both had won a victory, and they parted the best of friends.

Next day Monyebe called at the wagons and asked the missionaries to follow him into the valley stretching out below Inyati. The *induna* directed them to a spring pouring a steady flow of cool, clear water into the Ingwigwisi stream, southern boundary of the vast stretch of land Mzilikazi had set aside for the mission homes, gardens and grazing grounds. As they surveyed this beautiful valley, the missionaries rejoiced. In a flash all their doubts and fears were dispelled, and they joined in prayers of thanksgiving. Now they saw Mzilikazi not as a stubborn despot, but as a kindly, considerate King who had brought them from the impoverished cattle-post in the South to the great Inyati royal kraal and also the loveliest valley in Matabeleland. At the first opportunity they visited Mzilikazi to thank him for his generosity and to give him presents.

Building operations started in the valley of Inyati, and the first mission homes to be completed were thatch huts erected by a group of the King's servants. Meanwhile, Thomas and John Moffat were employed in building permanent European-style bungalows, and the materials they used for the walls and roofs were fetched in wagons drawn by Mzilikazi's oxen. Robert Moffat occupied a tent pitched beside his wagon, and although keenly interested in the activities of his fellow missionaries he devoted much of his time to doctoring Mzilikazi and attending to a variety of jobs demanding his skill in smithery.

During the first half of 1860, entirely owing to Moffat's influence, Mzilikazi drank less than had been his custom in previous years, and his health improved. Then traces of the hearty, engaging manner remembered by his closest associates began to reappear, and, whereas in the past it had been customary for him to spend long hours in the seclusion of his hut or wagon, now he resumed friendly chats with his courtiers and discussions about tribal affairs with his councillors.

When the missionaries asked to be allowed to conduct weekly services at Inyati, Mzilikazi not only agreed, but also provided the congregations by decreeing that the inhabitants of the kraal should gather in the royal cattle-fold on the white teachers' day of rest. To address these large gatherings of Matabele was a source of great joy to the missionaries, especially as Mzilikazi was always in attendance.

Seated in his old armchair, in the shade of a tree, the King would listen intently to the opening words of the interpreter translating the preachers' sermons into the vernacular. But soon his concentration would flag and he would grow fidgety. More often than not, his presence hindered the missionaries.

One Sunday morning Thomas Morgan Thomas was approaching the climax of his sermon when Mzilikazi remembered he had not yet drunk his coffee. The King rose from his chair, called for attendants to help him to his hut and vanished from the cattle-fold with the bulk of the congregation following him. On a subsequent occasion Thomas chose as his text the Sixth Commandment. His plea that the Matabele should honour their fathers and mothers brought the service to a dramatic close when Mzilikazi objected, declaring emphatically that as women never waged war they did not deserve to be honoured. In their early efforts to explain the principles of Christianity to the Matabele the missionaries were encouraged by the attentiveness of their listeners. They believed the day would dawn when their mission station would resound to the voices of black converts at worship, but neither their faith nor devotion to their calling induced them to aspire to seeking the redemption of Mzilikazi's soul.

In July Thomas and John Moffat completed their homes, and their families moved in. Apart from this achievement the missionaries also managed to prepare vegetable gardens, to commence a study of the vernacular, to visit the kraals outside Inyati over the weekends, and to attend to their wives, both of whom had recently given birth to sons.

Satisfied that the missionaries were comfortably settled, and that, with Mzilikazi's friendship, their work among the Matabele would thrive Robert Moffat decided to leave for Kuruman. On his last day in the valley he visited the royal kraal and found the King seated among a large group of harem women and councillors. Moffat and Mzilikazi sat chatting for a short while, and although at first the King seemed indifferent to the missionary's departure, he soon grew morose and confessed he knew there was nothing he could do to persuade his white friend to remain at Inyati.

Taking Mzilikazi by the hand, Moffat bade him good-bye, and exchanged with him wishes for good health and good fortune. The old King rose slowly, lifted his leathery face until his eyes met those of Moffat, and embraced with his palms the hand of the white man he had always admired and respected.

Mzilikazi's eyes followed Moffat as the missionary sauntered past the cattle-fold and then disappeared from sight beyond the rings of beehive huts. The Bull Elephant gazed reflectively across Inyati. He was alone, doomed to face, unaided by Moffat, the evil influences that had plagued him in the past and had threatened to drag him into the shadows of death.

CHAPTER 24

REPRISAL FOR WITCHCRAFT

An epidemic decimates Mzilikazi's herds
Intrigue among the indunas *— Destruction of Chief*
Makhobi's people — McKenzie refuses to doctor the
stricken King

THE year wore on. The crops were planted in the spring, and in midsummer the First-Fruits ceremony was celebrated. During this time and especially the first few months of 1861 Boer, British and Griqua traders and hunters streamed northwards, having learnt of the permanent settlement of missionaries in Mzilikazi's kingdom. The traders and hunters pestered Mzilikazi to allow them to enter Matabeleland, but the King refused: he feared that if he acceded to the requests of these strangers other adventurers would be encouraged to visit his domains, and eventually the Matabele tribe would be subjugated by powerful armies. However, he could not resist having two half-breeds from Kuruman escorted into the country. He was keen to exchange some of his elephant tusks for their wares.

These half-breeds spent several months in Matabeleland and returned to the South after concluding a series of lucrative transactions both with Mzilikazi and the missionaries. No sooner had the traders left Matabeleland than it was reported to the King that an epidemic of lung-sickness had broken out among the royal herds. Indeed, day after day messengers arrived at headquarters to tell Mzilikazi that the Matabele cattle were dying in great numbers, and that the mysterious scourge was spreading to cattle-posts throughout the land.

Mzilikazi was distraught. There was nothing he prized more than his cattle. He instructed his witch-doctors to prepare charms

251

and medicines to combat the evil spirits infesting the cattle-folds, while he himself conducted sacrificial ceremonies and called upon the ancestors for help. But the disease continued, claiming three out of every four of Mzilikazi's beasts.

Mzilikazi and his councillors met in the tribal court to discuss the crisis. Some of the King's advisers blamed not only the traders for bringing the epidemic to Matabeleland but also the missionaries, and demanded that the white men be punished. Then it occurred to Mzilikazi and a group of his closest associates that the missionaries' trek-oxen had suffered from the same disease two seasons before, and for this reason the white men had left them at Chief Makhobi's kraal on the border. According to Mzilikazi, this proved the missionaries were considerate people who deserved to be praised rather than condemned.

But as the debate continued, a certain section of the tribal court insisted that the missionaries should never have been allowed to settle in Matabeleland. Opposition mounted towards the white men, and at one stage of the proceedings it seemed their lives would be endangered. Fortunately Mzilikazi's great influence in the tribal court, coupled with his 'great sagacity and prudence', his 'large-heartedness' and 'noble spirit', saved the Inyati mission from disaster.[1] The old King believed resolutely that the missionaries would never seek to harm either him or the Matabele. His faith in the white men was rewarded, for soon after the close of the debate Mzilikazi was visited by Thomas, John Moffat and Sykes, who offered to inoculate all the royal herds in Matabeleland. Mzilikazi was happy to accept their help.

During the next few months the three missionaries struggled to save Mzilikazi's cattle from extinction, but so fierce was the onslaught of the disease that at the Inyati royal kraal and also the neighbouring settlements even the combined efforts of the Matabele, the dogs, the hyenas and the vultures failed to consume all the carcasses of the cattle.

And while this catastrophe tormented his mind, Mzilikazi was confronted by another – the sudden death of uLoziba, his favourite wife, senior Queen of the tribe. Bewildered and stricken with

1. T. M. Thomas, *Eleven Years in Central South Africa*, p. 320.

grief, Mzilikazi deserted the royal seraglio, now haunted by uLoziba's disembodied spirit. He called for his wagon and fled from Inyati. The Bull Elephant never returned to the great kraal of the Buffalo regiment.

The shock of these recent misfortunes drove the King to seek solace in beer. He started drinking more heavily than ever before, and soon the brew took toll of his already decrepit and ailing body. After leaving Inyati, Mzilikazi chose to lead the life of a wanderer. Confined to his wagon, and accompanied by his Buffalo regiment, he travelled hither and thither through the kingdom, remaining for a while at one or other of the kraals or cattle-posts, but always moving on in quest of new faces and new situations.

Towards the end of the year Mzilikazi entered the bush-clad approaches to the Matopos, some twenty miles south-west of Inyati, and reaching a royal kraal named emHlahlandlela he had his wagon brought into the seraglio. This settlement was still in the process of construction; it bore the name of the regiment garrisoning it, and that of the capital Mzilikazi's Bapedi slaves had built in the Magaliesberg in 1826. It was the home of Uku-giwe, new senior Queen of the tribe, and emHlahlandlela became known as the new headquarters of the King.

But Mzilikazi had hardly settled there when he resumed his rovings. So intense was his *Wanderlust* that even the missionaries at Inyati seldom knew his whereabouts.

The *indunas* of the tribal council had always accepted the policy that for security purposes the King should never spend too long a time in any particular kraal; but now they grew apprehensive of Mzilikazi's restlessness and associated it with other mystifying aspects of his recent behaviour. The King was undoubtedly be-witched, the *indunas* argued; what else could account for the change that had come over him in recent years? His swollen, palsied legs, his distended body, his prolonged indisposition – were these not symptoms of a sorcerer's curse? Even Mzilikazi's mind no longer resembled that of the Bull Elephant the *indunas* had known in the past, and who would have believed that in his old age Mzilikazi, the mighty warrior, the conqueror of tribes, the most fearsome ruler south of the Zambezi, would seek the company of harem women in preference to that of men? True, the royal wives comforted the King when he was ill and downcast. They fed him, dosed him with beer and carried him about in his chair. But why had Mzilikazi begun to heed women's advice in tribal matters when it had always been his custom to consult his councillors?

What baffled the *indunas* most was the fact that although the traders from Kuruman had been responsible for infecting the royal herds with the lung-sickness the King had since welcomed other strangers to Matabeleland. He had even allowed parties of white men headed by Jan Viljoen and Edward Chapman to hunt elephants. The *indunas* resolved to expose the sorcerer responsible for robbing the King of his reason and for tormenting his life with misfortune.

In the course of the discussions the *indunas* decided that Monyebe, the King's spokesman and closest confidant, was the person most likely to have planned Mzilikazi's decline. Monyebe, they recalled, was the man who in 1859 had warned Mzilikazi and his councillors that the white teachers should not be allowed to settle in Matabeleland for fear they might prepare the way for the white man's armies. Monyebe had been instrumental in prejudicing Mzilikazi against the missionaries, and even against Robert Moffat. And then, for some strange reason, this *induna* had suddenly changed his opinion and had pleaded with the King to fetch the stranded white men from the banks of the Bembesi and settle them in the valley below Inyati.

Indeed, of all the Matabele dignitaries Monyebe had eventually proved the most helpful to the missionaries, and Thomas described him as 'a noble fellow – a superior man, engaging and very social in his manners – far in advance of his fellow-countrymen in politeness and general demeanour'.[1] When, after uLoziba's death, Mzilikazi had left Inyati and the once flourishing royal kraal had become deserted, the missionaries were deprived of their congregations. Had it not been for Monyebe, who encouraged the missionaries to preach to the inhabitants of his kraal, the white men's

1. ibid., p. 251.

labours would not have extended beyond their own domestic servants. Thomas, Moffat and Sykes believed this enlightened *induna* would be among the first converts in Matabeleland.

Some of Mzilikazi's *indunas* disapproved of Monyebe, firstly because they were suspicious of his association with the missionaries, and secondly because they felt he was able to exercise too great an influence over the old King. The majority, however, were far more concerned about the many privileges Monyebe was enjoying, privileges which they themselves were denied. For, in the role of Mzilikazi's spokesman, Monyebe was in constant contact with visiting traders and hunters, who, in order to gain his favour, lavished on him gifts of horses, saddles, clothing and even firearms. No matter what personal reasons they had for disliking Monyebe, the *indunas* agreed unanimously to destroy him.

As a first step in their plot the *indunas* discreetly spread a rumour that Monyebe was practising witchcraft to oust Mzilikazi from the throne. Then, on an appointed day, they called on the King. They found him befuddled and indifferent to what they had to say. In vain they tried to explain that Monyebe was not to be trusted. They warned the King repeatedly that this dignitary was aspiring to the kingship of the tribe. Eventually the *indunas* left Mzilikazi, having accomplished nothing.

In due course they paid a second visit to the King, and reported they had evidence to prove Monyebe had been cohabiting with the harem women. The conspirators were amazed when Mzilikazi barely commented on the accusation, for in days gone by he would have reacted by ordering the immediate arrest, trial and skewering of the culprit. They returned to their kraals, sullen and not a little disconcerted.

It was then that Mzilikazi was involved in a mishap which led to Monyebe's doom. He was fiddling with a revolver given him by a hunter or trader when it exploded and wounded him in the hand. The *indunas* hurried to his side and blamed Monyebe for the injury, saying they had proof that Monyebe had recently caught a crocodile in the Bembesi river, had taken out its liver and prepared evil medicines to destroy the King. The Bull Elephant had been saved by the ancestral spirits, continued the *indunas*, but unless he ordered the immediate execution of Monyebe there would soon be another attempt on his life.

In his weak state of health and the helplessness of old age the King was compelled to sanction the step, in accordance with the law of the land. Next morning Monyebe, his wives, children and relatives were wiped out, their bodies flung to the hyenas and vultures, their huts fired and their belongings divided among Mzilikazi and the conspirators.

That Monyebe had conspired against the King caused consternation throughout Matabeleland, and perhaps the only people who failed to praise the *indunas* for the part they played in exposing the sorcerer were the missionaries. But neither Monyebe nor any other Matabele dignitary or commoner had ever contemplated assassinating the King. When one considers the tribal history of Southern Africa, and especially the conspiracies resulting in the downfall of famous potentates, chiefs and military leaders, one cannot but wonder how a tyrant like Mzilikazi succeeded in reaching old age unscathed by an assassin's assegai blade.

It is a tribute to Mzilikazi's greatness that in his seventy-second year he still enjoyed the devotion and respect of his subjects, and continued to command absolute authority despite both his mental and physical shortcomings. True, there were men who took advantage of him in his dotage to intrigue against fellow-tribesmen, but no one ever dared plot against the monarch of the Matabele tribe.

The year 1862 will be remembered as the time when famine threatened Matabeleland and when the economic stability of the tribe was in jeopardy. The Matabele were still bewailing the loss of their cattle, due to the lung-sickness, when another tragedy, even more serious, befell them. Drought wiped out their crops, and the harvests stored after the previous season were almost consumed.

The plight of the missionaries was even worse than that of the tribesmen. Since the departure of Mzilikazi from Inyati they had found nourishing food impossible to come by, for the few Mata-

bele who were occasionally to be found in the neighbourhood refused to barter with white men, lest they evoke the King's wrath
and bring disaster on their families. The missionaries' milch-cows
died during the lung-sickness, their vegetable patches shrivelled
up and their crops yielded not a grain of wheat or corn. Malnutri-
tion reduced them to listless, ailing individuals. Emily Moffat was
turning blind and had to be taken by her husband to the South,
while Mrs Thomas and her newly born baby contracted fever and
died.

As a result of the food shortage in Matabeleland Mzilikazi's
military leaders mobilized all available regiments, and prepared
them for a series of marauding expeditions into the territories of
neighbouring tribes. Mzilikazi approved of the scheme, and during the autumn three armies set out in different directions; the
first to Mashonaland, the second to the regions about Lake Ngami
and the third to Northern Bechuanaland, the country of Chief
Seghoma's Bamangwato.

The Mashona campaign proved particularly successful, for not
only did the army return with a valuable haul of grain and cattle,
but it also brought back an important Mashona chief who for
many years had evaded capture. When the royal prisoner was
handed over to Mzilikazi the warriors expected him to be sentenced to death. To their amazement the chief was treated kindly
by the old King and was allowed to return to Mashonaland on the
understanding that in future he would pay regular tribute to the
Matabele. While the warriors were marvelling at how lenient
Mzilikazi had become in his old age, the regiments of the second
expedition returned to report they had lost their way and had
therefore decided to abandon the search for Lake Ngami. Instead
of punishing the leaders for gross inefficiency, as indeed he would
have done in the past, Mzilikazi chose to ignore them. It was
whispered among the courtiers and fighting-men that the King's
authority was waning. But then, during the third army's invasion
of Bamangwato country, an incident occurred which convinced
the tribe that, although old and broken in health, Mzilikazi was
as fearsome a despot as ever he had been.

It has already been mentioned that the southern borders of

Matabeleland were guarded by a vassal chief named Makhobi. Traders, hunters, missionaries and black envoys wishing to visit Mzilikazi were obliged to report to Makhobi and explain the nature of their business in Matabeleland. It was the Chief's prerogative either to turn the strangers back or to detain them on the border until permission had been received from the King to escort them to headquarters. Robert Moffat and his fellow missionaries spoke well of Makhobi and regarded him as one of the most intelligent of Mzilikazi's senior officials.

When the third army reached the southern border, bound for Bechuanaland, it halted at Makhobi's kraal. The regimental captains visited the Chief and informed him that Mzilikazi had commanded that Makhobi assemble his warriors and join the expedition. Makhobi refused, explaining that he dared not leave the border unguarded. He added that he was only a vassal chief, one who had pledged allegiance to Mzilikazi, but he was also a kinsman of Seghoma, Chief of the Bamangwato, and it behoved him to remain neutral in the impending struggle. The Matabele captains swaggered out of Makhobi's kraal, fell in with their regiments and proceeded southwards towards Bechuanaland.

The Matabele army swooped down on the Bamangwato cattle-posts and villages, wiped out the inhabitants, rounded up the herds, emptied the granaries and struck on towards Shoshong, where they engaged a regiment consisting of the cavalrymen and musketeers of the tribe and drove it into the hills. Within the next few days the invading army accomplished its mission and was marched triumphantly back towards Matabeleland.

Before returning to Makhobi's kraal the commander-in-chief of the army sent word to Mzilikazi that the vassal chief had refused to fight against the Bamangwato. Messengers returned saying that the King was angry and demanded the death of the disloyal keeper of the southern borders. The army leaders acted swiftly. They invited Makhobi to meet them in a valley outside the village, informing him at the same time that Mzilikazi wanted a section of the looted Bamangwato herds to be left in his care. Later in the day, when Chief Makhobi and his men arrived to fetch the looted cattle the Matabele fell upon them and killed them.

The regiments advanced on Makhobi's kraal, sacked it, and butchered the inhabitants. Fired with a lust for killing, the warriors careered into the veld and set about destroying the settlements of Makhobi's subjects. They massacred the men and youths, captured some of the women, and drove the rest, together with their children, into thé lion-infested hills. The army remustered at Makhobi's kraal and set out for headquarters.

The campaigns of 1862 saved the Matabele tribe from the hazards of famine, and the slaughter of Chief Makhobi and his followers served to remind both the Matabele and their tributaries of the doom awaiting anyone who dared disobey the commands of the King.

In 1863 prosperity returned to Matabeleland. The rains fell frequently throughout the summer and the harvests were plentiful; the regiments undertook raids into Makalanga and Mashona country and returned with large herds of tribute cattle.

In the previous year John and Emily Moffat had left Inyati by ox-wagon, and had travelled through Bechuanaland to Kuruman. They continued through the Orange Free State into Natal, and by the beginning of the new year had returned to their parents' mission station. Emily, whose failing health once had caused her husband great concern, benefited considerably by this long trek, and was growing impatient to return to her home at Inyati. At the end of April Emily and John, with Livingstone, their baby son, took leave of Robert and Mrs Moffat and commenced the arduous journey back to Matabeleland.

En route the Moffats tried unsuccessfully to buy grain from the tribes of Bechuanaland. Therefore, on reaching the Marico district, they visited Jan Viljoen, Pieter Jacobs, Louw Pretorius and Dantjie Botha, four prosperous farmers living in the country once occupied by Mzilikazi's tribe. Receiving a load and a half of grain, ground for them at Jan Viljoen's water-mill, the Moffats returned to the Missionaries' Road and continued the journey into Northern Bechuanaland.

At Shoshong John and Emily met the Rev. John McKenzie, a colleague who, during the Matabele attack on the Bamangwato, had fled from his mission station and had hidden in a cave in the near-by hills. So difficult had mission work among the Bamangwato become that McKenzie decided to accompany the Moffats to Matabeleland and settle at Inyati. He was soon to realize that decisions such as this could only be taken with Mzilikazi's consent.

The missionaries trekked northwards and on the Matabele border discovered the charred ruins of Makhobi's kraal. When, only a year before, the Moffats had passed this way they had found the Chief and about a thousand of his subjects living peacefully along the border. John and Emily were shocked at the devastation they encountered everywhere. They feared for the lives of the fugitives still living in the neighbouring hills.

The missionaries departed from the ruins. They had barely entered Makalanga country when their wagons were intercepted by two Matabele warriors, sent from headquarters to report that Mzilikazi wanted no additional teachers among his people and refused to allow McKenzie into Matabeleland. For several days the missionaries were delayed in the bush while the two warriors returned to Mzilikazi to assure him that McKenzie merely wished to visit the white teachers of Inyati. On learning that McKenzie was prepared to leave the country after one full cycle of the moon, the King gave permission for the missionaries to proceed and ordered the white stranger to report at headquarters.

McKenzie's introduction to Mzilikazi took place in a modest kraal situated at the base of a hill. The white man was taken to a sheep-pen where, in the company of warriors, royal women and a little captive-boy, the King sat enjoying the warmth of a fire. When McKenzie shook Mzilikazi's hand the warriors bellowed 'Great King ! Man-eater !'[1] in accord. McKenzie seated himself on the ground and peered into Mzilikazi's face, searching in vain for signs betraying the tyrannous career the despot had followed. Mzilikazi's life was ebbing swiftly, thought McKenzie, for the King was so frail he could neither walk a single step nor even stand. Furthermore, '... his arms moved with difficulty, and in a

1. John McKenzie, *Ten Years North of the Orange River*, p. 304.

spasmodic manner; his head was grey, and his face bore the wrinkles of old age'.[1]

From this small kraal McKenzie and the Moffats set out for Inyati. During the next three months McKenzie enjoyed the beauty and the quietude of the mission station, but concluded that if he remained permanently among the Matabele he would establish a place of his own.

Learning in December that Mzilikazi had moved to emHlahlandlela, McKenzie, accompanied by Sykes and John Moffat, set out for the capital. The great royal kraal swarmed with warriors being prepared by the witch-doctors for raids into neighbouring territories. While the missionaries were being conducted to Mzilikazi they were approached by a courtier who warned them that as the King was unable to lift his arms they must not attempt to shake hands with him.

The white men found the Bull Elephant lying back languidly in his chair. Mzilikazi looked haggard, bland, helpless. He greeted his visitors with the remotest flicker of a smile. An attendant lifted a beer-pot to the King's lips. He drank long and thirstily.

Then, his voice feeble and shaky, Mzilikazi addressed McKenzie. He had no objection to McKenzie's remaining for ever among the Matabele, and if the missionary wished to found a new mission station a suitable site would be selected for him. But, continued the King, the white teachers must not attempt to teach the Matabele to read or write. They must be careful not to turn his people into traitors.

After a week spent at the royal kraal the missionaries returned to Inyati. McKenzie lost interest in Matabeleland, realizing that while Mzilikazi dictated the course mission work should take in the country there could be no scope for converting the Matabele to Christianity. McKenzie longed to be back at Shoshong, where in the past he had been free to pursue his teaching, free of interference from the ruler of the tribe.

In January 1864 the missionary saddled his horse and rode to emHlahlandlela to thank Mzilikazi for offering him a site for a

1. ibid

261

mission station, and also to tell the King of his decision to return to the Bamangwato.

Mzilikazi was not in the slightest concerned about McKenzie's desire to leave Matabeleland, mainly because he was too ill. Discreetly dismissing the subject, the King begged for medicines to relieve his pain. McKenzie refused. He said he had brought no medicines, but was sure that, if asked, the Inyati missionaries would assist Mzilikazi as they had done in the past. And as Mzilikazi continued to plead, McKenzie reflected that in any case he dared not risk attending to the King. Mzilikazi's malady was beyond cure; and if by chance his condition deteriorated the *indunas* of the tribe might conclude that the King had been poisoned or even bewitched by the white teachers.

McKenzie declared he was 'heartily sorry for the stricken King, but insisted he had no medicines which would make him better'.

'Would you tell that to your own father, if he were in my position today?'[1] implored Mzilikazi.

The missionary evaded the question. He left emHlahlandlela, never to see the Bull Elephant again.

1. ibid., p. 348.

CHAPTER 25

GOLD

Henry Hartley discovers gold in Mashonaland
Mzilikazi plagued by hallucinations
A witch–doctor predicts disaster for Matabeleland

AT the beginning of the reaping season a procession of traders
and hunters approached the Matabele border from the South.
They were admitted into Matabeleland, except a few whom Mzilikazi and his councillors did not trust. The King derived great
pleasure from the visits of the white men, for he took advantage
of his position to pester them for presents. Invariably on reaching
Mzilikazi's kraal the traders and hunters were compelled to wait
for days before the King condescended to see them. Mzilikazi
delighted in keeping his white visitors in suspense, continually
sending messengers to inform them that he was still making up
his mind whether he should allow them to trade and hunt, and
reminding them that his decisions would be greatly influenced by
the number of presents he received. Although in 1864 Mzilikazi
ceased to regard the white strangers as spies, he was careful to
keep them out of his raiding-grounds in Mashonaland, lest they
supply his vassals with fire-arms.

Mzilikazi's favourite traders and hunters were John Lee, George
Westbeech, George Phillips and Jan Viljoen. These men enjoyed
great privileges in Matabeleland. Each had travelled extensively
among the tribes of Southern Africa, each had mastered at least
one of the vernacular languages and each had acquired a sound
knowledge of tribal etiquette. It was undoubtedly these attributes,
coupled with a knack of providing Mzilikazi with the gifts he
cherished most, that acquired for these white men the Open
Sesame to all sections of Matabele territory except Mashonaland.

But during 1865 even greater numbers of adventurers gained access to Matabeleland, and within a short while Mzilikazi's hunting-grounds were divided into sections to prevent congestion among the rival parties. Jan Viljoen arrived with a group of hunters and pleaded with the King to allow him to cross into Mashonaland. After prolonged discussion Mzilikazi agreed, and the Boer set out with his two sons, Org and Tienie, accompanied by Pieter Jacobs the famous lion-hunter from the Marico district.

Barely had Viljoen's hunting-party left when another, led by Henry Hartley, arrived at headquarters. Swarthy, thick-set and club-footed, Hartley was a man of fifty. During the past thirty years he had traversed the entire territory of South Africa and had acquainted himself with the customs of most of the indigenous peoples, including those inhabiting the remotest parts of the Kalahari desert and also the forest regions of the Zambezi. Mzilikazi liked Hartley, especially as the hunter was prepared to pay handsomely for privileges. The King did not hesitate to grant him permission to hunt in Mashonaland, but nevertheless appointed an *induna* to accompany the wagons, fearing that Hartley and his party might be tempted to sell guns to the subjugated tribes.

The members of Jan Viljoen's party shot about two hundred elephants in Mashonaland and collected five tons of ivory. During this trip they sold five guns to one of Mzilikazi's vassal chiefs. When this transaction was reported to the King he was furious and sent a regiment to destroy the tribe concerned. Mzilikazi regretted he had ever allowed the Boers into Mashonaland, and was determined never to trust Jan Viljoen again.

Hartley and his companions travelled as far north as the Umfuli river, to the regions that Fernando, the Portuguese explorer, had visited three and a half centuries before. Hartley discovered that many parts of the countryside were scarred by pits, shafts, shallow trenches and rock dumps. He inspected some of these strange excavations and concluded they were abandoned mines. He was intrigued when, on speaking to local tribesmen, he learned that in centuries past both Arab and Portuguese traders had frequented the country in quest for gold. Hartley continued hunting, and, when the winter drew to a close and his wagons were heavily laden with tusks, he returned to Matabeleland, took his leave of Mzilikazi, and then set out for the Transvaal. In every way this had been a successful trip and he was more than satisfied. His happiest thought was that Mzilikazi had agreed to his returning to Mashonaland for the coming hunting-season.

And while Hartley was travelling southwards with his large haul of ivory he chanced to meet a young German named Karl Mauch, who had but recently arrived in the country, eager to explore the interior. Learning that Mauch was a student of geology and mineralogy, the hunter told him about the abandoned workings in Mashonaland and invited him to join the next hunting-expedition to the north. Mauch gladly accepted Hartley's offer.

Incredible as it may seem, Mzilikazi's health at the end of 1865 was much the same as it had been four years earlier. Indeed, the old King's iron constitution was holding out, despite his incessant drinking and the fact that he was never free of pain. In the autumn of 1866, when the white men again started streaming into Matabeleland for the new hunting-season, one of them described Mzilikazi as 'a frail, palsied old man, in his second childhood, unable to move a yard';[1] but he also mentioned that Mzilikazi enjoyed the company of the white strangers and delighted in calling them to his side and depriving them of handkerchiefs and other knick-knacks that chanced to catch his eye.

In June 1866 scores of hunters and traders, among them Henry Hartley and Karl Mauch, found Mzilikazi living in a dilapidated kraal, one of the many places the King chose to visit in the course of his wanderings. Usually when they interviewed Mzilikazi he was confined to an armchair given him by Robert Moffat, a soiled blanket and a leopard-skin kaross wrapped about his body and a Balmoral cap perched on his head. Sometimes the harem women carried the King to the entrance of one of the huts, and sometimes to the goat-pen where the royal medicine-men treated his

1. J. P. R. Wallis (ed.), *Southern African Diaries of Thomas Leask*, p. 64.

illness. Here, as Mzilikazi rested in his chair, a pot of boiling medicines was placed between his feet, and several blankets were draped over his body and head. The King endured the steam until it almost suffocated him. Then, struggling with the blankets, he would free his head and gasp for breath, burst into fits of coughing and sneezing and sink back into his chair to listen to the voices of his doting courtiers as they echoed: 'King! Big King! Above all men! Black Bull! Khumalo!'[1] And always royal women were at his side administering the one opiate he craved above all others – beer.

Towards the end of July, some weeks after Hartley and Mauch had moved off to hunt and prospect among the disused mines in Mashonaland, chaos almost descended upon Mzilikazi's temporary kraal.

The King's illness took a sudden turn for the worse and his mind became prey to the most fearsome imaginings. Befuddled, Mzilikazi saw visions of enemies approaching Matabeleland, hordes of fighting-men marching to destroy the tribe and to steal its cattle. He raged over the inadequacy of the Matabele defences. He called his *indunas* together and commanded them to send messengers to summon the regiments to headquarters. He insisted there was no time to be lost, for clearly he could see the Zulu, his oldest foe, approaching Matabeleland.

Meanwhile one of the *indunas* had hastened to Inyati to tell Thomas that Mzilikazi was desperately ill. The missionary inspanned a wagon and, travelling southwards, he noticed the kraals he passed were deserted of tribesmen, who were already answering the King's call to arms.

Thomas arrived at Mzilikazi's settlement after sunset. Thousands of frenzied warriors were dancing and singing in the vicinity of the huts; a group of men was spearing oxen; another group was skinning and dismembering beasts already slaughtered, while a third was to be seen seated beside a chain of fires, roasting beef in the embers. Long lines of women streamed in from outlying kraals carrying pots of beer for the regiments. During the entire

1. ibid., p. 101.

night the countryside resounded to a tumultuous confusion of voices, and Thomas could not sleep a wink.

When dawn broke Thomas strode towards Mzilikazi's quarters. He passed long, makeshift shelters erected for the warriors, and row upon row of crudely constructed homes resembling haycocks. He found Mzilikazi reclining in a wagon; he greeted the old King and tried to engage him in conversation. But Mzilikazi was in no mood for talking. During the entire day he lay in his wagon in a half-stupor and refused to utter a word.

Early next morning Thomas was summoned by Mzilikazi. He was sick and wanted medicines. On two occasions during the day the missionary dosed the King with the mixtures, but still Mzilikazi refused to talk.

On the third day, after Mzilikazi had gulped down more of Thomas's medicine, he turned to the missionary to announce that he had decided to leave Matabeleland and trek to Lake Ngami. At that moment a bevy of royal wives appeared, but before they could approach the King ordered them to return to their huts and prepare for the journey to the west. Some of the *indunas* sauntered towards the wagon. They halted as, with menacing voice, Mzilikazi commanded them to arrange for all the cattle of the tribe to be collected and for all the people to be advised that soon they would be moving to Lake Ngami. The *indunas* turned about and left the kraal.

Next moment Mzilikazi was shouting for his wives to carry him to another of his wagons, the one which was to take him to the Lake; the bewildered *indunas* were calling the members of the tribal court together; and the regiments, headed by their commanders, were pouring into a near-by cattle kraal.

A hush fell over the settlement when the assembly was called to order. A group of dignitaries, pensive and obviously afraid, stood beside the royal wagon. The Matabele waited for their King to speak.

Mzilikazi gazed at the multitude before him. As loudly as he could he addressed his people. He told them the Zulu armies were surging into Matabeleland, and he, Mzilikazi, knew his own forces could not match their might. Shaka, personally, was in command of the invaders, therefore the Matabele must collect their families, their possessions, and their animals and prepare to follow their King to a new land, to Lake Ngami, before it was too late.

The Matabele throng glared at Mzilikazi interrogatively. The old ringheads of the tribe shook their heads in dismay. What talk was this of Shaka? What evil influences possessed the Bull Elephant causing him to believe that the Zulu tyrant, now forty years dead, had risen from the grave?

Thomas stepped forward to remonstrate with Mzilikazi, fearing that unless he could dispel these hallucinations from the old man's mind, the Matabele would soon be subjected to untold hardship and suffering.

Thomas assured the King that it was unlikely the Zulu would invade Matabeleland. Discreetly the missionary avoided mentioning that Shaka had been assassinated when Mzilikazi was a young man. The Matabele must not flee, at least not until scouts had been dispatched to ascertain whether in actual fact the enemy was on the advance. Matabeleland was a beautiful fertile country, continued Thomas, one in which both cattle and men thrived. It would therefore be a shame to abandon it for the waterless Kalahari desert and regions infested by hostile tribes.

Thomas's words penetrated the mist of Mzilikazi's thoughts. The King agreed that the journey to the Lake would be far too perilous for the Matabele to undertake, but suggested that instead they should move to the Zambezi.

At that moment the *indunas* took charge of the situation. Striding to and fro before the regiments, they took turns in relating episodes out of the life of their monarch. They referred to the days when, in the thick of battle, Mzilikazi was the bravest warrior in the regiments; they recalled that when eventually he moulded the Matabele into a powerful tribe he became the most feared of all black conquerors. They extolled Mzilikazi for the part he had played in delivering his people from the many hazards that had confronted them. They reminded the assembly that, had it not been for the great Bull Elephant, the Matabele might never have survived to enjoy the prosperity their country now afforded them. Mzilikazi would always be honoured, always be obeyed, and always protected, and it was the duty of every man to see that the King was always happy.

The crowd roared in approval and hailed Mzilikazi with all his praise-names. A group of wizened old warriors, dressed in full battle attire, paraded between the wagon and the cattle-fold. In a series of slow, deliberate movements they demonstrated how, in the old days, they had fought the Zulu, the Boers, and the other enemies of the Matabele. Steeped in reverie, Mzilikazi watched them. Tears welled up in his eyes. Mzilikazi was weeping.

Some of the old *indunas* and warriors, seeing the King's distress, were so moved that they too broke into tears. A greybeard, sobbing bitterly, ventured to Mzilikazi's side. He begged the Bull Elephant not to lead the Matabele away from their homeland. Instead, Mzilikazi must muster the army to repulse the foe. The old *induna* implored his King not to be afraid, saying if by chance the Matabele were defeated by the invaders, they would never allow their father, the great Mzilikazi, to come to harm.

These were comforting words, for immediately Mzilikazi agreed to cancel the trek to the west. The *indunas* dried their tears and praised him; the regiments stamped their feet on the dung floor of the cattle-fold, beat their shields with their assegai shafts and broke into song.

For a while Mzilikazi enjoyed peace of mind. Scouts were sent out to scan the southern reaches of the country for signs of the Zulu army, and finding no trace of invaders, returned to report the good news to their King. Mzilikazi was carried to the goat-kraal, where he watched one of his senior *indunas* spear twelve beasts to death and sacrifice the carcasses to the ancestors. The *indunas* called on the spirits to deliver the Matabele from misfortune, and implored the ancestors always to provide the tribe with rain, with rich harvests, with healthy herds and with power to overcome any enemy seeking to destroy it.

After a half-hour of prayers the *induna* stood in obeisance before Mzilikazi and reported that the spirits were grateful for the sacrifices and prayers offered, and that all would be well in Matabeleland.

Then Mzilikazi was brought to his hut, where three of his

indunas waited to tell him of their visit to a witch-doctor captured during one of the Matabele raids. This wise man had cast his bones, said the *indunas*, and had seen by their positions that enemies would be entering Matabeleland from the South. But, reassured by the reports that there was no Zulu army in the country, and that the ancestral spirits had promised to protect the Matabele from adversity, Mzilikazi and his advisers paid little attention to the witch-doctor's predictions.

Little did they know that, in the years to come, the Matabele would indeed be conquered by white men from the South and that the two people fated to pave the way for this disaster were at the moment hunting elephant and prospecting for gold in Mashonaland.

CHAPTER 26

THE FALLING OF A MOUNTAIN

Gold fever – Rival claims to goldfields
Mzilikazi's death and entombment

MEANWHILE, Henry Hartley had taken Karl Mauch into Mashonaland, to the abandoned workings discovered in the previous year. The hunter persuaded a Mashona tribesman to act as guide to conduct the German to the old mines situated between the Sebakwe and Bembesi rivers. Hartley dared not openly assist Mauch in searching for the gold reefs, for included in the party was a man named Nyoka – the Snake – an *induna* assigned by Mzilikazi to the task of both keeping a constant check on the white men's movements and reporting anything suspicious to headquarters. And while Karl Mauch busied himself with crawling in and out of excavations and with examining rock-faces and fragments of stone, the *induna* became inquisitive and repeatedly asked the prospector what business he had with mines when, in fact, he had only sought permission from Mzilikazi to hunt elephants.

Fortunately the Snake eventually took Mauch for a simpleton, and paid less attention to his movements. In due course the prospector came upon gold-bearing seams of quartz in outcrops of diorite and granite, and he forecast that soon parts of Mzilikazi's domain would be resounding to the clanking of diggers' spades and picks. When the hunting-season ended and Mauch and Hartley returned to the South, the German was satisfied with the results of his labour. He resolved to return to Mashonaland in the following year and continue his investigations.

Mzilikazi was not suspicious of Mauch's activities in Mashonaland. The Matabele dignitaries were far too concerned about the King's failing health and far too preoccupied in tribal affairs to attach importance to the tales they heard of the German's unusual pursuits. The young regiments were engaged in cattle-raids; the older warriors grumbled about the King's senility, which they claimed deprived them of donning the headring and settling down to married life. Mzilikazi's closest associates were finding him increasingly unapproachable, and they became reconciled to the fact that soon the old King would die and a successor to the throne would then be selected from among his sons. Indeed, no one gave undue thought to Mauch, not even the white traders and hunters who, although amused by the foreigner's devotion to the study of natural phenomena, could not but regard him as unbalanced of mind and incapable of taking part in the manly sport of hunting.

In March 1867 Hartley and Mauch returned to Matabeleland and received Mzilikazi's blessing to proceed to any part of the country. Instead of travelling directly to Mashonaland the white men decided to hunt in the regions about the Tati river, in the borderland separating the Bechuana and Matabele tribes. Gradually the hunting-party moved northwards, reaching the Umfuli river and the old mining sites examined the previous year.

Mauch followed a chain of excavations among the outcrops and in July, on a tributary of the Umfuli, he struck an auriferous reef which he proceeded to trace for about twenty-two miles. Greatly encouraged, Mauch and Hartley returned to the Tati area. In this borderland the German came upon a gold-bearing reef eighty miles long and two miles broad. He was jubilant. Karl Mauch hurried to Pretoria, capital of the South African Republic, to announce his discovery.

Towards the end of the year a letter written by Mauch appeared in the *Transvaal Argus*. He described in extravagant language the beauty of the Tati and the potential of the Mashonaland goldfields. He claimed that the reefs were so vast that they presented ample scope for thousands of mines. This letter aroused the interest of the political leaders of the Republic, but it failed to impress the rank and file, who were essentially farmers.

Mauch then trekked to Natal, where his pioneering achievements were warmly acclaimed by the newspapers. The citizens of this British colony were instantly smitten with gold fever, and adventurous men dreamt of the fortunes awaiting them beyond the Limpopo. And there was to be even greater excitement when eventually the assay results of Mauch's samples were described as excellent.

Mauch arrived in Cape Town, where he was fêted by the Lieutenant-Governor of the Colony, and other senior British officials. In the meantime *The Times* and other London newspapers were giving prominence to the Tati goldfields, and a pamphlet was published for the specific purpose of encouraging miners to migrate to South Africa and travel to Mzilikazi's country by way of Natal.[1] It quoted Mauch as saying that the Tati area would yield more gold than either California or Australia. The people of South Africa and England were dazzled by the reports, especially from acknowledged authorities, suggesting that Mauch had discovered King Solomon's mines of Ophir. Mining syndicates were formed, and in Australia and California diggers were booking their passages for South Africa.

Mzilikazi and his councillors learned of Mauch's discoveries and the pending goldrush from the traders, hunters and missionaries. They were thunderstruck. In the kraals and cattle-folds, at the open hearths and in the cornfields, there was talk of white men, accompanied by soldiers, criminals and lawless desperadoes, marching from the South to the goldfields. The daily sitting of the tribal court turned into turbulent demonstrations against Hartley and Mauch's treachery and indignant *indunas* demanded that the hunter and his friend be arrested and brought to trial.

The Matabele seized the Tati district. Their right to ownership was challenged by the Bamangwato, who insisted that from time immemorial they had herded their cattle in those parts, and that therefore the borderland belonged to them. Tension mounted between the two tribes. The Bamangwato appealed to the Cape Governor for help, and offered to place their country, together with the Tati area, under a British Protectorate. Nothing came of

1. Richard Babbs, *The Goldfields of South Africa, and the Way to Reach Them.*

this scheme and, realizing that alone they could never hope to wrest the goldfields from the grip of the Matabele army, the Bamangwato withdrew their claim.

In the early months of 1868 a Boer delegation headed by Jan Viljoen, the elephant hunter, arrived in Matabeleland. Viljoen interviewed Mzilikazi and told him he had been sent by the Government of the Transvaal Republic to buy the Tati district from the Matabele. Viljoen warned the King there would soon be a rush of diggers to the goldfields and explained that if the Republic bought the area, and settled some of its Boers there, it would prohibit the influx of strangers into Matabele territory. The thought of having the Boers or any other white men share even a small portion of his country horrified the King. Mzilikazi dismissed Viljoen and summoned the *indunas* to a sitting of the council.

Several days later the Boer hunter received Mzilikazi's reply. The King would neither sell any part of his dominions nor would he grant permission for any other nation to settle within his borders. Mzilikazi was convinced that two kings would never rule the same country, and that if black and white men were brought into close contact with one another they would never live in peace.

The Boer delegation departed, and ten days later there was an uproar at emHlahlandlela when the wagons of Henry Hartley hove into sight. Ten thousand angry warriors surrounded the hunter's party and threatened to exterminate it. Hartley, who until recently had been one of Mzilikazi's favourites, could not understand why the Matabele should have grown hostile towards him. He asked to be conducted to Mzilikazi, but the crowd of gesticulating warriors refused to allow him to move. The officers accused Hartley of betraying the Matabele, and told him a white man had informed them that hundreds of gold-diggers were surging northwards to conquer the tribe, and that he, Hartley, was plotting to murder the King. Hartley was arrested. The warriors awaited Mzilikazi's command to execute him.

Hartley awaited his doom with fortitude. During the course of the day he and his companions were startled by the tumultuous roar of the warriors heralding the sudden appearance of Mzilikazi in their midst. The old King, his body worn and distorted by age and suffering, his face drawn, his eyes feeble and watery, was carried in his armchair to the wagons. Mzilikazi looked glassily at the hunter. He was happy to see Hartley again, and wanted no harm to befall him. Mzilikazi instructed an *induna* to send the warriors back to their barracks. He called Hartley to his side, exchanged a few words of greeting with him, and bade him go about his business of hunting in Matabeleland.

In June Mzilikazi was living at Ingama, a small kraal situated a few miles south-west of the capital. His days of wandering were over. He had grown so weak that he was permanently confined to his hut. The missionary Sykes, learning that the King was bedridden, travelled from Inyati to see him. This was 'a sad and painful visit', wrote Sykes in a letter to the director of his Society, 'I shall never forget how he looked at me ... and how affectingly he said to me with a feeble, stammering voice, "I am very ill." I endeavoured to comfort him, but the only words which seemed to create any interest in his mind were in a message from Mr Moffat, senior, that he was praying for him and his people ... The moment I spoke of Moffat his countenance beamed with interest, but he said nothing ... It was manifest that he himself supposed, as well as others, that one foot was already beginning to glide towards the grave.'[1]

Old uMncumbata, chief *induna* of the tribe and Mzilikazi's lifelong friend, was brought to the capital to act as regent. His appointment signified the approaching death of the King. The Matabele conducted sacrifices, and offered prayers to the ancestors, imploring them to spare Mzilikazi's life. But apparently the spirits were offended, for they neither assisted the royal medicine-men to resuscitate the King nor breathed a word of another tragedy, far greater than the death of Mzilikazi, due to befall the tribe.

For had the spirits possessed the power to talk to the people they would have warned the Matabele that their country would soon be overrun by white diggers, that the Tati district and Mashonaland would quake beneath the rumble of stamping and

1. J. P. R. Wallis (ed.), *Matabele Mission of J. S. and E. Moffat*, p. 246.

crushing machines, that Mzilikazi's kingdom would eventually be invaded by British troops, that the Matabele warriors would be mown down by rifle and machine-gun fire and that the tribe would become the servants of colonists who would build their towns and lay out their farms where once Mzilikazi's kraals had stood.

During the months of July and August Mzilikazi lay struggling with death. Thomas was brought from Inyati to the Ingama kraal and was asked to administer medicines to save the King. 'I therefore remained with him for fifteen days,' wrote Thomas in his memoirs, 'doing all in my power to restore his strength, to arrest the progress of the disease, and feeding him with the best in our wagon.'[1]

But Thomas's efforts proved to no avail. The King was sinking fast. Day after day, in the gloom of a hut, a few of Mzilikazi's senior queens, principal *indunas* and kinsmen of the original Khumalo clan sat watching in silence over the Bull Elephant. On the afternoon of 5 September the small group saw that the King was close to death. The men who had known Mzilikazi since childhood and had served him loyally in all his conquests were so overcome with grief that they crawled out of the hut and stood sobbing outside. About half an hour later Mzilikazi breathed his last. A tremulous wail rose from the hut as the queens announced his death. The people of the Ingama kraal wept hysterically. The *indunas* returned to the hut and formed a circle about Mzilikazi's corpse. A great mountain had fallen, the loftiest mountain in all Matabeleland.

When night fell the *indunas* wrapped the royal corpse in a pile of blankets and skins three feet high, lifted it on to a wagon, and in the cover of darkness took it to emHlahlandlela, where they placed it in one of the principal huts. Then the inhabitants of the capital mourned the passing of their patriarch and, in addition to the many taboos they would be compelled to observe, they undertook to keep Mzilikazi's death a closely guarded secret until the *indunas* decided to announce the burial day.

1. T. M. Thomas, *Eleven Years in Central South Africa*, p. 284.

Twelve of the royal widows took turns at watching over the body, and a group of *indunas* slept at the door of the hut lest wizards or hyenas attempted to enter it. By day and by night the women kept a solemn vigil beside the bulky pile of skins. They plugged their nostrils with sweet-smelling leaves in an effort to overcome the stifling stench that eventually filled the hut.

On the seventh day many of the queens and princes collected their belongings and fled, for they had often been told that in Zululand, Mzilikazi's birthplace, a mass slaughter of relatives by ambitious aspirants to the throne invariably followed the death of a king. The commoners, seeing the flight of members of Mzilikazi's family, were apprehensive and guessed that the King had died.

The last traces of winter faded. The October sun blazed down on Matabeleland, and still the dozen faithful widows continued to sit beside Mzilikazi's decaying body. Towards the end of the month the King's death was announced officially throughout the land, and the regiments of every military kraal were summoned to the capital.

At cockcrow on the morning of 1 November Mzilikazi's corpse, now in an advanced state of decomposition, was carried from the hut where it had lain for fifty-six days and was placed in a wagon. A second wagon was loaded with all the articles the King had used in his declining years – his garments, his utensils, his sleeping-mats and a vast collection of beads, ornaments, brass rings and other items he had received from European friends. The wagons drew out of emHlahlandlela and, followed by the army in full panoply and also a slow stream of *indunas* and subjects, they proceeded eastwards towards the Matopos.

Eight miles from the capital the cortège descended into a valley and moved slowly over the veld through thatching-grass and thorny shrubs, streams, rocks and fallen tree-trunks. It approached enTumbane – the Little Hill, a section of the Matopos range – followed its base and climbed laboriously into its slopes. But when the wagons could proceed no farther, the *indunas* called a halt, lifted the royal corpse from the hearse, carried it to an outcrop of mammoth boulders, and laid it to rest in a granite-walled cave. Then they sealed the mouth of the sepulchre with stones and returned to the throng awaiting them on the slopes of enTumbane.

The *indunas* then had Mzilikazi's wagon dismantled, and all its parts, together with the King's personal belongings, were taken into a second cave. The *indunas* left an armed guard in charge of the sepulchre, and then set out with the procession of mourners for emHlahlandlela.

Reaching the royal kraal, the army sang anthems. Fifty black bullocks were speared to death and sacrificed to the spirit of Mzilikazi and to the spirits of his father and grandfather. A priest called upon the shades of the tribe to receive the departed King into the spirit world, and begged them to have compassion on the grief-stricken Matabele by providing them with a new monarch – one as wise, just and fatherly as the great Mzilikazi.

The praise-singers came out, paraded before the throng and raised their voices in adoration of the departed King.

Mzilikazi, the young Khumalo warrior who in distant times had defied the mighty Shaka, had fled from Zululand with a tiny clan and had crossed the Drakensberg to blaze a trail through the highveld and lowveld of the Transvaal and the regions stretching westwards into Bechuanaland and the Kalahari desert; Mzilikazi, the young Chief, who had routed the tribes of central South Africa, had occupied their territories, had destroyed their settlements, had captured their cattle, their women and children, and had converted their menfolk into Matabele warriors; Mzilikazi, the conqueror who, on three occasions, had saved his growing tribe from Dingane's invading armies and had defeated the mounted forces of the Griqua, the Koranna and the Bergenaars; Mzilikazi, the Bull Elephant, the King who had evacuated his people from the Marico district when Hendrik Potgieter's commando had threatened to exterminate the tribe; Mzilikazi, King of Black Kings, who had united the Matabele in the Matopos, had subjugated all the indigenous peoples between the Zambezi and the Limpopo and had seen his subjects multiply and prosper while he himself struggled with the sickness and pain tormenting his body and mind; Mzilikazi, the Matabele's greatest son, the tyrant who had conquered half a million square miles of Southern Africa and yet had outlived all other black tyrants of his time; Mzilikazi, who in life had been the father of the Matabele and, in death, was the tribe's most illustrious ancestor.

There is a road which leads out of the picturesque suburbs of the present-day city of Bulawayo and proceeds south-westwards to the bushy regions where Mzilikazi spent the last three months of his life. This road skirts the Matopo Railway Terminus, cuts across the site where the hedges, the circles of beehive huts, the seraglio and the cattle-fold of emHlahlandlela once stood, hurries away towards Fort Usher and branches off through the Matopo Reserve and the bald-headed hills extending almost to Gwanda.

This is a quiet road, a dirt-road. Today it is used mainly by pedestrians, descendants of Mzilikazi's Matabele tribe, black men and women dressed in European fashion, some conversing in English, others in their mother tongue.

At a point where the road reaches the site of Mzilikazi's former emHlahlandlela kraal, the present-day Matabele tread lightly, for this is sacred ground. Here their attention is drawn to a spreading uMgugudo tree and a massive granite boulder standing in its shade.

Fixed to the boulder is a plaque, erected by the white men of the Colony, as a tribute to Mzilikazi, founder and King of the Matabele tribe.

An inscription reads:

MZILIKAZI, SON OF MASHOBANE,
KING OF THE MATABELE—
A MOUNTAIN FELL ON THE 5TH OF SEPTEMBER, 1868.
ALL NATIONS EXCLAIM: BAYETE!

EPILOGUE

THE passing of the great Mzilikazi was followed by a prolonged period of political confusion, brought about by the failure of the royal councillors to reach agreement on the choice of a suitable candidate for the vacant throne. Some of the younger *indunas* demanded that Kulumane, rightful heir to the throne, be installed as the new king. They refused to believe he had been murdered at Mzilikazi's command, insisting that he had been exiled to Zululand to avoid being assassinated by conspirators. They were strongly opposed by old uMncumbata, regent of the tribe, who declared that, thirty years before, he had himself supervised the killing of Kulumane and another young prince named Ubuhlelo. Lobengula, known to all the *indunas* as one of Mzilikazi's favourite sons, would also have died if his mother had not taken him into hiding.

Determined that there should be no undue delay in the choice of a new king, uMncumbata nominated Lobengula as Mzilikazi's successor. This nomination gained the immediate support of a large section of the council of *indunas*, but it was bitterly opposed by Mbigo Masuku, influential commander-in-chief of the Zwangendaba regiment. Lobengula was little impressed by the sudden honour about to be thrust on him. He was reluctant to accept nomination, for he feared that his assassination would be plotted by unsuccessful aspirants to the throne.

There seemed no hope of reaching a unanimous decision in the council, so uMncumbata dispatched a party of Matabele dignitaries, headed by *indunas* Mhlaba and Mangwana, to search for Kulumane in Zululand and Natal. The question of the succession was postponed for a short while, and political tension was eased.

In due course the Matabele delegation returned to report the failure of their mission, and at the next meeting of the council uMncumbata proposed that Lobengula be installed immediately. Mbigo, now supported by the Induba and Inqobo regiments, again objected; firstly, because he was convinced Kulumane was still alive and, secondly, because Lobengula was the son of an inferior royal wife of Swazi origin. He predicted that Kulumane would shortly return to occupy his father's throne. If, therefore, the *indunas* insisted on appointing Lobengula king, they would be exposing the Matabele to civil war.

Two of the *indunas*, growing weary of Mbigo's attitude, accused him of intrigue. They warned him that if he continued to ignore the majority vote of the council, he would become the confirmed enemy, not only of Lobengula, but also of the Matabele tribe. Not even his outstanding record, as one of Mzilikazi's greatest military leaders, would save him and his followers from destruction.

Shortly after this eventful meeting, news reached emHlahlandlela that Theophilus Shepstone, Secretary of Native Affairs in Natal, had a groom in his service who claimed to be Kulumane, heir-apparent to the Matabele throne. uKhanda, as he was then known, was determined to be proclaimed King of the Matabele. He journeyed upcountry as far as Northern Bechuanaland, where he strove to persuade the Bamangwato to invade Matabeleland and place him at the head of the kingdom. However, when he received no real support from the Bamangwato he realized his ambitious plans were doomed, so he returned to the South where, presumably, he resumed the role of uKhanda, a domestic servant.

On 17 March 1870, eighteen months after the death of Mzilikazi, Lobengula was formally installed at emHlahlandlela. The tribe rejoiced, with the notable exception of Mbigo's faction and, in accordance with Zulu custom, Lobengula set about building a new capital, the great Gibixhegu, which was to become Bulawayo in later years.

Meanwhile, Mbigo grew increasingly defiant of the King's authority, and the *indunas* of the royal council demanded his death. Mindful, however, of the great part played by Mbigo and the Zwangendaba regiment in the conquest of the territories between the Limpopo and Zambezi rivers, Lobengula was reluctant to take drastic action. He sent councillors to confer with the rebel commander, and to explain that the Matabele could never be a united tribe while he and his people refused to cooperate. Mbigo responded by having the messengers thrashed, and he instructed them to tell their King that henceforth the Zwangendaba regiment would be prepared to talk only with stabbing-spears.

Lobengula mustered his regiments and led them against Mbigo, whose military kraal lay fifty miles to the north. In this brief but bloody 'civil war' Lobengula's forces were twice repulsed, but eventually they defeated the powerful Zwangendaba regiment and put Mbigo to death.

Eighteen months after the death of Mzilikazi the Tati goldfields, discovered by Hartley and Mauch, were occupied by white diggers. Exclusive mining rights were granted, by uMncumbata, to the Limpopo Mining Company, a London firm headed by Sir John Swinburne. Permission to mine gold was also given to Thomas Baines, who established the Northern Goldfields in the region of the Zambezi river.

During the next eighteen years few other significant changes took place in Matabele territory. Following in the footsteps of his father, Lobengula ruled with absolute authority, executing all whom he suspected of disloyalty and butchering any of the subjugated tribes who failed to provide the tribute demanded by him. He was always intensely suspicious of strangers, but was kind to the missionaries, and cooperated with white hunters and traders, provided that they obeyed the laws of his kingdom. Lobengula had the sincerest respect for the British nation and even ventured to propose marriage to Queen Victoria.

In 1888 Lobengula took the first step towards the overthrow of his power when he sold the mineral rights of Matabele territory to parties of white men. This led to the founding of the British South African and Chartered Companies, and eventually to the occupation of Mashonaland by white settlers who built a string of forts garrisoned by strong armed forces. As villages sprang up in the former hunting-grounds of the Matabele, Lobengula grew apprehensive. Within four years of their arrival in Mashonaland the white settlers became involved in a series of clashes with parties of marauding Matabele, and in 1893 war broke out.

It was mid-October when the troops of the Chartered Company, commanded by Majors Forbes and Wilson, advanced on Bulawayo, destroying kraals along the route as they scanned the countryside for a sight of Lobengula's army. Towards the end of the month the first major battle took place on the banks of the Shangani river, resulting in the withdrawal of the Matabele. Early in November the Matabele attacked the advancing enemy as it approached the Bembesi river, but so fierce was the onslaught of the white men's machine-guns that two powerful regiments, the Imbezu and Ingubo, were wiped out almost to a man. What remained of the Matabele army retired in confusion. Lobengula ordered the sacking of Bulawayo and, accompanied by his subjects, fled towards the Zambezi river in the North.

With the discovery that Bulawayo lay in ruins, the white forces returned to the Shangani river. On 3 December Major Wilson set out with a small party of cavalrymen in search of Lobengula. On the following day the King was located beyond the Shangani with a large body of warriors. As Wilson approached him the warriors surged forward, surrounded the party and massacred it.

Meanwhile, the Matabele army was gradually being crushed by Forbes's column, supported by a contingent made up of Bechuanaland border police and men drawn from the British South African Company. Lobengula sued for peace, but it was only in January 1894, when he contracted fever and died, that the war drew speedily to a close.

Thus, with the death of the second and last of the Matabele kings, the territories between the Limpopo and Zambezi passed into the hands of the white conquerors to become known as Southern Rhodesia. Villages and towns rose in the bush and on the plains; schools, churches, businesses, factories and Government offices sprang up where in former years many a bloody battle had been waged.

And with the establishment and subsequent growth of Southern Rhodesia the white man learnt to pay tribute to the greatest of all Matabele – Mzilikazi ka Mashobane.

APPENDIX I

The Southern Bantu (Ethnic Groups)

Hundreds of Negroid tribes, classified ethnically as the Bantu, inhabit Central and Southern Africa. This is a vast territory, bounded on the north by a line running roughly from the Gulf of Guinea, in the west, to the east coast of the continent.

The Bantu form three major groups: Western and Eastern Bantu inhabit the area bordered, to the south, by two great rivers – the Zambezi and the Kunene; the third major group, the Southern Bantu, is spread over the rest of Southern Africa, extending from the Moçambique channel in the Indian Ocean to the Kalahari desert, and southwards to the tip of Africa.

The Southern Bantu of South Africa, from among whom rose Mzilikazi's powerful Matabele (Zulu: *Ndebele*) tribe, are further subdivided into the following ethnic groups:

1. *The Sotho*

They are scattered over an extensive part of Southern Africa: from the Zambezi to the Orange river and from Lesotho to Botswana. Although related languages are spoken by the Sotho peoples, three main groups are distinguishable.

(a) *The Southern Sotho* (founded by Moshesh) who inhabit Lesotho, the Orange Free State, the regions adjoining the Northern Transkei and the western section of Natal.

(b) *The Western Sotho* (or Tswana-speaking tribes) who occupy a belt of country in the west extending from the Orange river to the Zambezi. This sub-group includes the Barolong and Batlhaping of the Northern Cape, the Bangwaketsi, Bakwena, Bamangwato, Bakgatla, Batawana, and Bakgalagadi of Botswana, and, finally, the Bahurutsi of the Transvaal. Branches of the Bakwena and Bakgatla are to be found in the Western Transvaal.

(c) *The Northern Sotho*. This sub-group, of which the Bapedi of

Sekukuniland are the largest and most influential tribe, is spread over several districts of the Northern Transvaal.

2. *The Bavenda*

This tribe occupies the Zoutpansberg regions and the Louis Trichardt and Sibasa districts of the Transvaal. Essentially mountain-dwellers, the Bavenda are closely related to the neighbouring Bantu tribes of Rhodesia, having migrated across the Limpopo sometime during the sixteenth and eighteen centuries.

Residing among the Bavenda are the Lemba people, whose customs, in many respects, are distinctly Semitic. Their facial features are less Negroid than other Bantu tribes of South Africa.

3. *The Shangana-Tsonga*

These are an offshoot of the peoples of Portuguese East Africa, and are found in large numbers in the North-eastern Transvaal and Vendaland.

4. *The Bantu of South-West Africa*

(a) The *oHerero*. They live mainly in areas north-west, north-east and south-east of Windhoek. Predominantly pastoralists, their cultural activities are hampered by the precarious rainfall of the country.

(b) The *oVambo* and *oKavango*. These tribes form by far the largest population of South-West Africa. Their territories include a great strip of tropical country south of the Angola border. Here the rainfall is relatively plentiful and agriculture plays an important part in their economic activities.

5. *The Nguni*

Mzilikazi's small Khumalo clan, and the Matabele tribe that grew from it, belong to this influential ethnic group of the Southern Bantu.

The Nguni peoples are settled mainly along the east-coast belt of South Africa, bounded on the west by the Drakensberg ranges. Their territories extend from Swaziland in the north to the Great Fish river of the Cape Province in the south.

There are four distinct Nguni sub-groups:

(a) *The Swazi*. Their language and customs closely resemble those of the Zulu. The Swazi, like all major tribes of Southern Africa, are made up of clans, each controlled by a separate chieftain. Swaziland is the homeland of this tribe, but almost half the population lives outside its borders in the adjoining eastern districts of the Transvaal.

(b) *The Xhosa-speaking peoples* are made up of twelve tribes. Their territories lie roughly in the eastern section of the Cape Province, between the Great Fish river and the southern border of Natal. During the eighteenth and nineteenth centuries the Xhosa were involved in a series of bloody wars with the forces of the British Cape Colony. Although they speak a language similar to the Swazi and the Zulu, they do not resemble these tribes physically.

(c) *The Zulu Group*. Between 1816 and 1828 Shaka, once a petty chief of the insignificant Zulu clan, conquered the hundreds of other clans of present-day Zululand and Natal and moulded them into the powerful Zulu tribe. His reign was blemished by incessant warfare, by the slaughter of tens of thousands of Southern Bantu tribesmen and by the extermination of incalculable numbers of his own subjects. Shaka was assassinated in 1828 by Dingane, his half-brother.

Dingane's reign, although less turbulent, ended abruptly in 1837 when he plotted the murder of Piet Retief and a large party of Voortrekkers at the Zulu capital of emGungundlovu. Dingane's treachery led first to the defeat of the Zulu army, at the Battle of Blood River, and then to the flight of the royal house beyond the Pongolo river.

Dingane was succeeded by his brother Mpande, a weakling by Zulu standards. Mpande's reign was marked by royal intrigues and subsequent internecine wars waged among the Zulu clans.

Mpande died in 1872 and Cetshwayo, a tyrant in the Shakan pattern, came to the throne. A redoubtable conqueror, Cetshwayo in 1879 wiped out a formidable British force under Lord Chelmsford at Isandlwana. Later in the same year Chelmsford defeated the Zulu army at Ulundi, and the captured Cetshwayo was exiled to the Cape. In due course the Zulu King arrived in England where he was accorded an interview with Queen Victoria. He was allowed to return to Zululand but, shortly after, he had to flee for his life from the army of his erstwhile general, Zibebu. His health broken, Cetshwayo died in 1884.

Dinizulu, next of the Zulu kings, was soon involved in hostilities with the British of the Cape Colony. In 1888 he was arrested, found guilty of high treason and deported to St Helena. Ten years later he was permitted to return to the Zulu throne, but in 1907 he was one of the prime movers in the Bambata rebellion. Recaptured, he was again tried for high treason and banished to the Transvaal. He died, in exile, in 1913.

Dinizulu was the last of the warfaring Zulu kings. He was succeeded by Solomon ka Dinizulu, who was followed by Nyangayezizwe Cyprian Bekhuzulu, present-day Paramount Chief of the Zulu.

(*d*) *Ndebele*. This influential Nguni sub-group traces its origins to Zululand and, especially, the homeland of Mzilikazi's small Northern Khumalo clan. At the time of their surge into the interior of South Africa, Mzilikazi's followers were exclusively of Nguni stock. Mzilikazi's progress through the highveld and lowveld regions of the Transvaal and, later, his devastating campaigns against the tribes of Bechuanaland resulted in the introduction of 'foreigners' into the Matabele regiments and habitations.

By 1826 the Matabele had become a heterogeneous tribe, composed of a Nguni nucleus and two large groups of Northern and Western Sotho captives. However, in the same year, batches of Nguni warriors, fugitives from Shaka's despotic régime, arrived at emHlahlandlela in the Magaliesberg area. With this increase of Zulu-speaking members, two distinct social classes evolved: a Nguni *élite* and a Sotho proletariat. Mzilikazi's Sotho subjects were obliged to learn the Zulu language and adapt themselves to Nguni customs.

In 1836, at the time of the Battle of Vegkop, the Matabele tribe probably included members of all the Sotho-speaking groups of South Africa except the Batlhaping (whom Mzilikazi never attacked) and the newly founded Basuto tribe, whom he failed to dislodge from Thaba Bosiu.

In 1837, with the dispersal of the Matabele by the Boers, the Sotho-speaking elements of the tribe were reduced. The subjugated peoples of the Transvaal and Bechuanaland regained their freedom, and many of Mzilikazi's Sotho captives flocked back to their villages.

On reuniting his people north of the Limpopo, Mzilikazi embarked on the subjugation of the Makalanga and Mashona peoples of Southern Rhodesia. In this way a new ethnic group of Bantu was assimilated by the tribe, and within ten years of their flight from the Transvaal the Matabele were once again a powerful people. As a result of this increase in the numbers of Mzilikazi's subjects, the Sotho section, now considered old members of the tribe, rose in status. Although they were themselves still inferior to the Nguni nucleus, the Sotho treated the newcomers with contempt. At this stage of the development of the Matabele, Mzilikazi was elevating Sotho members to comparatively responsible military and political posts. Nevertheless marriage or even sexual intercourse between Nguni and non-Nguni subjects was forbidden.

The privileged Nguni, aristocrats of the tribe, were known as *Abezansi* – 'those from down-country'. They held the most important posts in Matabeleland and were recognized by the rest of the tribe as the superior class. The Sotho group were the middle class, the *Abenhla*, or 'people from up-country'. Both the Abezansi and Abenhla regarded the Makalanga and Mashona captives as *Amaholi* – serfs.

Today, the Ndebele of Rhodesia, the Matabele, as they were first named by the Sotho-speaking peoples of the Transvaal, are settled in reserves. Their language, siNdebele, differs little from the Zulu spoken by their forefathers.

APPENDIX II

A. Matabele Kraals

1. *Choice of Sites*. Sites for kraals were usually chosen on sloping, dry ground where drinking-water and firewood were plentiful, where the soil was fertile and the pasturage good. Tall thorn-bush hedges encircling the beehive huts served as protection from beasts of prey. Entrance to the kraal was through a large gap in the hedge known as *isango*. The hedge and the huts embraced a large cattle-fold (*isibaya*), sheep-pens (*izilupi*) and small enclosures (*izibayana*) for housing cows and calves.

2. *Huts*. Matabele huts were built of thatching-grass supported by sturdy frameworks of wattle sticks. The entire structure was held in position by a stout pole planted upright in the centre of the floor. Between this pole and the small doorway of the hut the family hearth was situated. This was merely a hollow about eighteen inches in diameter. The hut-floor was prepared from a mixture of moist clay (or ant-heap) and cowdung, pounded into a hard surface and then rubbed with flat river stones until it became as smooth as marble.

Foodstuffs were stored at a point farthest from, and directly opposite, the doorway. Clothes were packed on a wooden platform raised on poles to a height of about two feet. Other items such as cooking utensils, firewood, beer-pots, sleeping-mats, karosses and calabashes were packed along the sides, leaving the central section of the hut clear.

The Matabele hut had no chimney, the smoke from the hearth escaping through the thatch, until the roof became coated with a thick layer of greasy soot. The members of the family slept in a circle about the hearth, their bodies wrapped in karosses or ox-hides and their heads resting on 'pillows' carved from wood.

3. *Diet*. The Matabele enjoyed a healthy, balanced diet. Stews were prepared from pumpkin, soft, green calabash, sorghum corn, maize, and a variety of edible roots and leaves gathered from the veld. They

also ate boiled beef, mutton and venison as well as a thick porridge made from ground corn or maize. Milk, both fresh and curdled, and beer were drunk through the day.

4. *Beer brewing*. Beer, the most popular Matabele beverage, was consumed in large quantities. Brewing followed a traditional pattern. Sorghum was soaked in water for a day. Then the water was poured away and the seeds were covered and kept moist. During the next few days the resulting germination produced a yeast which was gathered, laid out to dry, and eventually ground on a grinding-stone. Water-soaked sorghum or maize was then ground, husks and all, into a coarse meal. This meal, together with a handful of yeast, was poured into pots. The pots were filled with boiling water and the mixture stirred thoroughly. When it cooled, more yeast was added and the beer-pots then left untouched overnight. The following morning the mixture was brought to the boil and held there for some hours. During the afternoon the murky liquid was poured into fresh pots and again left to cool. More yeast was added so that, during the night, fermentation took place. By morning the beer, so greatly relished by the Matabele, was almost ready for drinking. It was poured, finally, through cylindrical, woven sieves in order to remove the husks. Then the beer-pots were carried to a cool spot, there to be visited regularly by those members of the tribe whose task it was to keep drinking-pots replenished at the gathering place of men.

5. *Snuffing and Smoking*. During the last ten years of Mzilikazi's reign tobacco-growing became increasingly popular among the Matabele. The people prepared snuff by grinding dry tobacco leaves between two stones and mixing bark-ash into the coarse tobacco powder. Snuff-boxes were made from small horns, calabash shells, bones and even tree-pods. Both men and women snuffed. Indeed, according to the missionary Thomas (*Eleven Years in Central South Africa*, p. 179) 'scarcely one in a thousand is found without this box, generally stuck in the ear-hole, hanging by the neck in a small bag, attached to a string, or rolled in the waist-belt'.

Unlike some of the tribes of South Africa, where women smoke pipes, only men were allowed this privilege in Matabeleland. Tobacco was smoked in crudely fashioned clay pipes (*ingiti*), but by far the most popular smoke was the flower of wild hemp (*insangu*), generally known in South Africa as *dagga*, and in other parts of the world as *marijuana*. The pipe used for this intoxicating smoke was the traditional *igudu*, a koodoo horn containing a quantity of water through which the strong *insangu* fumes were drawn. Habitual *insangu* smokers could be detected at a glance, for their bodies trembled and their minds were stupefied.

B. Dress and Ornaments

On the whole the Matabele were a clean-living people who washed daily and who took pains to ornament their bodies.

Infants played naked about the huts, but during childhood the girls were compelled to wear small skin aprons, decorated with beads, and the boys a similar garment, though not decorated, made from the pelts of wild animals.

On entering puberty girls discarded the small apron for a larger skin garment covering the buttocks and the front of the body between the knees and waist. Unmarried girls wore nothing from the waist upwards, except a few strings of multi-coloured beads tied round the neck and wrists.

After marriage women dressed in heavy ox-hide skirts, softened inside and smeared with fat and charcoal. Women of the royal harems wore a piece of flat clay, about the size of a penny, on the crown of the head to distinguish them from the wives of commoners. All married women had bead necklaces and bracelets, the most popular colours being blue, yellow, pink, white and black. However, the large type of bead, brought by traders into Matabeleland, was used only by the King's most senior wives.

Teenage boys wore a medium-size loin-skin hanging, in strips, about their thighs, and adult men a kilt-like loin covering (*idumbu*) made from strips of wild cat and jackal skin. Secured about the waist, this garment almost extended to the knees.

The full battle-dress of a Matabele warrior included a headdress of plumes (*indhlugulu*), a charm worn around the neck (*intebe*), a light cape (*isigulu seNxwala*), armlets (*izigetsho*), a kilt of wild cat and monkey tails (*umtika*), leglets (*amadhloli*), a knob-headed stick (*induko isitshingo*) assegais (*imikhonto*), a shield (*isihlangu*) and a shield stick (*umgobo*).

C. Matabele Craftsmanship

In common with all other Bantu tribes of Southern Africa the Matabele were skilled craftsmen. From reeds and grass both the men and women wove baskets, sleeping-mats, beer-strainers and eating-mats. The moulding, decorating and baking of clay pots, bowls and other household utensils was left largely to the women, while the men saw to the tanning of skins, the making of clothes and ox-hide shields, the working of iron and the carving of wooden food-bowls, milk-pails, spoons, ladles, stirring sticks and head-rests. The crudest of tools were used for carving – home-made knives, adzes, axes and chisels, but the standard of workmanship was outstanding.

By virtue of their experience in smelting iron ore and manufacturing iron implements the Mashona captives were appointed the blacksmiths of the tribe. With their primitive hammers, tongs, bellows and stone anvils they turned out blades for stabbing-spears, hatchets, battle-axes and a variety of bangles and other ornaments.

Among the most talented Matabele craftsmen were the men who, with the aid of long eyeless needles and thread prepared from the sinews of the ox, made beautiful karosses from the pelts of the wild cat. Finally, from horns, skins, sinew, reeds, wood and calabashes the Matabele made string, wind and percussion musical instruments.

D. Hunting and Trapping

Organized hunting in Mzilikazi's dominions usually took place when the regiments were inactive, after returning from the plundering excursions into enemy territory. Thousands of warriors took part in the hunt. They proceeded, with their commanders, to the grazing-grounds of the game, there to spread out and form a circle several miles in circumference. Then, at the command of the supervisors of the hunt, the warriors moved slowly forward chanting, hissing and stamping the ground with their feet. As they progressed towards the centre of the circle the Matabele drove the game before them. Soon a confusion of animals, both large and small, both timid and aggressive, started running hither and thither, all bent on finding a way of escape through the menacing ring of hunters. In due course lions, rhinos and buffalo became so desperate with fear that they charged blindly, and escaped to freedom through passages conveniently provided for them by the warriors.

The slaughter of the remaining animals followed swiftly, but often hunters were injured, or even killed, by the onslaught of the horns and hooves of the larger species of antelope. The hyena, if trapped, was never killed, for the Matabele believed it possessed supernatural powers. When the excitement was over, the warriors carried the carcasses to Mzilikazi's kraal. The meat was divided among the regiments, and days of feasting followed.

Much of the tribe's supply of venison was derived from trapping. Game-pits, hidden beneath branches and grass, were dug throughout Matabele country. An animal falling into one of these traps met a cruel death, for planted at the bottom was a sharp wooden stake.

The most destructive game-traps in Matabeleland were the *umhopo*, large concealed pits situated in the vicinity of rivers. Reaching out on either side of this type of pit, in the shape of a funnel, were two thorn-bush hedges. Animals approaching, or leaving the river, were driven between the hedges and then forced to flee in the direction of the pit. There were occasions when the pit filled so rapidly with game that the bodies formed a 'bridge' over which the animals, still trapped between the hedges, were able to gallop to safety.

E. Witchcraft and Magic

Magic and witchcraft played a dominant role in the way of life of all the Matabele. Unable to understand most of the mysteries of nature, or to account for the tragedies that befell their homes, families, herds and crops, they believed certain people, animals, birds, and reptiles possessed evil and destructive supernatural powers.

The subsistence economy, as practised by the Matabele, lent itself to fluctuating fortunes. When the harvests were abundant and the herds healthy, the people attributed their good fortune to the magnanimity of the ancestral spirits. When disaster came in the form of hail, drought, locust swarms, lightning and disease, they believed they were in disfavour with the spirit world. However, when individual tribesmen met with misfortune while their kinsmen enjoyed prosperity, they blamed this on witchcraft and sought the help of a medicine-man, an influential member of the tribe reputed to possess special magical powers.

There were two types of medicine-men – diviners and witch-doctors. The diviner's greatest attribute was his ability to predict events. He practised good or 'white magic'. When visited by an ailing tribesman, not only did he diagnose the cause of the disease, but he also decided whether his patient had been bewitched or, on the other hand, whether he was merely being punished by an ancestral spirit. Whatever his decision the diviner had to find a remedy. If, in his opinion, the culprit was a sorcerer, then it was necessary to 'smell him out', to expose him and destroy his evil medicines. The highly specialized task of 'smelling out' was the prerogative of the witch-doctor, a person who, in royal circles, enjoyed great prestige and political influence.

Undoubtedly the most widely used method for diagnosing diseases and predicting events was bone-throwing. Each diviner owned a leather bag in which he kept the ankle-joints of a goat, sheep, ant-bear, hyena, monkey, baboon, wild boar, leopard and a few species of antelope. He also had the knuckle-joints of a lion, the beak of a vulture, stones taken from the stomach of a crocodile, cowries and other shells, a piece of tortoise-shell, pips of certain indigenous fruits, the tips of an ox-hoof and small squares of ivory marked with varying numbers of black dots.

Each of these magical objects had a meaning and served to guide the bone-thrower in his predictions. For example : the ankle-joints of goats represented people – the commoners of the tribe – while those of the sheep stood for the Chief and important members of the royal family. The hyena's bones signified the councillors, but also sycophants, and those of the ant-bear meant the ancestral spirits and the power of death. The knuckle-joint of the lion was the king of the tribe, and in later years, the white man. The vulture's beak indicated direction, shells and cowries pointed to the position of boundaries, and the tortoise-shell, depending upon which way it fell, designated either peace or misfortune. A bone falling in an upright position meant that the diviner's patient would be healthy and able to take part in normal activities. If, however, it settled upside down, this was a bad omen – a sign of impending illness, general misfortune or even death.

Many Matabele medicine-men were also herbalists whose expert knowledge in the medicinal qualities of herbs, roots, seeds, leaves, tree-bark, bulbs and insects had been passed on to them by their forebears. Most of the remedies prepared by herbalists were effective in the treatment of sores and wounds and in the curing of simple bodily disorders.

The Matabele believed in the existence of witches and wizards, people who used supernatural powers to harm fellow tribesmen. During the day they were ordinary, normal individuals, but after dark their souls became disembodied and turned into evil creatures that roamed the countryside carrying disaster into the kraals.

Witches and wizards were said to be in league with the hyena, an animal dreaded by the Matabele. Together they visited the graves of the ancestors, bewitched innocent tribesmen by sprinkling medicines and ox-blood near the huts, and vanished before daybreak. People 'smelt out' and then found guilty of witchcraft were sentenced to gory deaths, and their corpses were fed to the hyenas.

A similar fate awaited the sorcerer, a person who, both by day and by night, was occupied in diabolical practices. He was intensely despised for, unlike the witch or wizard whose nocturnal activities were dictated by disembodied souls, he was in full control of his actions.

Witches, wizards and sorcerers practised evil or 'black magic'.

APPENDIX III

1. *Mzilikazi's Regiments*

REGIMENT	COMMANDER (*Induna*)
Amagogo	Maqekeni Sithole
Amatshetshe	Sifo Masuku
Babambeni	Dagamela Ncube
Dibinhlangu	Mletshe Tebe
Eguqeni	Mletshe Ndeweni
Godlwayo	Tambisamahubo Mafu
Indinana	Mfangilele Matshazi
Induba	Lotshe Hlabangana
Ingwegwe	Mkanyeli Masuku
Inhlambane	Tambo Ndeweni
Inqama	Somhlolo Matema
Inqobo	Mazwi Gumede
Insinda	Tshuwe Gwebu
Insingo	Somabulane Dlodlo
Intemba	Mjojo Mlotshwa
Intunta	Mhabahaba Mkwanazi
Inyati	Ntabene Gwebu
Inxa	Ntshumane Kanye
Inzwananzi	Mpiliwa Magutshwa
Isiphezi	Maqundela Sigola
Mabugudwane	Mayege Mthethwa
Mahlokohloko	Mbambelele Hlabangana
Makoloza	Mankanyana Tebe
Mbuyazwe	Mhlipi Ndeweni
Mhlahlandlela	Gwabalanda Mathe
Mzinyati	Majijili Gwebu
Nyamayendlovu	Mkoki Masuku
Oyengweni	Mlota Khumalo
Sizinda	Mapisa Fuyane
Zimnyama	Mtshamayi Ndeweni
Zwangendaba	Mbigo Masuku

2. Zulu *isibongo* or praise-song sung by Dingane's army, presumably after its third clash with the Matabele. (As recited to the author by Princess Magogo uZulu ka Dinizulu, Kwa Phindangene royal kraal, Zululand.)

Bantu nezihlobo laph' eSigweni
People and relatives of Sigweni
Bikelani abakwaMashobane
Report to the Mashobane people (the Matabele)
Nithi lukhulu luyeza luyanyelela,
Say something tragic is stalking them,
Lufana noPhunga waSoyengweni
It is like Phunga of Soyengweni
Ngilufanisa noPhunga noMageba.
I liken it to Phunga and Mageba.
Abakw Maashobane belelesile
The Mashobane People have committed a crime
Basibukule itshe linemamba,
They unearthed a rock that hid a mamba,
Sebejiyele nokulisibekela.
Now they do not know how to return it (the rock).
Isihlangu sika Mashobane
Mashobane's shield
Sasala entabeni ende eMpama,
was left at a high mountain named Mpama,
Saswela nendoda esithathayo.
There was no man prepared to carry it.
Wadla uGundane kumitha kwa Mashobane,
He (Dingane) defeated Gundane at Mashoban's (kraal)
Wadla umlomo wezinqaba kwa Mashobane,
He conquered the stronghold at Mashobane's (kraal),
Wadla insimba insila ulugaju kwa Mashobane,
He took the booty tails of the genet at Mashobane's
    (kraal).
Wadla Nsimbakazana unina ka Mzilikazi,
He killed Nsimbakazana mother of Mzilikazi,
Wadla uKhwababa embathi'mpaka kwa Mashobane,
He killed Khwababa of the wizard's cat-skin at
    Mashobane's (kraal),
Weza nodwendwe lwamaqhikiza kwa Mashobane,

He brought a crowd of maidens from Mashobane's
    (kraal),
Weza noNtanase kwa Mashobane,
He brought Ntanase from Mashobane's (kraal),
Weza noNozinyanga kwa Mashobane,
He brought Nozinyanga from Mashobane's (kraal),
Weza nomhabulangwebu isashisa kwa Mashobane,
He brought a beer-taster from Mashobane's kraal,
Weza nenkomo ekulala kulukhuni kwa Mashobane.
He brought a cow which sleeps with difficulty from
    Mashobane's (kraal).

BIBLIOGRAPHY

African Notes and News, 1947–9, vols. V–VI; 1949–51, vols. VII–VIII.

Arbousset, T., and Daumas, F., *Narrative of the Exploratory Tour to the North-east of the Colony of the Cape of Good Hope*, Bishop, 1852.

Baines, T., *The Gold Regions of South Eastern Africa*, Stanford, 1877.

Becker, Peter, *Sandy Tracks to the Kraals*, Dagbreek, Johannesburg, 1956.

Bird, John, *The Annals of Natal, 1495–1845* (two volumes), P. Davis and Sons, Pietermaritzburg, 1888.

Bond, John, *They were South Africans*, Oxford University Press, Cape Town, 1956.

Broadbent, Samuel, *A Narrative of the First Introduction of Christianity Among the Barolong Tribe of the Bechuanas, South Africa*, Wesleyan Mission House, 1865.

Bryant, A. T., *Olden Times in Zululand and Natal*, Longmans, 1929.

Bryant, A. T., *The Zulu People*, Shuter and Shooter, Pietermaritzburg, 1949.

Bullock, Charles, *The Mashona and the Matabele*, Juta, Cape Town, 1950.

Campbell, J., *Travels in South Africa*, Westley, 1822.

Casalis, E., *The Basuto*, Nisbet, 1861.

Chase, J. St. C. (ed.), *The South African Quarterly Journal*, no. IV, July–September 1830.

Clinton, Iris, *These Vessels ... The Story of Nyati, 1859–1959*, Stuart Manning, Bulawayo, 1959.

Ellenberger, D. F., *History of the Basuto*, Caxton Publishing Co., 1912.

Gibson, J. Y., *Story of the Zulus*, Davis, Maritzburg, 1903.

Gronum, Commandant Carl (Sendelingspos, Mosega), unpublished records.

Harris, Captain W. C., *The Wild Sports of Southern Africa*, John Murray, 1839.

Herrman, L. (ed.), *Travels and Adventures in Eastern Africa*, by Nathaniel Isaacs (two volumes), Van Riebeeck Society, Cape Town, 1937.

Hole, H. M., *The Passing of the Black Kings*, Philip Allan, 1932.

Hyatt, S. P., *The Northward Trek*, Andrew Melrose, 1909.

Isaacs, Nathaniel, *Travels and Adventures in Eastern Africa* (two volumes), Edward Churton, 1836.

Journal des Missions, 1833 and 1856.

Kirby, P. R. (ed.), *The Diary of Andrew Smith, Director of the 'Expedition for Exploring Central Africa'*, 1834–1836 (two volumes), Van Riebeeck Society, Cape Town, 1939–40.

Krige, Eileen J., *The Social System of the Zulu*, Longmans, 1936.

Lister, Margaret H. (ed.), *Journals of Andrew Geddes Bain*, Van Riebeeck Society, Cape Town, 1949.

Livingstone, David, *Missionary Travels and Researches in South Africa*, Harper and Brothers, New York, 1858.

Macgregor, J. C., *Basuto Traditions*, Argus Co., Cape Town, 1911.

McKenzie, John, *Ten Years North of the Orange River, 1859–1869*, Edmonston and Douglas, Edinburgh, 1871.

Mhlagazanhlanzi, *My Friend Kumalo*, Sidelights on Matabele Tradition, Rhodesian Printing and Publishing Co. Ltd., Bulawayo, 1946.

Moffat, John S., *The Lives of Robert and Mary Moffat*, T. Fisher Unwin, 1885.

Moffat, Robert, *Missionary Labours and Scenes in Southern Africa*, John Snow, 1842.

Moffat, R. U., *John Smith Moffat, C.M.G., Missionary: A Memoir*, John Murray, 1921.

Moodi, D. C. F., *The History of the Battles and Adventures of the British, the Boers and the Zulus, etc., in Southern Africa*, Murray and St Leger, Cape Town, 1888.

'Mziki' (A. A. Campbell), *Mlimo: The Rise and Fall of the Matabele*, Natal Witness, Pietermaritzburg, 1926.

Pellissier, S. H., *Jean Pierre Pellissier van Bethulie*, J. L. van Schaik, Pretoria, 1956.

Posselt, F. W. T., *Fact and Fiction, a Short Account of the Natives of Southern Rhodesia*, Rhodesian Printing and Publishing Co. Ltd., Bulawayo, 1935.

Potgieter, Dr Carel, and Theunissen, N. H., *Kommandant-General Hendrik Potgieter*, Afrikaanse Pers Bpk, Johannesburg, 1938.

Proceedings of the Royal Geographical Society (London), vol. XII, 1867–8.

Bibliography

Ritter, E. A., *Shaka Zulu*, Longmans, 1955.

Shooter, J., *The Kaffirs of Natal*, Stanford, 1915.

Smith, Edwin W., *The Life and Times of Daniel Lindley, 1801–80*, Epworth Press, 1949.

Steedman, A., *Wanderings in Southern Africa*, Longmans, 1835.

Stow, G. W., *The Native Races of South Africa: a History of the Intrusion of the Hottentot and Bantu, etc.*, Swan Sonnenschein, 1905.

Stuart, J., *uTalasizwe*, Longmans, 1923.

Stuart, J., *uBoxoxele*, Longmans, 1924.

Tabler, Edward C., *The Far Interior*, A. A. Balkema, Cape Town and Amsterdam, 1955.

Theal, G. M., *History of South Africa, 1795–1875* (five volumes), George Allen and Unwin, 1908.

Theal, G. M., *South Africa*, T. Fisher Unwin, 1899.

Thomas, T. M., *Eleven Years in Central South Africa*, John Snow & Co., London; James Wood, Cardiff, 1872.

Walker, Eric A., *A History of South Africa*, Longmans, 1957.

Walker, Eric A., *The Great Trek*, A. and C. Black, 1938.

Wallis, J. P. R. (ed.), *Matabele Journals of Robert Moffat* (two volumes), Chatto and Windus, 1945.

Wallis, J. P. R. (ed.), *Matabele Mission of J. S. and E. Moffat*, Chatto and Windus, 1945.

Wallis, J. P. R. (ed.), *The Northern Goldfields Diaries of Thomas Baines* (three volumes), Chatto and Windus, 1946.

Wallis, J. P. R. (ed.), *Southern African Diaries of Thomas Leask, 1865–70*, Chatto and Windus, 1954.

Whiteside, J., *History of the Wesleyan Methodist Church of South Africa*, Stock, 1906.

Williams, A. F., *Some Dreams Come True ... the Discovery of Copper, Diamonds and Gold in Southern Africa*, Howard B. Timmins, Cape Town, 1948.

Willoughby, W. C., *The Soul of the Bantu*, Doubleday, Doran, New York, 1928.

REFERENCES

For full details of the books referred to, see preceding Bibliography

CHAPTER ONE

Bryant, *Olden Times*: 62–9, 73–7, 83, 95–100, 119–20, 162–5, 419–20, 421. Bryant, *Zulu People*: 464, 490, 511–15, 523, 731. Gibson: 11–19, 30. Krige: 73–4, 78–80, 252–5. Thomas: 155–6. Shooter: 249–55.

CHAPTER TWO

Bryant, *Olden Times*: 172–3, 174, 202–3, 204–9, 212, 422, 586. Isaacs: I, 73. Herrman: I, 61. Ellenberger: 203–4. 'Mziki': 26. Hyatt: 64–5. Shooter: 255–67. Thomas: 157. Ritter: 150–51, 152, 228–30.

CHAPTER THREE

Bryant, *Olden Times*: 422–3. Bird: I, 680. Ellenberger: 203–4. 'Mziki': 27–30, 34–7. Ritter: 231–4.

CHAPTER FOUR

Stow: 373, 409, 436, 473, 481, 532. Arbousset: 64. Ellenberger: 248, 252–3, 264–7, 280–7, 295. Livingstone: 55–9. Becker: 68–71. Willoughby: 209. Campbell: 233, 237–8, 291.

CHAPTER FIVE

Theal, *South Africa*: 169. Theal, *History*: I, 456. Moffat, Robert: 544–5. Ellenberger: 204–5. Bryant, *Olden Times*: 424. 'Mziki': 42–4. Posselt: 163. Gibson: 30.

References

CHAPTER SIX

Bryant, *Olden Times*: 136–40. Macgregor: 8, 16–17, 27–35. Ellenberger: 39–48, 217–26, 227. Arbousset: 58, 60, 62. Theal, *History*: II, 27, 34, 442–3. Stow: 460, 461–2, 506, 523, 526, 540. Moffat, Robert: 340–1, 346–7, 354–65. Becker: 15. *Journal* (1856): 92–4.

CHAPTER SEVEN

Bryant, *Olden Times*: 425. Stow: 551, 555. Moffat, Robert: 524, 525–8, 555. Kirby: I, 117–18, 143, 169, 191; II, 75, 133, 134, 138, 145–6, 169, 171–2, 174–5, 189, 194, 220, 258. Ellenberger: 155. Arbousset: 268. Shooter: 135, 306.

CHAPTER EIGHT

Walker, *History*: 176. Lister: 3, 11, 12–15. Whiteside: 32. Macgregor: 66. Ellenberger: 51–70, 173, 180. Livingstone: 99. Steedman: II, 183–7.

CHAPTER NINE

Moffat, Robert: 203–4, 210. Stow: 300, 308, 311, 375, 381–2, 515. Kirby: I, 158–9, 378–9; II, 98.

CHAPTER TEN

Stow: 516, 555. Chase: 402–7. Steedman: II, 176–9, 180, 183–5. Kirby: I, 25, 266; II, 10. Wallis, *Matabele Journals*: I, 4.

CHAPTER ELEVEN

Chase: 402–7. Kirby: I, 263, 266–7. Wallis, *Matabele Journals*: I, 4. *African Notes*: V and VI (1947–9), VII and VIII (1949–51). Steedman: II, 185–7.

CHAPTER TWELVE

Kirby: I, 237, 382; II, 101. Moffat, John: 1–7, 11–14, 16–20, 25, 26, 28–33, 35, 38, 43, 44, 46, 47. Moffat, Robert: 511–19, 522–3, 525, 528–30. Wallis, *Matabele Journals*: I, 1, 2, 4, 5, 6, 7, 10–11, 12, 13, 14. Steedman: II, 187–8. Bond: 72, 209. Chase: 407. Broadbent: 176.

3 3

CHAPTER THIRTEEN

Wallis, *Matabele Journals*: I, 13–17, 20–31. Moffat, Robert: 531–8. Moffat, John: 158–64.

CHAPTER FOURTEEN

Bryant, *Olden Times*: 425, 429, 430, 431–2, 658–63, 665–8, 674, 675. Ellenberger: 207, 208–9. Kirby: I, 350; II, 38, 75, 101, 120, 138, 179, 190. Stuart, uTulasizwe: 69. Casalis: 22. Macgregor: 15–19. Becker: 15, 16. Theal, *History*: I, 462–6.

CHAPTER FIFTEEN

Wallis, *Matabele Journals*: I, 59. Kirby: I, 381–4; II, 64–5. Bryant, *Olden Times*: 430. Ellenberger: 207. Stow: 389–91. Harris: 223–4, 351. Theal, *History*: I, 482.

CHAPTER SIXTEEN

Theal, *History*: I, 475. Stow: 542. Pellissier: 107, 109–10, 112–13, 116–19, 121–3. *Journal* (1833): 13–15. Wallis, Matabele Journals: I, 76–7. Posselt, 167–8. Kirby: II, 53, 56.

CHAPTER SEVENTEEN

Harris: 86, 111. Gronum. Posselt: 167–8. Lister: 132, 140–5. Stow: 497. Theal, *History*: I, 484; II, 298. Kirby: I, 18, 35, 37, 49, 79, 205, 270, 293, 294, 307, 328, 331, 333, 335–6; II, 13–15, 17, 141, 161, 167, 218, 240, 243, 244, 247, 251. Wallis, *Matabele Journals*: I, 59, 62, 66–7, 73, 75, 78–9, 83, 85, 91–2, 94, 95–6, 101, 103, 123–4, 128.

CHAPTER EIGHTEEN

Kirby: II, 14, 16–18. Theal, *History*: II, 276, 277, 284–5, 290–92, 298, 302. Theal, *South Africa*: 194–5, 197. Smith: 54. Potgieter: 52, 54, 57, 61–2. Harris: 87–9. Walker, *Great Trek*: 122. Moodi: I, 374–80.

CHAPTER NINETEEN

Harris: 120–23, 136–7, 144, 180. Theal, *History*: II, 294, 296, 303. Gronum. Potgieter: 70, 81, 85, 88–9. Walker, *Great Trek*: 118–28. Smith: 108–9. Bryant, *Olden Times*: 436. Stuart, uBoxoxele: 110. Moodi: 380–85. Bird: 325, 331–2, 333.

References

CHAPTER TWENTY

Mhlagazanhlanzi: 8, 9, 13, 15. Posselt: 10–11, 174, 175. Clinton: 20. Livingstone: 100. Hole: 84, 103–5, 109–10. Wallis, *Matabele Journals*: I, 233, 239–40. Bryant, *Olden Times*: 439. Bullock: 10, 28, 166. Tabler: 118–20.

CHAPTER TWENTY-ONE

Potgieter: 98, 102, 114–15, 116, 118, 125–7, 141, 146, 154–5, 172, 177–8, 256–8. Theal, *South Africa*: 204–7, 209, 211, 375. Theal, *History*: II, 401, 506. Livingstone: 44, 52–76. Wallis, *Matabele Journals*: I, 217, 220, 225, 229–30, 232–5, 243, 249, 251, 254–5, 263, 267, 272, 290, 299, 296–7, 316, 321–2, 326–7, 329, 365. Bird: 211–15.

CHAPTER TWENTY-TWO

Wallis, *Matabele Journals*: II, 1, 2, 4, 5, 9, 59, 67–8, 74, 76–8, 83, 86–7, 104, 107, 112, 119, 120–21 139–40, 159. Theal, *History*: V, 14. McKenzie: 1–4.

CHAPTER TWENTY-THREE

Moffat, R. U.: 55–8. Wallis, *Matabele Mission*: xxxi–xxxiii, 11–56, 75, 106. Wallis, *Matabele Journals*: II, 204, 224, 227–30, 236, 246, 264. Thomas: 65, 68–9, 70–71, 84, 271, 311–12. McKenzie: 1–4.

CHAPTER TWENTY-FOUR

Thomas: 251–3, 318–20, 323–6. Wallis, *Matabele Mission*; 93, 96, 100, 107–9, 114–15, 135–7, 150–51, 153, 155–7, 162, 164, 188, 211, 220, 222–3. McKenzie: 293–7, 303–4, 326–7, 348–9.

CHAPTER TWENTY-FIVE

Gronum. Wallis, *Matabele Mission*: 233, 236, 242–6. Thomas: 392–4, 343–5. Hole: 113–15. Wallis, *Southern African Diaries*: 69, 97–8, 100, 102. Theal, *History*: V, 3–4. Williams: 443. Wallis, *Northern Goldfields Diaries*: I, 26; III, 616, 776. Baines: 12–13.

Baines: 2–3, 13–20, 120–21. Wallis, *Northern Goldfields Diaries*: I, 62; II, 461, 469, 472, 498, 503, 511, 533; III, 776. *Proceedings of the R.G.S.*: 268–73. Tabler: 283, 287–94. Thomas: 284–7, 394–5. Hole: 115–20. Wallis, *Matabele Mission*: 246–7. Mhlagazanhlanzi: 20.

Route taken by Mzilikazi's Matabele through Southern Africa
(1822–40).

Positions of the main tribes affected by Mzilikazi's rise to power.

INDEX

309

prepare way for envangelists,
138; preaches to Matabele,
233–4; effects Truey's release,
and departs, 234; asked to
intercede for Matsheng, 239;
tends Mzilikazi's health,
240–41; gets his agreement to
missionaries, 242; obtains
release of Matsheng, 242;
accompanies Matabele mission
to Mzilikazi, 243–4; witch
doctor purifies, 244; taken to
Mzilikazi, 244; snubbed by
him, 245–6; helps to establish
Inyati mission, 247–8; leaves
Mzilikazi again, 249; opinion
of Makhobi, 258; message to
Mzilikazi in his last illness,
275

Moffat, Robert, Jr, 241
Mokgatla, Chief of the
Bahurutsi, 136–7, 145, 170;
orders execution of Matabele
spies, 173
Mokotoko, Chief of the
Maphuthing, 66–8; killed by
impalement, 69–70
Moletsane, Chief of the Bataung,
98–9; determination to crush
Mzilikazi, 107, 114
Molopo River, 100, 116, 180, 182,
183
Mondane, 233
Monyebe, Matabele *induna*, 246;
plot against, 247–8; killed,
254
Mooi River, 223
Moordkop, Matabele attack at,
167
Morema, 93
Moroko, Chief of the Barolong,
196–7
Mosega, 135, 136; mission station
at, 170, 171, 188; Matabele
spies in, 173–4; becomes

official headquarters of
Matabele, 178; epidemic in,
183, 191; flight of Matabele
from, 198
Moshesh, founder of the Basuto,
74 *and* n., 82; and Mantatisi,
74, 82; drives out Matiwane's
people, 102; settles at Thaba
Bosiu, 159–60; repels Matabele
invaders, 161–2; gives them
cattle, 162
Mothibe, Chief, 100
Mountain Men, *see* Bergenaars
Mpande, King of the Zulu, 286
Mpangazita, Chief of the Hubli,
71; invades the Basia, 72–3, 75;
slain, 82, 91
iziMpangele Regiment, 200
Mpebane River, 133
iziMpohlo Regiment, at
enTubeni, 43–5
Mthethwa clan, 27; army, 28;
Shaka settles affairs of, 36
Murder Hill, Matabele attack at,
167
Murray, Mungo, 225
Mwari, worship of, 215
Mzilikazi, King of the Matabele:
meaning of name, 23n.; birth,
23; childhood with
grandfather, 23–6; coming of
age, 26; hatred of Zwide's
atrocities, 34; installed as Chief
of the Khumalo, 35
life with Shaka: surrenders to
Shaka and begs for protection,
35; appointed group captain,
36; in Zulu-Ndwandwe
campaign, 38–9; broods over
Shaka's success, 39–40; C.-in-C.
of expedition against Ranisi,
40; refuses to surrender spoils
of battle to Shaka, 41, 42–3;
and Matabele, 287–8
wanderings with the Khumalo:

Index